Raphael
Masterpieces of Art

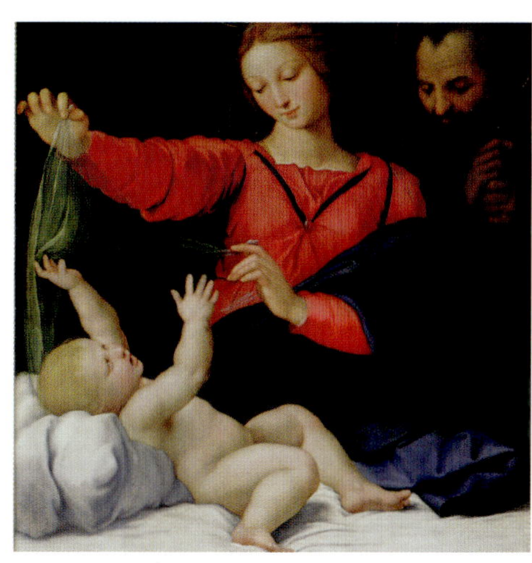

Publisher & Creative Director: Nick Wells
Commissioning Editor: Polly Prior
Senior Project Editor: Catherine Taylor
Copy Editor: Anna Groves
Art Director: Mike Spender
Layout Design: Jane Ashley
Digital Design & Production: Chris Herbert

Special thanks to Dawn Laker, Helen Snaith, Frances Bodiam.

FLAME TREE PUBLISHING
6 Melbray Mews
Fulham, London SW6 3NS
United Kingdom

www.flametreepublishing.com

First published 2020

20 22 24 23 21
1 3 5 7 9 10 8 6 4 2

A copy of the CIP data for this book is available from the British Library.

Image credits: Courtesy of **Bridgeman Images** and the following: 1 & 35 Musee Conde, Chantilly, France; 3 & 119, 120 Villa Farnesina, Rome, Italy; 6 & 45, 32, 46, 57 Galleria degli Uffizi, Florence, Tuscany, Italy; 8 Mondadori Portfolio/Electa/Sergio Anelli; 9l Musee des Beaux-Arts, Caen, France ; 9r & 67 Pinacoteca di Brera, Milan, Italy; 10 & 73, 11, 124 Royal Collection Trust © Her Majesty Queen Elizabeth II, 2019; 12 & 34, 42 & 58, 54, 91, 68 Louvre, Paris, France; 14 & 60 & 76 Galleria Borghese, Rome, Lazio, Italy; 16 & 110, 38, 100, 101, 108, 109, 111 Vatican Museums and Galleries, Vatican City; 17 & 105 Basilica di Sant'Agostino, Rome, Italy; 18 & 78 Rijksmuseum, Amsterdam, The Netherlands; 19 & 90 Pinacoteca Nazionale, Bologna, Emilia-Romagna, Italy; 22 & 53, 27 & 36, 30, 74 & back cover National Gallery, London, UK; 23 & 81, 82, 84, 85, 86, 88, 89 Victoria & Albert Museum, London, UK; 24 Photo © Raffaello Bencini; 26 & 123, 94 & 116, 102, 103, 117, 118, 122, 125 Vatican Museums and Galleries, Vatican City/Photo © Stefano Baldini; 28 & 39, 40 & front cover Gemaeldegalerie Alte Meister, Dresden, Germany/© Staatliche Kunstsammlungen Dresden; 31 Kunsthistorisches Museum, Vienna, Austria ; 41 Palazzo Pitti, Florence, Italy/Photo © Raffaello Bencini; 48, 49, 50, 52, 55 & 128 Palazzo Pitti, Florence, Italy; 51 Palazzo Ducale, Urbino, Italy; 59 Palazzo Barberini, Gallerie Nazionali Barberini Corsini, Rome, Italy; 62 Pinacoteca Tosio Martinengo/ Photo © Luisa Ricciarini; 63 Photo © Luisa Ricciarini ; 64, 65 Rome, Pinacoteca vaticana/Photo © Luisa Ricciarini; 66 National Gallery, London, UK/ Photo © Fine Art Images; 71 Alte Pinakothek, Munich, Germany/Tarker; 75, 80 Prado, Madrid, Spain; 77 , 93 Ashmolean Museum, University of Oxford, UK; 98 Vatican Museums and Galleries, Vatican City/Photo © Luisa Ricciarini; 104, 106, 114 Vatican Museums and Galleries, Vatican City/De Agostini Picture Library/G. Cigolini. Courtesy of **Shutterstock.com** and the following: 7 marcociannarel; 21 Anna Pakutina. Courtesy of **National Gallery of Art, Washington** and the following: 13 & 72, 37 Andrew W. Mellon Collection; 56 Samuel H. Kress Collection; 79 Gift of W.G. Russell Allen. Courtesy of **Wikimedia Commons**: 15 & 96; 25 & 92 Alvesgaspar/CC BY-SA 4.0. Courtesy of **SuperStock** and the following: 4 & 47 Iberfoto; 20 De Agostini Picture Library/G. Cigolini; 33 Peter Barritt; 69 A. Burkatovski/Fine Art Images; 70 4X5 Collection. Courtesy of **akg-images** and the following: 44 Heritage Images/Fine Art Images; 112 Mondadori Portfolio/Archivio Lensini/Fabio E Andrea Lensini.

Raphael
Masterpieces of Art

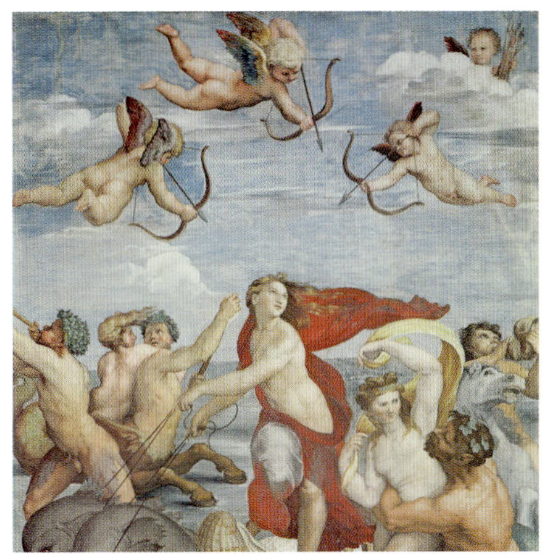

Julia Biggs

FLAME TREE
PUBLISHING

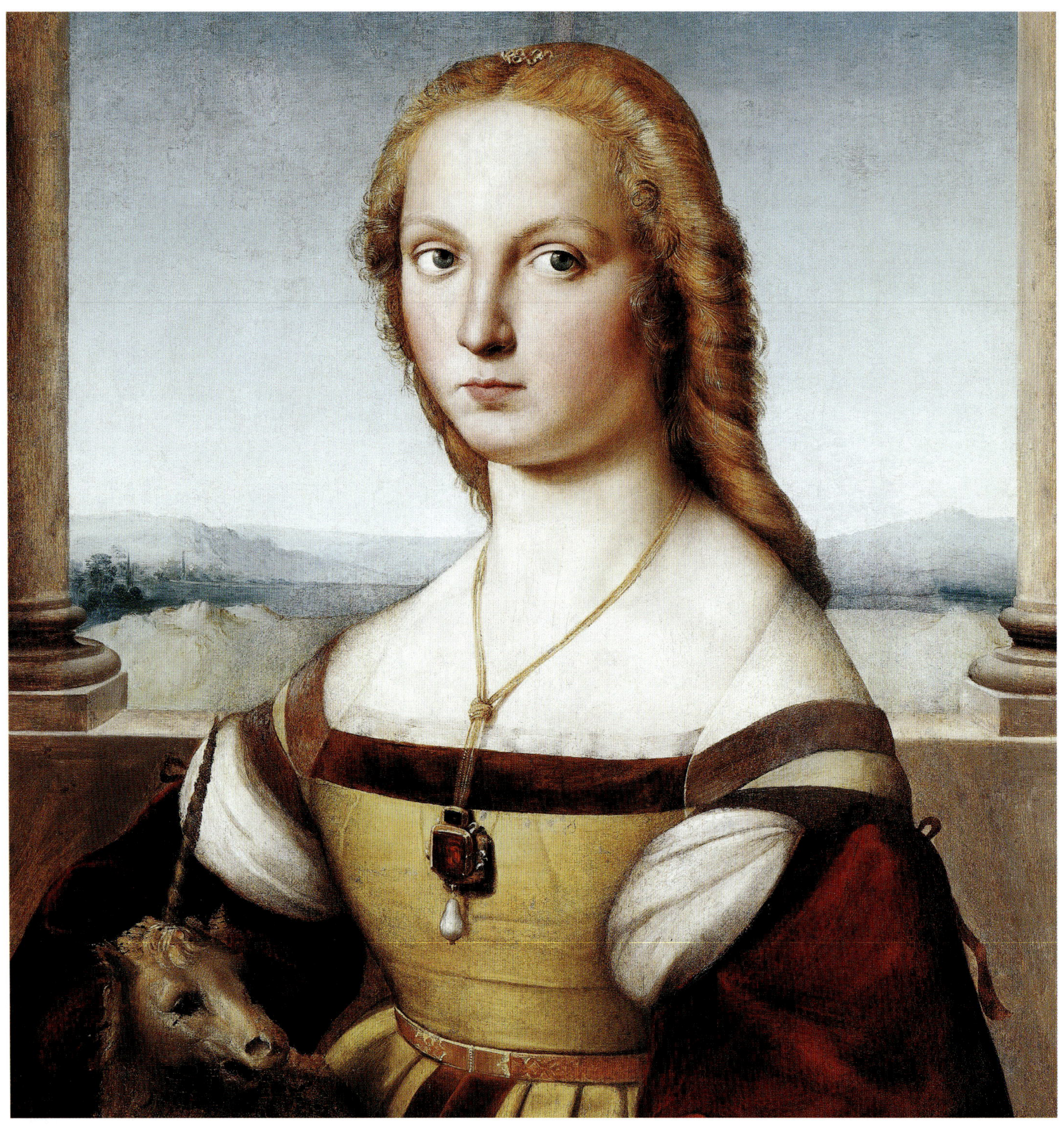

Contents

Raphael: Renaissance Poster Boy

Raffaello Santi or Sanzio (1483–1520), known simply as Raphael, has for centuries been considered one of the greatest artists who ever lived. As part of the supreme trio of Italian High Renaissance artists, along with Leonardo da Vinci (1452–1519) and Michelangelo Buonarroti (1475–1564), Raphael stands at the centre of the story of the development of European culture.

A painter, architect, archaeologist and entrepreneur, Raphael was a trailblazer, whose refined and graceful works acted as devotional aids, love tokens and diplomatic gifts. Legendary for his passionate affairs, good looks, luxurious lifestyle (he counted popes, cardinals, dukes and the literati amongst his friends) and early death, Raphael was also reputedly extraordinarily precocious and determined. This book explores his brilliant career and creativity, mapping his artistic journey from Urbino to Rome via Perugia, Siena and Florence. It reveals how Raphael's self-assurance, talent for friendship, technical prowess and ability to combine the sublime and sensual propelled him to fame.

A Gossipy Biographical Portrait

Much of what we know about Raphael comes from the Florentine painter Giorgio Vasari's (1511–74) groundbreaking tome, *Lives of the Artists*, published in 1550 and revised in 1568. In this work, the first art history book, Vasari coined the term 'Renaissance' (*rinascita*) to describe the cultural rebirth that he thought was happening in Italy, and to explain how some of the glories of antiquity were now being recreated in painting, sculpture and architecture.

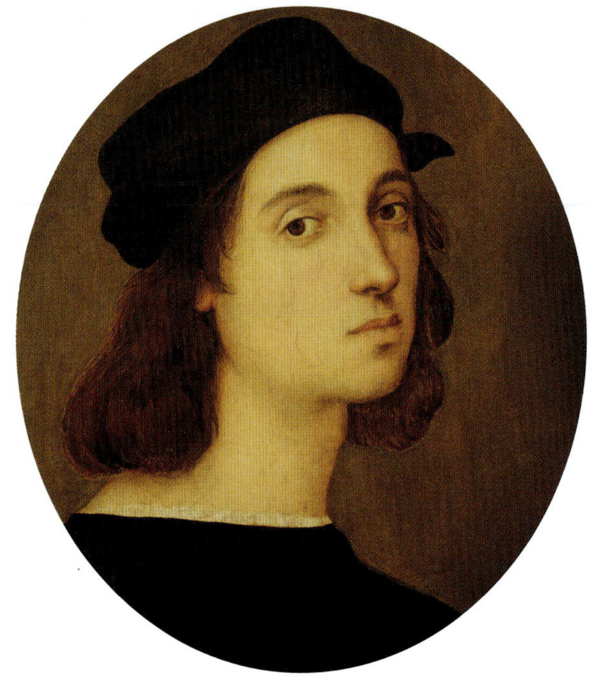

The text is full of professional insight, juicy anecdotes and vivid biographical portraits of major (and minor) artists, including Cimabue (Cenni di Pepo, *c.* 1240–1302), Leonardo, Sandro Botticelli (1445–1510), Titian (Tiziano Vecellio, 1488–1576), Michelangelo and Raphael. Although Vasari is hardly what one would call impartial or disinterested, and despite some inaccuracies and rhetorical overstatement, scholars still turn to him and his biography of Raphael as a primary source for understanding the artist's career, commissions and patrons. Vasari's more or less heroic account of Raphael's life, in which he enthusiastically presents his subject as the epitome of elegance and gentility (Vasari seems to not only want to paint like Raphael, but to be Raphael!), was intended as a parable for young artists. Vasari stresses that Raphael's talent was brought about by hard work and study, and that by learning from his example, others 'may rise superior to disadvantages as Raphael did by his prudence and skill'.

At Home in Urbino

Italy during the Renaissance was not a united country but a ragged
patchwork of city-states: there were republican oligarchies, the
popes and their family clans in Rome and numerous princely courts,
including the small and prosperous duchy of Urbino, where Raphael
was born. This hilltop town was ruled by members of the Montefeltro
family, famous both as mercenary commanders (*condottieri*) and as
discerning art patrons. Federico da Montefeltro (1422–82) had built
an impressive palace (*see* right) based on strict geometric rules, filled
its library with humanist manuscripts, and employed painters such as
Piero della Francesca (*c.* 1415–92) and Justus of Ghent (*c.* 1410–80)
to work for him.

Although Vasari characterized Raphael's father, Giovanni Santi (*c.*
1435–94), as a 'painter of no great talent', he was the head of a
respected and successful workshop in Urbino. He executed paintings
for the court as well as churches in Urbino and neighbouring towns.
Devoted to literary pursuits, including playwriting and poetry, we
know him above all as the author of a rhymed chronicle, dedicated
to Duke Federico da Montefeltro, in which he shows himself to be
a connoisseur of the contemporary art scene. He perceives Andrea
Mantegna (*c.* 1431–1506), Giovanni Bellini (*c.* 1430–1516), Luca
Signorelli (*c.* 1445–1523), Leonardo and Perugino (Pietro Vannucci,
c. 1446–1523) to be the leading masters of his day, but also mentions
the great Netherlandish artists Jan van Eyck (*c.* 1390–1441) and
Rogier van der Weyden (*c.* 1399–1464).

Raphael probably received his earliest lessons in drawing and painting
from his father, and must have watched him at work and instructing his
assistants in the preparation of materials for painting on walls, canvas
and panel. According to Vasari, while still a child Raphael aided his father
in commissions for the state of Urbino. Raphael was 11 when his father
died in 1494 (his mother, Magia di Battista Ciarla, died in 1491), and his
training and experience between this date and 1500 are not documented.
His modern biographers disagree about whether he remained in the
Santi workshop after his father's death, joined Perugino's in Perugia or
Florence, or perhaps spent some time in all three places.

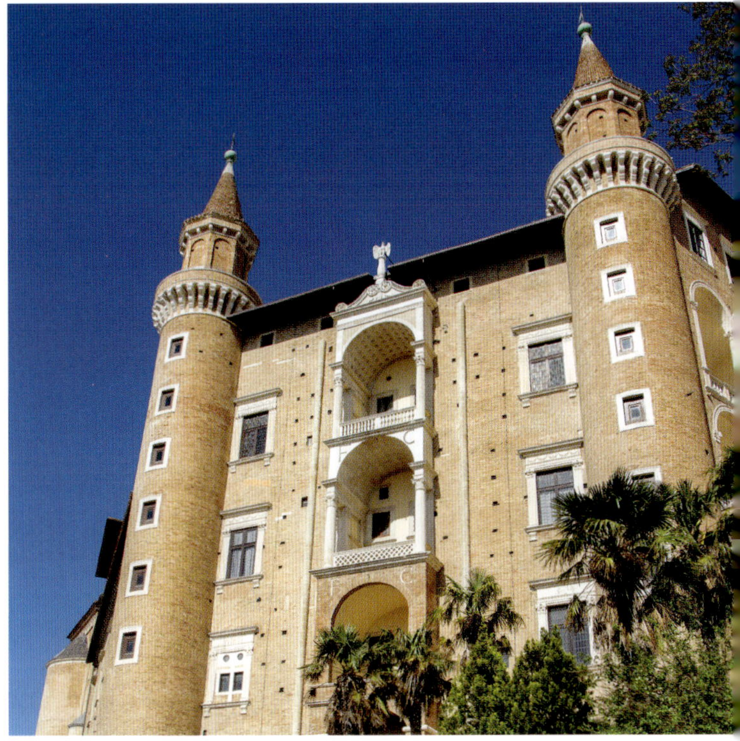

The Young Master

Raphael may have taken over control of his father's workshop in 1500
– an early indication of his artistic and business skills. By the age of
17 he must already have acquired a reputation, since in December
1500 he was described in a contract as a *magister* – a fully qualified
master of a painter's guild. Raphael had received a commission with
Evangelista da Pian di Meleto (*c.* 1460–1549), his father's senior and
loyal assistant, to execute a very large altarpiece of the *Coronation
of Saint Nicholas of Tolentino* (1501, *see* page 62). The work, which
survives only in fragments, was created for the church of Sant'Agostino
in Città di Castello, a small city midway between Urbino and Perugia.
The techniques used in this work are compelling evidence that Raphael
trained in his father's workshop.

Città di Castello's artistic scene was dominated by Signorelli, and his
work made a deep impression on Raphael as he began to undertake
commissions of his own there. Raphael studied Signorelli's altarpieces

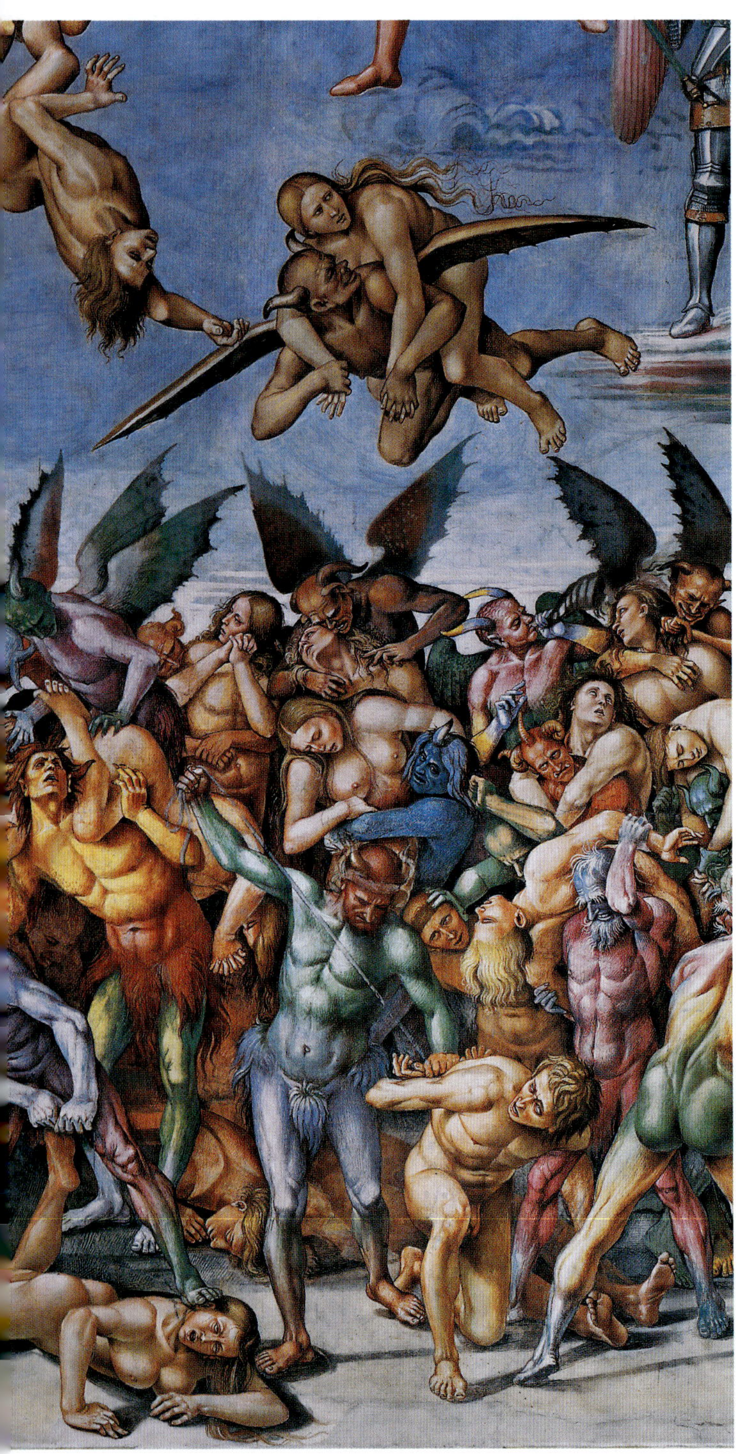

in the city and learned how to paint the male nude in action, giving it vigour and movement. He was also inspired by some of Signorelli's bold foreshortenings, and he visited the artist's dramatic frescoes of the *End of the World* and the *Last Judgement* (1499–1502, *see* left) in the Cappella Nuova of Orvieto Cathedral.

However, Raphael's most significant artistic experience was his association with Perugino, who was one of the most admired and influential painters working in Italy at the turn of the sixteenth century. Perugino was highly successful in commercial terms and fulfilled commissions in Rome for the papal court. His style was praised in his lifetime as exhibiting an 'angelic and very sweet air', and this is likely to have referred both to the facial expressions of his graceful figures and his delicate rendering of atmospheric perspective. Perugino's system of preparing a painting by means of compositional sketches (*schizzi*), drawings from models, detailed studies (*studii*), presentation drawings (*modelli*) and finally full-size drawings (known as cartoons or *cartoni*) and their transfer to the required medium, was one that Raphael followed throughout his career.

Competing with Perugino

Raphael's tactics in his interaction with Perugino were ones he employed again and again. The young painter demonstrated the ability to make contacts with older leading artists and major workshops from whom he could learn. He would develop his skills and assimilate what others could do, not in order to repeat it, but to go beyond it and, as a result, receive prestigious commissions. Raphael's familiarity with Perugino's style and technique is evident from the altarpieces he painted for churches in Umbria, such as *The Mond Crucifixion* (1503, *see* page 66) and the *Coronation of the Virgin* (1502–04, *see* page 64). The latter work, also known as the *Oddi Altarpiece*, was the first project in which Raphael appeared in open competition with Perugino's workshop. It was created for the chapel of the Degli Oddi family in the church of San Francesco al Prato in Perugia. Conforming to the preferences as well as the social and devotional expectations and aspirations of his paymaster (as did all artists eager to please patrons and win commissions in a fierce marketplace), Raphael prepared the altarpiece with laborious precision, creating a number of preliminary drawings.

The textbook comparison of Raphael's and Perugino's interests has always been their two versions of the *Betrothal of the Virgin (Lo Sposalizio)*, and Vasari chose Raphael's 1504 picture (*see* below right and page 67) to show how the younger artist had surpassed Perugino. Painted for the chapel of Saint Joseph in the church of San Francesco in Città di Castello, Raphael's altarpiece obviously depends on Perugino's work (1500–04, *see* right). The repetition of subject was determined not by the artist but by his patron, who may have instructed Raphael to outdo Perugino's image. Such 'better than' clauses were common in contracts. Taking everything and changing everything, Raphael focused on details such as the display of perspective, the grouping of the figures and the more

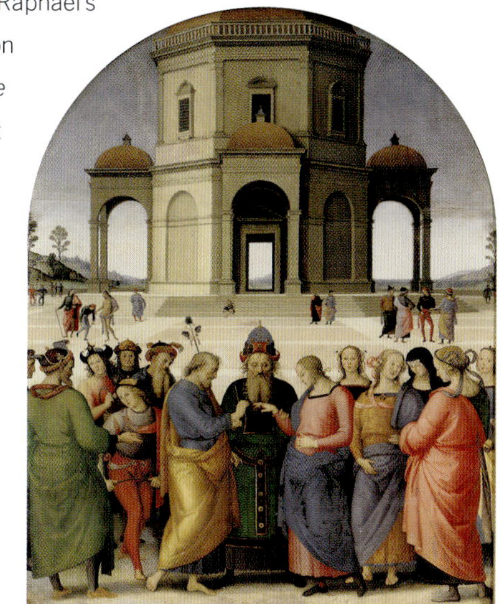
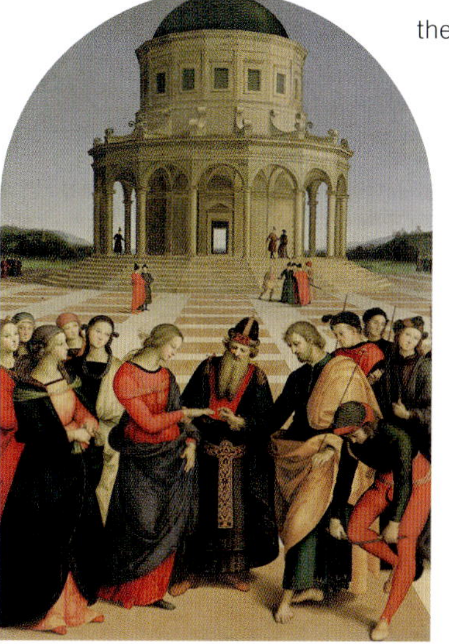

precise physiognomies. Raphael's ostentatious signature, engraved in the cornice of the temple at the very heart of the composition (his earliest surviving work to be both signed and dated), is a conspicuous declaration of authorial pride and indicates professional self-awareness and the recognition that the altarpiece marked a watershed in his career.

A Sensation in Siena

Along with Perugino, Pinturicchio (Bernardino di Betto, *c*. 1454–1513) counted as the most important painter in central Italy. During the 1480s and 1490s he had completed major works in Rome, including frescoes in the Sistine Chapel and the Borgia Apartments of the Vatican Palace. In 1502 Pinturicchio was commissioned to paint the fresco decoration celebrating episodes in the life of Pope Pius II (1405–64) in the new Piccolomini Library (attached to the cathedral in Siena), founded by Cardinal Francesco Piccolomini

(1439–1503), Archbishop of Siena and for a very brief period Pope Pius III. The contract legally bound Pinturicchio to produce all the preparatory drawings and cartoons himself. However, according to Vasari, Pinturicchio, 'being a friend of Raphael and knowing him to be a draughtsman of the finest quality', invited him to Siena to work with him on the frescoes.

Despite being Pinturicchio's junior by almost 30 years, Raphael provided the much more experienced artist with detailed compositional drawings for the project (possibly as many as five), of which two survive. Taking the inventive lead, Raphael cemented his reputation as a prodigy, and his work in Siena was key to his later career in Rome, where, as we shall see, he renewed the contacts he established there with powerful men in the papal court, including Agostino Chigi (1466–1520).

In the Cradle of the Renaissance

At the turn of the sixteenth century Florence was at the height of its artistic supremacy. A hub of humanist scholarship and the seat of a technological and scientific flowering, the rapid pace of creative innovation in the city had been set in the days of Donatello (Donato di Niccolò di Betto Bardi, 1386–1466), Lorenzo Ghiberti (1378–1455), Filippo Brunelleschi (1377–1446) and Leon Battista Alberti (1404–72), with public competitions and theoretical debates.

Armed with a letter of recommendation from Giovanna Feltria della Rovere (1463–1513), sister of Guidobaldo da Montefeltro (1472–1508), Duke of Urbino, to Piero Soderini (1450–1522), head of government of the Florentine Republic, Raphael moved to the Tuscan city at the end of 1504. However, he continued to travel back and forth to Urbino and Perugia to look after his business interests there.

Raphael arrived at a heady moment. Michelangelo's *David* (1501–04) had just been installed in the Piazza della Signoria, and he was working on the cartoon for the *Battle of Cascina* fresco (never completed) for the large council chamber inside the Palazzo Vecchio. In direct competition with him, Leonardo, at the pinnacle of his career, was creating a gigantic painting (now lost) of *The Battle of Anghiari* (1504–05) for the same room in the Palazzo Vecchio. The carefully rendered heroic naked men in Michelangelo's picture, and the violent

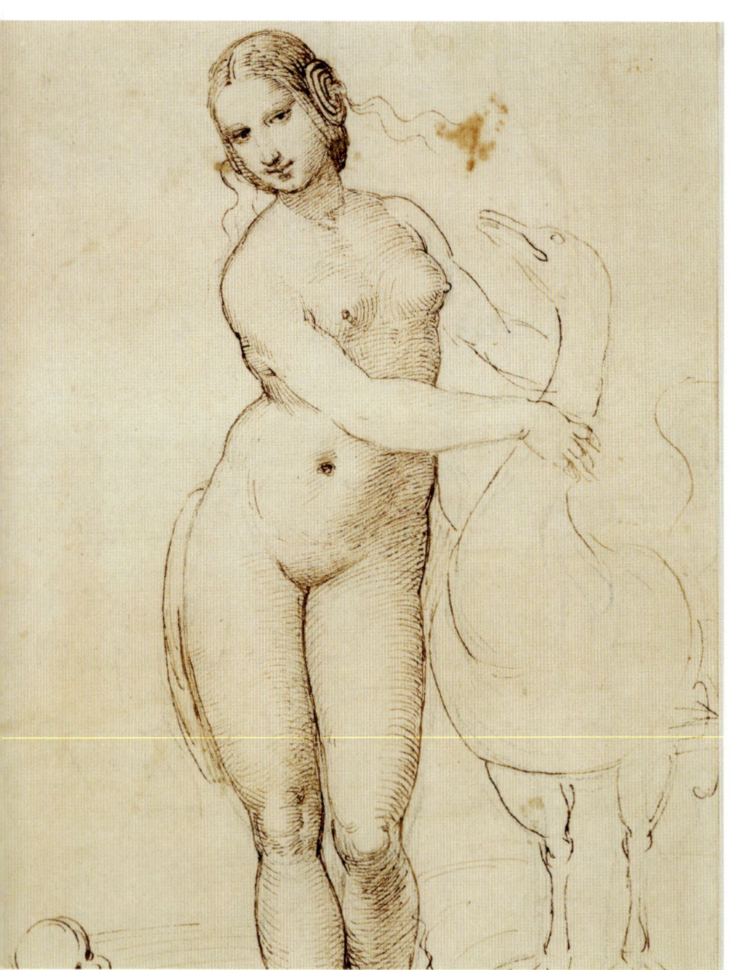

clash of Leonardo's, were unlike anything seen before. Spurred on to familiarize himself with, and master, the new style and requirements of Florentine art, Raphael rigorously scrutinized the depiction of figures in dynamic movement, the expression of intense emotion through facial features and gesture, the effects of light to give forms three dimensions and the construction of complex narrative. His course of study is made clear in his drawings of Michelangelo's *David* (*c.* 1504–05) and Leonardo's lost sinuous *Leda and the Swan* (*c.* 1507, *see* below and page 73), as well as a later series of sketches of fighting nudes (*c.* 1508–10, *see* page 77).

Raphael also studied the works of fifteenth-century artists. Vasari mentions that he looked at 'the old things by Masaccio' (Tommaso di Ser Giovanni di Simone, 1401–28) – above all, the frescoes in the Brancacci Chapel of Santa Maria del Carmine (*c.* 1425–27). Raphael's drawings show that he paid close attention to Donatello's sculptures on the façade of the church of Orsanmichele too.

Florentine Friends

Aligning himself with Florence's vibrant artistic community, Raphael made friends with young painters in the city, such as Bastiano da Sangallo (known as Aristotle, 1481–1551) and Ridolfo Ghirlandaio (1483–1561), and he frequented the studio of the woodcarver, sculptor and architect Baccio d'Agnolo (1462–1543). He was particularly attached to the talented artist and draughtsman Fra Bartolommeo (Baccio della Porta, 1472–1517), who had abandoned art to become a Dominican friar (and a follower of the fiery, charismatic preacher Girolamo Savonarola, 1452–98), and had only just taken it up again as head of the small workshop at the convent of San Marco.

Fra Bartolommeo was deeply influenced by Leonardo, whose spiritual feeling, *sfumato* (the softening of edges and surfaces of forms so that they appear to fuse into one another) and keen response to nature he incorporated into his smoothly harmonious compositions. Fra Bartolommeo in turn inspired the young Raphael. Vasari said Raphael 'associated constantly with him, wishing to paint in the manner of the friar because he liked his management and blending of colours'. Learning from the purity and simplicity of lines and forms in Fra Bartolommeo's paintings and drawings, Raphael may well have seen his friend as a 'middle way' between the inventions and artistic achievements of Leonardo and Michelangelo.

Drawing: Ambition and Experimentation

Drawing drove Raphael's creativity. He used drawing as a means of observation and as a mode of experimentation (numerous sheets of paper show the artist testing and brainstorming). Raphael's drawings include rapid preliminary sketches (studies of individual figures and figure groups, as well as smaller details such as heads, hands, feet, drapery, architecture and landscape), and more finished compositional drawings. He never wasted any of his creations, as he would generate new contexts for his discarded preparatory studies and rework or cut out motifs to replace them with others.

Frequently, Raphael would make a cartoon of a finalized design by pricking the outlines of the composition with a needle to transfer it to the working surface by pouncing charcoal dust through the holes (*spolvero*). These types of drawings provided artists, copyists and artisans with the possibility of efficiently producing multiples of designs. Once the images had been transferred, Raphael would add some freehand additions to the underdrawing. In larger works, he used a grid to scale up a squared design.

Raphael's early cartoon practice was often close to that of Perugino. His cartoons for easel paintings from before his arrival in Florence and shortly thereafter were small and drawn rather schematically in pen and brown ink. A major turning point in his approach to drawing cartoons was his encounter with Leonardo, who explored the potential uses of centring marks, axis lines, plumb lines and framing outlines. This body of marks became ubiquitous in Raphael's underdrawings and pricked drawings, as he calculated the geometry of form and its visual effect. Alongside this methodical process, Raphael developed his virtuosity in handling every Renaissance drawing technique, from metal point to pen and ink and black and red chalk, but by far the largest proportion of his known Florentine drawings are in pen. There is

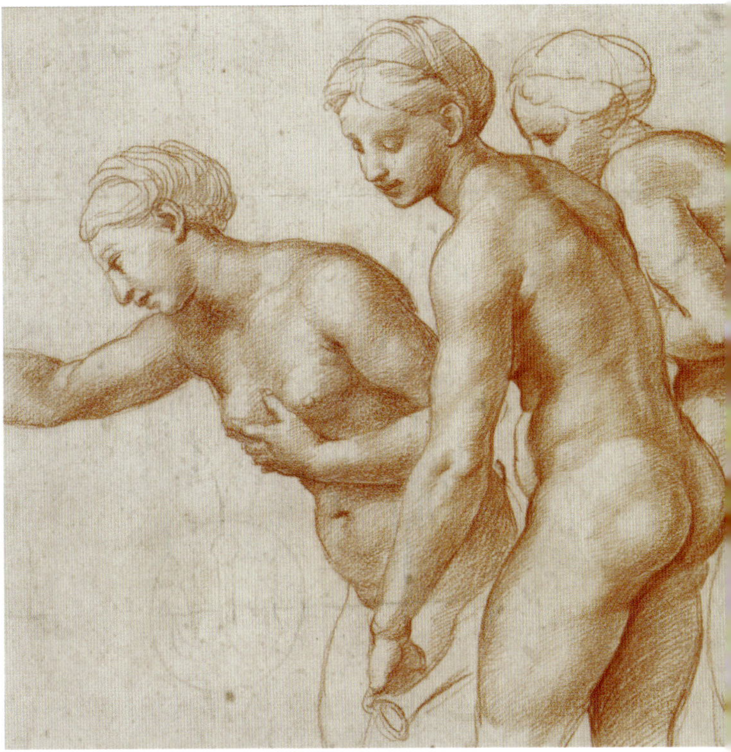

a real sense of energy about many of these drawings, as Raphael raced at his studies with growing confidence, forging his artistic identity and acquiring an increasingly sophisticated graphic language.

Multiple Madonnas

The painting of small devotional pictures of the Madonna and Child, suitable for private contemplation in the home, became the proverbial 'bread and butter' supporting Raphael's career in Florence between 1504 and 1508. (He is known to have painted at least 17 Madonna images during this period.) In great demand in the city from the fifteenth century, panels depicting the Madonna and Child were also popular wedding gifts and they attracted collectors as well.

Combining the humanly sympathetic (tender sentiment) with the appropriately divine, Raphael depicted the Madonna in every possible combination with other holy figures, playing with new compositional forms as he absorbed the lessons of Leonardo. For example, in the tiny *Madonna of the Pinks* (*c.* 1506–07, *see* page 33), Raphael closely followed Leonardo's Benois Madonna (1478). Similarly, in the *Madonna of the Meadow* (1505–06, *see* page 31) and *La Belle Jardinière* (1507, *see* below and page 34), depicting the Madonna and Child with the infant Saint John the Baptist (and one of the most ambitious of the Madonnas he painted in Florence), Raphael borrowed enthusiastically from works by Leonardo. In particular, he employed Leonardo's pyramidal structure or grouping of figures. Fundamental for Raphael was a famous (lost) cartoon by Leonardo showing the Madonna and Child with Saint Anne, which had drawn huge crowds when it was publicly displayed at the

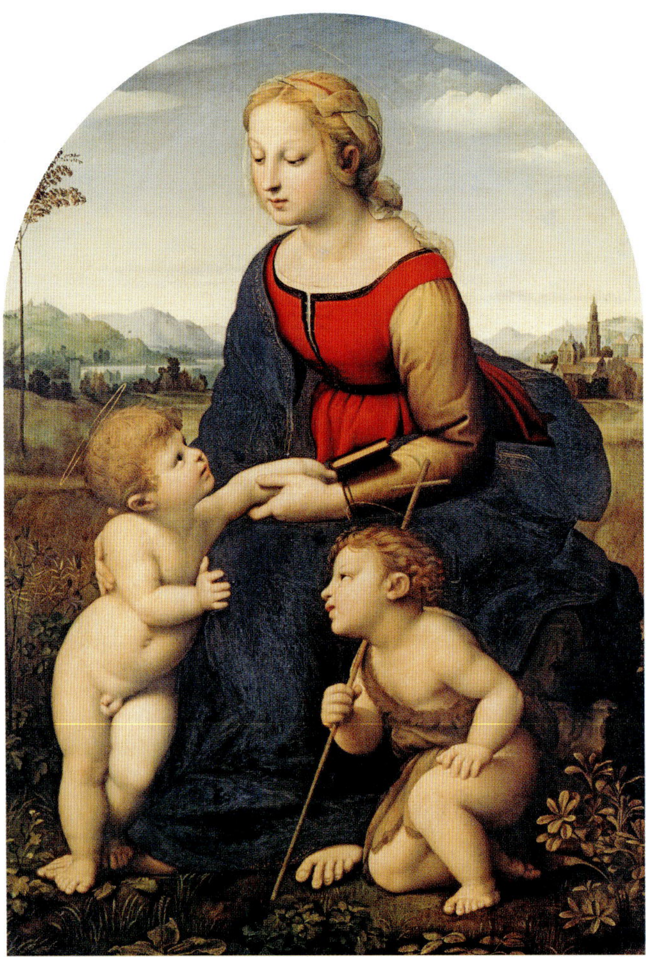

church of Santissima Annunziata in 1501. Vasari describes how the composition 'left Raphael amazed and entranced'. It seems likely that Raphael's emulation and absorption of Leonardo's innovations, motifs and *chiaroscuro* techniques of modelling (contrasting areas of light and shade) were based on some direct access not only to Leonardo's most recent preparatory drawings or cartoons, but also to his notes and research materials for his intended painting treatise, the *Trattato della Pittura*, posthumously issued in 1651 in Italian and French.

Raphael's Madonnas rapidly gained him access to Florence's wealthiest and most influential families. He executed paintings for Domenico Canigiani (1486–1548), the prominent merchant Taddeo Taddei (1470–1528), and for the marriage of his friend Lorenzo Nasi (1485–1547) he made the *Madonna of the Goldfinch* (or the *Madonna del Cardellino*, *c.* 1505–06, *see* page 32). However, for the prosperous cloth merchant Agnolo Doni (1474–1539) and his young wife, noblewoman Maddalena Strozzi (1489–1540), Raphael produced a pair of portraits (1506, *see* pages 48 and 49), which have their roots in Netherlandish models and Leonardo's *Mona Lisa* (*c.* 1503–05).

Painting Techniques

The way Raphael applied paint in his early works originated from the mid-fifteenth-century Central Italian tradition. His paintings were worked up gradually and evenly, and he applied colour in several layers rather than by mixing. He usually covered the larger and substantial areas, such as the sky and background, with a single layer of oils, applied with broadly horizontal strokes that often left a slightly textured surface. In contrast, the draperies in Raphael's pictures tend to be more thickly painted, because specific colour and saturation effects were sought, or the use of particular pigments dictated a multi-layered technique. In this period, Raphael commonly applied a final layer of modelling to draperies by using dark, hatched brushstrokes to reinforce an area of shadow, and he would add a layer of glazing to enhance brilliance. Flesh paints (including a faintly greenish-brown underpaint) were applied in thin layers, and Raphael's method closely followed the way in which the Perugino workshop painted. This had its basis in the technique practised by Andrea del Verrocchio (*c.*

1435–88) and his followers, and it can also be seen in the works of Fra
Bartolommeo and in other Florentine paintings.

Whether in his Madonnas or his other smaller works made for the court
at Urbino (such as his *Saint George and the Dragon*, c. 1506, *see* right
and page 72), Raphael attempted to bring together Umbrian painting
(with its rich colours and idealized faces) and Tuscan art (famous for
its naturalism and classicism).

From Leonardo to Michelangelo

Raphael's painting *The Deposition* (or *The Entombment*, 1507, *see*
overleaf and page 76) represents a critical moment in his development.
He moved from taking compositional formulas wholesale from
Leonardo to selectively appropriating ideas from Michelangelo. *The
Deposition* was Raphael's first major commission since his move to
Florence, that is, his first altarpiece. The patron was not Florentine,
however, but from Perugia. Atalanta Baglioni commissioned the
painting in memory of her son Grifone, killed in 1500 in a family feud.
Vasari says that in composing this picture 'Raphael imagined to himself
the sorrow harboured by the nearest and dearest relatives when
carrying the body of a loved one – one in whom truly the wellbeing
and reputation and functioning of an entire family had consisted'.
Vasari's account is sweet but unverifiable. We do not know how much
Raphael empathized with the family events he was commemorating
in the Baglioni chapel in San Francesco al Prato, and the only
existing correspondence between the patron and artist is a note about
remuneration – a complaint from Raphael that payment for his work
was overdue.

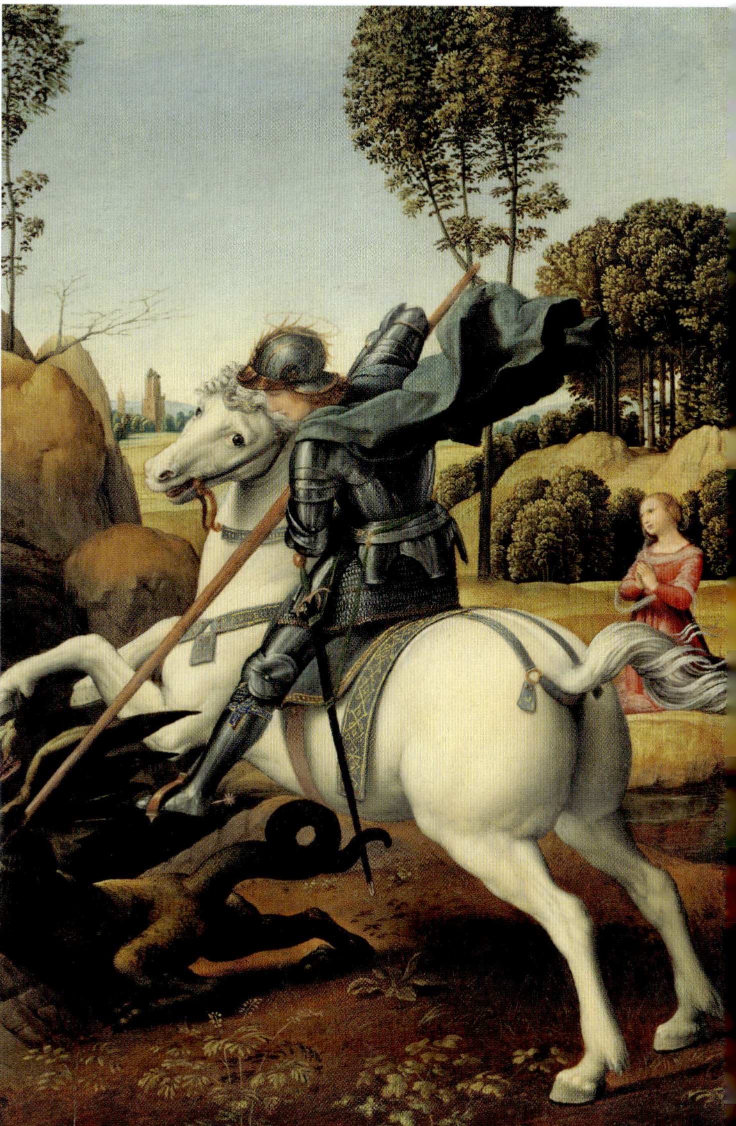

Raphael's serious approach to this prestigious assignment is
demonstrated in the large number of surviving preparatory studies
(early sketches reflect the static assembly of figures in Perugino's
1495 *Lamentation over the Dead Christ*), the complex creation
of a dramatic design and subject, and the quality of the finished
altarpiece. Raphael followed Alberti's guidelines for narrative painting
contained in his 1435 handbook *De Pictura* (*On Painting*), and he
drew inspiration from prints by Mantegna and an ancient sarcophagus

relief depicting the dead hero Meleager being carried away for burial.
However, the altarpiece is almost a manifesto of Raphael's admiration
for Michelangelo. The kneeling young woman on the right who twists
round was inspired by Michelangelo's *Doni Tondo* (1505–06); Joseph
of Arimathea was based on Michelangelo's unfinished statue of *Saint
Matthew* (c. 1506); and the pose Raphael selected for the dead Christ,
with his arm hanging down, is very close to Michelangelo's *Pietà*

(1498–99) in Saint Peter's Basilica in Rome. The altarpiece attests to Raphael's skill and ingenuity in creating such a moving image, but it also denotes his transition from Leonardo to Michelangelo, from Florence to Rome.

Arrival in Rome

The papal court in Rome was the most powerful and prestigious centre of artistic patronage in the land, where leading theologians rubbed shoulders with outstanding humanists and the most learned scholars of the arts and Classical antiquity. In 1508, Raphael was summoned to this intellectual and cultural powerhouse by Pope Julius II (Giuliano della Rovere, 1443–1513), a lover of war, who led his own armies, and a lover of art, who had launched a campaign to redecorate the new papal apartments known as the *Stanze* in the Vatican Palace. The Pope's original idea may have been to assign the whole task to Perugino, but when the ageing master refused such a huge commission, other painters from far and wide were brought in to help.

Vasari reports that Raphael was recommended to the Pope by Donato Bramante (1444–1514), one of the most influential architects in Rome and, like Raphael, from Urbino. However, Julius could also have learned of the painter through the Della Rovere family members based at Urbino. Whatever the case, Raphael's name was not completely unknown in Rome, where some of the artists he had previously collaborated with were also recipients of papal commissions.

As painter to the papal court, Raphael had, quite literally, arrived. It was here that he would achieve celebrity status, serving successive popes as they sought to bolster their power and authority and illustrate the spiritual and temporal mission of their pontificates.

A Magisterial Creative Outpouring

For Raphael, inexperienced in large-scale, multi-figured decorations and in the technique of wall-painting, the Vatican commission presented a considerable challenge. He started work in the

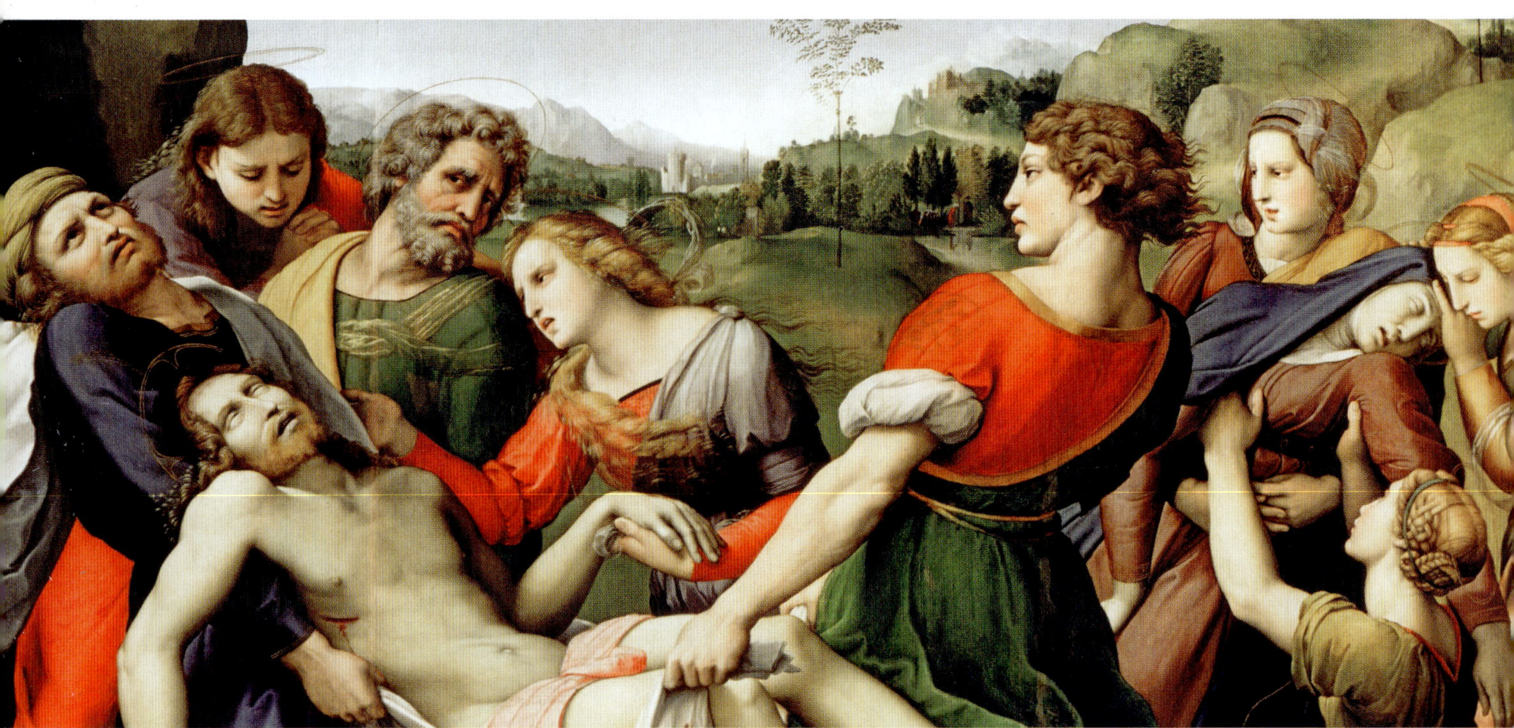

central room, the Stanza della Segnatura (1509–11), originally the Pope's library, making use of his colleagues' assistants. Below personifications of the four 'faculties' or branches of learning (Theology, Poetry, Philosophy and Jurisprudence) in the vault, Raphael began painting the *Disputa* fresco, in which theologians debate the mystery of the Holy Sacrament (*see* right and page 96). Distinguished by its elegant compositional partitioning of earthly and heavenly zones, the figures of the *Disputa* were chiefly inspired by the works of Leonardo and Fra Bartolommeo. Vasari claimed that on seeing this first fresco, the Pope was so overawed that he dismissed the other artists, had their works destroyed and entrusted Raphael exclusively with the decoration of the *Stanze*, but this view is no longer plausible. Raphael's success and complete control over the apartments actually grew far more gradually.

On the north wall, Raphael depicted poets gathered around Apollo and the Muses on Mount Parnassus, a famous Greek mountain above the city of Delphi (*see* page 98). He combined likenesses of his contemporaries, such as Ludovico Ariosto (1474–1533), with imaginary portraits of significant ancient poets and the figures of of Dante Alighieri (1265–1321), Petrarch (Francesco Petrarca, 1304–74) and Giovanni Boccaccio (1313–75). To the south, beneath Jurisprudence (in the guise of Justice), are the three other cardinal virtues: Fortitude, Prudence and Temperance (*see* page 104).

The most celebrated of all the frescoes is *The School of Athens* (*see* page 100), in which a group of philosophers and sages surround Plato (*c.* 427–*c.* 347 BC), pointing up to a higher and eternal reality, and Aristotle (384–322 BC), gesturing downwards, because in his philosophy the only reality is the one that we can see and experience by sight and touch (*see* page 101). The impressive grandeur of the architecture in this work (evident in the perspectival foreshortenings of the coffered barrel-vaulted ceilings) no doubt reflects Bramante's plan for St Peter's, and the balding architect himself appears as Euclid (*c. 325–c.* 265 BC), explaining the laws of geometry to his pupils (*see* page 103).

Raphael's extraordinary artistic evolution is on full display in this influential cycle of monumental narrative paintings: the brushstroke is

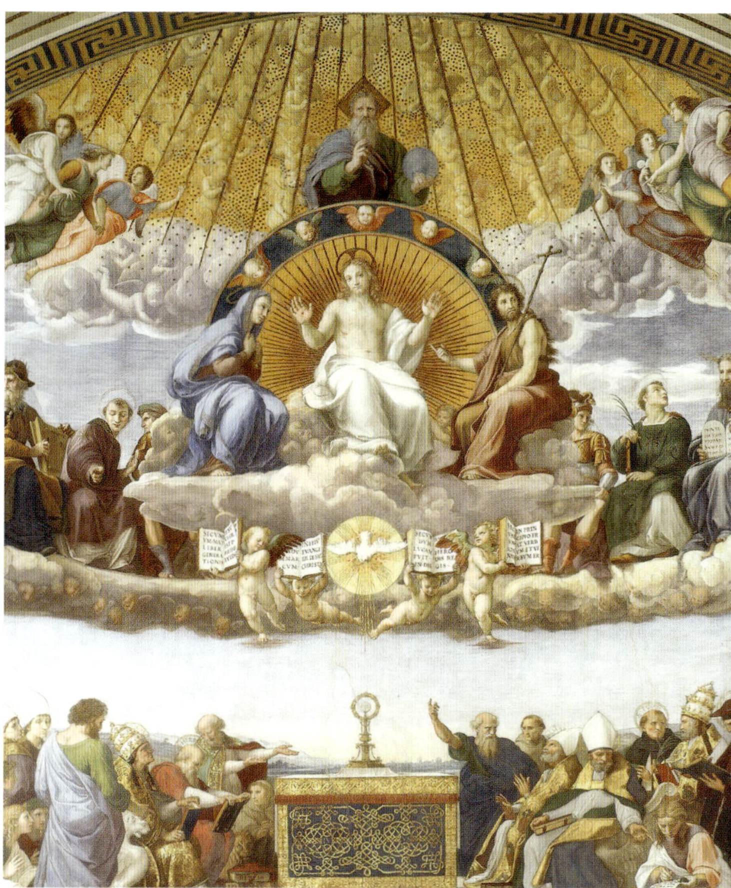

confident, the figures weighty, the palette harmonious and the system of design unambiguous, enlivened by sparkling details.

Painting Political Concerns

Raphael's work in the papal apartments continued with the decoration of the room that came to be known as the Stanza di Eliodoro (1512–14), an audience chamber. Here the Pope wanted his immediate political anxieties expressed – the liberation of northern Italian territories from French occupation was essential to save the papacy. Julius was also threatened by a hostile faction of cardinals demanding the convocation of a Church Council. Raphael was therefore commissioned to paint episodes from the second book of Maccabees, the Acts of the Apostles and relatively recent Church history, united

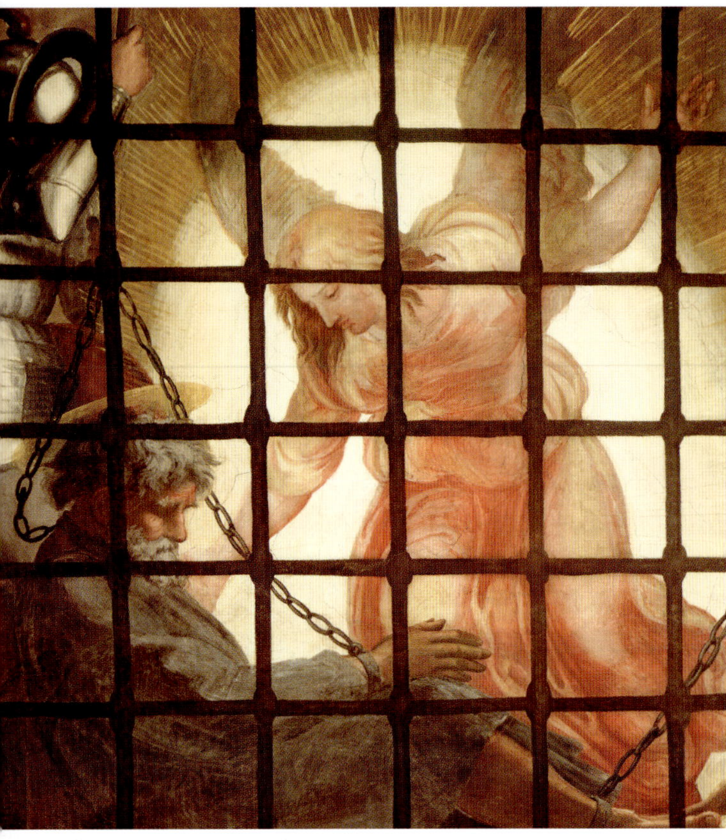

by the common theme of God coming to the aid of His people even in seemingly hopeless situations. Into the paintings, the bearded Pope and his court were inserted, as participants or witnesses.

The first three frescoes, probably completed before Julius's death in February 1513, seem to have been executed in the following order: *The Expulsion of Heliodorus from the Temple* (*see* page 106); *The Mass at Bolsena* (*see* page 108), singled out for special praise by Vasari on account of his belief in Raphael's ability to force the viewer to feel what the figures portrayed are feeling; and *The Liberation of St Peter* (*see* above and pages 109 and 110). Raphael used fewer and larger figures in these scenes than in the Stanza della Segnatura, but the key aspect in his stylistic progression here is the breakthrough to a different role for colour and light. This is most obviously the case in the dramatic, visionary and highly charged *Liberation of St Peter*.

Adopting lime-based glazes to suggest the dense atmosphere of the night air, Raphael represented the various effects of moonlight, the divine light of an angel, the smoke of a torch and light striking metal. This innovation raises the issue of Raphael's familiarity with (or direct knowledge of) contemporary Venetian painting, resulting from a possible visit made by the artist to Venice.

The Stanza di Eliodoro was finished under Julius II's successor, Pope Leo X (Giovanni de' Medici, 1475–1521), whose features appear in the tumultuous *Meeting of Leo the Great and Attila* (*see* page 111). Under his patronage, Raphael would be called upon to exert all his powers of invention and originality.

Rivals

Raphael thrived on the competitive rivalry that existed among so many artists working alongside each other at the papal court, with Vasari attributing his transformation and grander style to the study of antiquity and Michelangelo's Roman works. Raphael and Michelangelo had come to know each other in Florence, and there is evidence that the relationship was cordial, at least in the beginning. These two artists could not have been more different: Raphael was gentle, courteous, diplomatic and obliging; Michelangelo, the opposite – difficult, melancholic, neurotic and prone to violence. Raphael always appeared elegant. Michelangelo, Vasari tells us, cared nothing for his appearance and slept in his boots.

Michelangelo had preceded Raphael to Rome, and in 1508 had embarked upon painting the Sistine Chapel ceiling. By the time he completed it (1512), Raphael had concluded his work in the Stanza della Segnatura and on most of the Stanza di Eliodoro cycle. However, much to Michelangelo's annoyance, Raphael had managed, with Bramante, to creep into the Sistine Chapel for a sneak preview. It had a great effect on Raphael's subsequent paintings, as is clear from his *Prophet Isaiah* fresco (1512, *see* opposite and page 105) in the church of Sant'Agostino in Rome, and his insertion of the figure of Heraclitus (*c.* 535–475 BC), a portrait of Michelangelo, represented in Michelangelo's figure style, into his completed *School of Athens* fresco (*see* page 102).

Michelangelo complained that everything Raphael had in art 'he had from me', but even Vasari, who viewed Michelangelo as 'divine', noted that Raphael's friends 'maintained that his works were more strictly in accordance with the rules of art than Michelangelo, affirming that they were graceful in colouring, of beautiful invention, admirable in expression, and of characteristic design; while those of Michelangelo, it was averred, had none of those qualities with the exception of the design. For these reasons, Raphael was judged, by those who thus opined, to be fully equal, if not superior, to Michelangelo in painting generally, and … decidedly superior to him regarding colouring in particular.'

Learning and stealing from each other, and working in opposition to each other, the artistic personas of Raphael and Michelangelo developed along distinct lines, but together they are credited as fathers of a new, monumental and psychologically incisive approach to art – the High Renaissance. This was the period in which the creative aims and goals of the Renaissance arguably reached their greatest application.

Expansion Plans: The Artist's Workshop

Following the enhancement of his reputation due to his work in the Stanza della Segnatura, Raphael accommodated all the demands placed upon him by gradually taking on a widening circle of talented assistants and establishing an efficient workshop. (It is difficult to say where it was located, but after 1517 Raphael was living in the Palazzo Caprini, so he is likely to have had his studio there as well.) Although the workshop expanded and contracted depending on the work at hand, there seems to have been a variety of casual affiliations. Specialists and independent mature artists such as Giovanni da Udine (also known as Giovanni Nanni, 1487–1564) worked there as collaborators, alongside Raphael's permanent colleagues, referred to collectively as *garzoni* (also known as 'Raphael's boys'). Raphael's two principal assistants and pupils were Gianfrancesco Penni (*c.* 1496–1528) and Giulio Romano (Giulio Pippi, *c.* 1499–1546, whose fresco *The Battle of Ostia* is shown here), who entered his studio at a young age and worked with him continuously thereafter.

Raphael used his assistants to copy rough sketches, keep records of drawings and make life studies (a novel departure in workshop practice). These workshop drawings show the skill of Raphael's assistants at imitating his formal vocabulary – it is often impossible to differentiate them from Raphael's own sheets. Depending on the prestige or complexity of a commission, Raphael also delegated the work of preparation and execution. Reducing his personal contribution

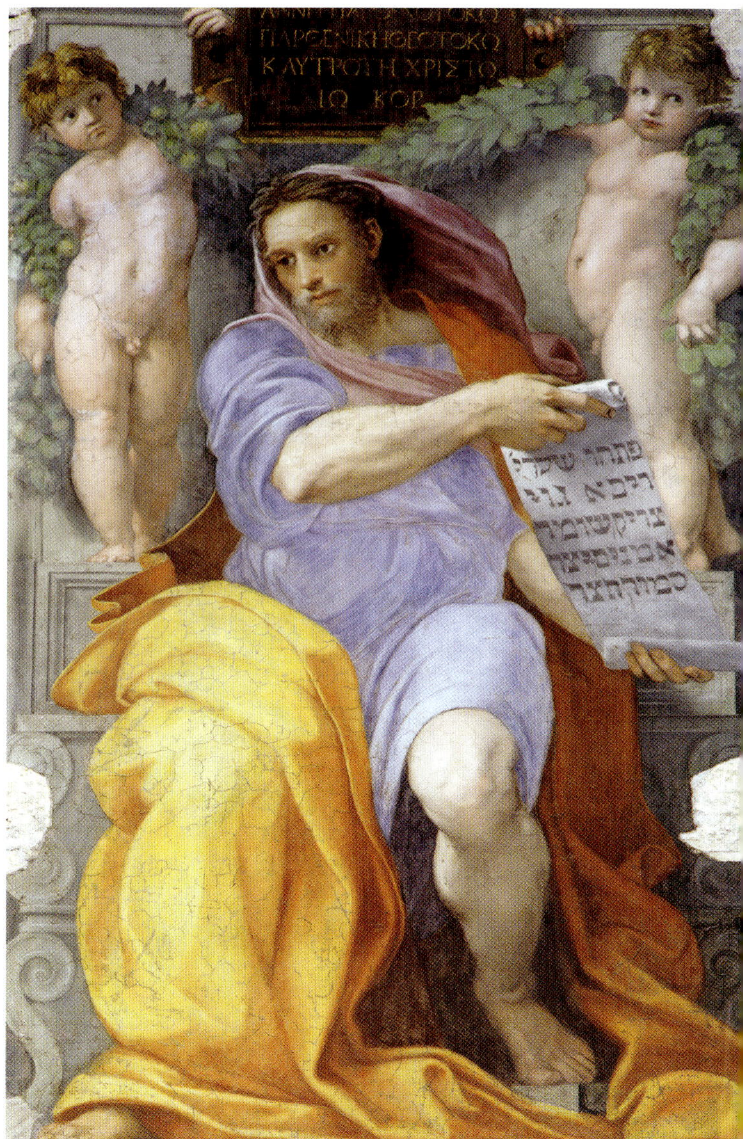

to concentrate on invention, management and supervision, he turned his studio into a large-scale enterprise, something that could almost be called a firm. According to Vasari, 50 painters followed Raphael daily to the papal court! Raphael's name on a work of art was often now a seal of his approval, rather than an autograph.

Engravings and Prints

Raphael's reputation continued to grow and his fortune increased, in part due to the prints made after his designs which began to appear in his early years in Rome as a result of his collaboration with the Bolognese engraver Marcantonio Raimondi (*c.* 1480–*c.* 1534). Raimondi had made his name in Venice as an exact imitator,

and on occasion forger, of Albrecht Dürer's (1471–1528) prints. He has long been considered the leading figure in a print revolution that transformed the visual arts in the Renaissance. Harnessing the technical achievements of copperplate engraving and the printing press – two modern inventions only about 50 years old at the time – he was instrumental in driving a proliferation of images.

Raphael mainly gave Raimondi drawings related to his painted projects, but some of Raimondi's more spectacular plates – for example, the carefully choreographed *Massacre of the Innocents* (*c.* 1515, *see* below and page 78) and *Il Morbetto* (or *The Plague*, *c.* 1515–16, *see* page 79) – were likely made from drawings especially intended for the purpose.

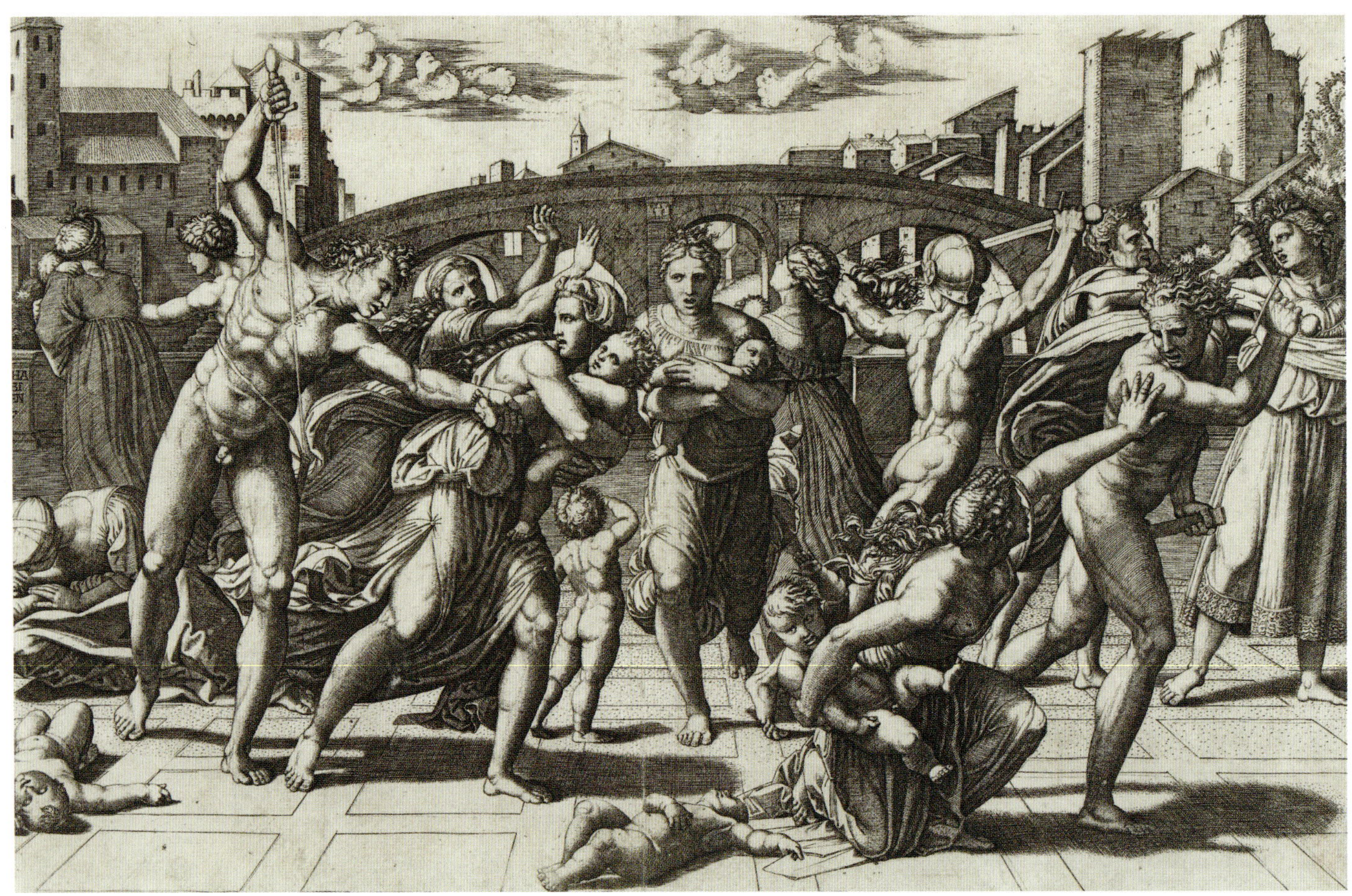

Raimondi was translating some of Raphael's designs into engravings at a time when relatively few artists worked with print media, as it required the co-operation of several participants (including the artist themselves, an engraver and a *stampatore* who was entrusted with the printing) and significant financial investment (copperplates were very expensive). To moderate the costs, artists usually joined forces with one or more publishers. According to Vasari, Raphael appointed one of his apprentices to supervise the printing and sale of prints produced after his designs. Raimondi's engravings placed art in the hands of new audiences, broadening the circulation of Raphael's art far beyond the palaces and churches of Rome.

More Madonnas and a Musical Altarpiece

Throughout the period he was working in the Vatican, Raphael also managed to complete other commissions, including two small, circular devotional images – *The Alba Madonna* (*c.* 1510, *see* page 37) and the *Madonna della Sedia* (or Seggiola, *c.* 1513–14, *see* page 41) – and major altarpieces such as the *Madonna di Foligno* (*c.* 1511–12, *see* page 38), with its cloud cherubs, painted for the church of Santa Maria in Aracoeli in Rome. Around the same time, Raphael created probably the most famous of all his altarpieces, the visionary *Sistine Madonna* (*c.* 1512–13, *see* page 39), for the church of San Sisto in Piacenza. In this work, the Madonna and Child seem to float forwards out of the painting, while two bored-looking cherubs at the bottom of the picture help to bridge the gap between this world and the next (*see* page 40).

Another of Raphael's outstanding paintings is *The Ecstasy of St Cecilia* altarpiece (*c.* 1518, *see* right and page 90), commissioned by Antonio Pucci (1485–1544), Bishop of Pistoia, for a chapel in the church of San Giovanni in Monte, in Bologna, belonging to Elena Duglioli dall'Olio (1472–1520). The latter, revered by her contemporaries for her devotion to a chaste and saintly life in emulation of Cecilia, was famed for her frequent visions. In Raphael's painting the enraptured Cecilia (flanked by saints partly chosen for their attitude to chastity) is shown with her eyes turned towards heaven, as if listening to celestial voices. Vasari quotes a verse that had been dedicated to the work: 'Others merely paint with colours, in Cecilia's face Raphael reveals her soul.' Contemporary texts

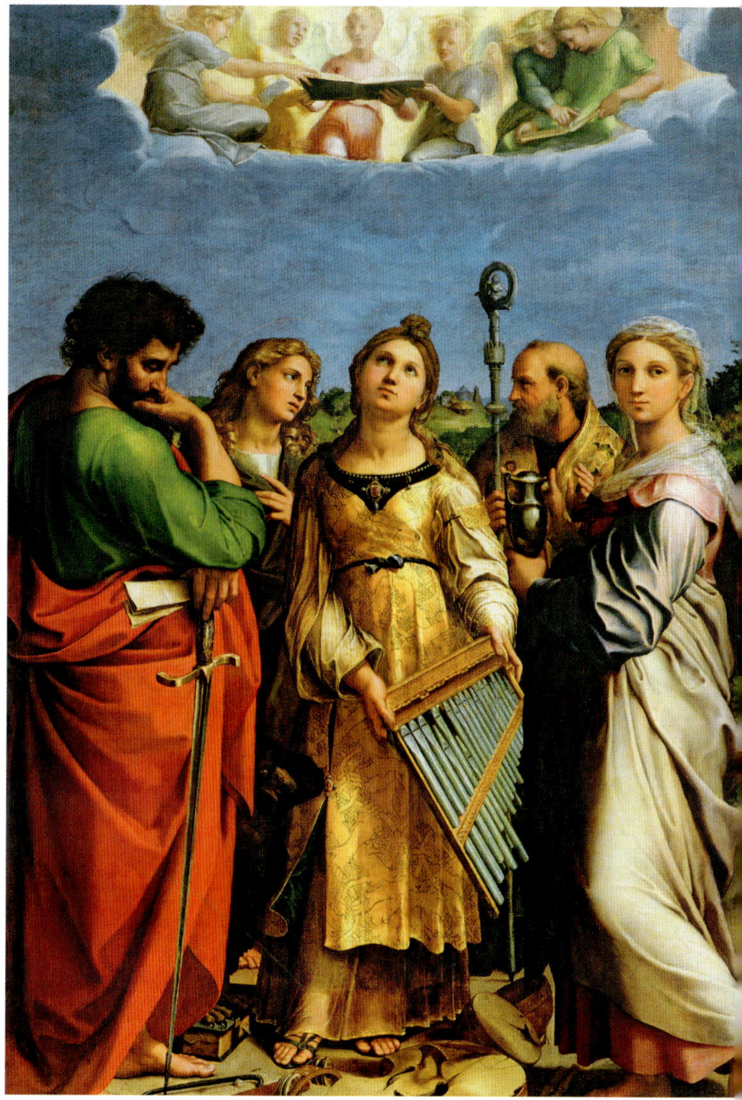

suggest Raphael himself had enjoyed a form of imaginative inspiration in painting the work – an idea probably sparked by the altarpiece's association with Elena, who claimed she could hear heavenly music in front of the picture. Stylistically, the image signals a transition. The twisting form of Mary Magdalene and Cecilia's beatific face anticipate Mannerist features (that date from the 1520s to 1600). The altarpiece also prefigures Baroque representations of self-absorbed, ecstatic visions, especially those by the Bolognese painter Guido Reni (1575–1642).

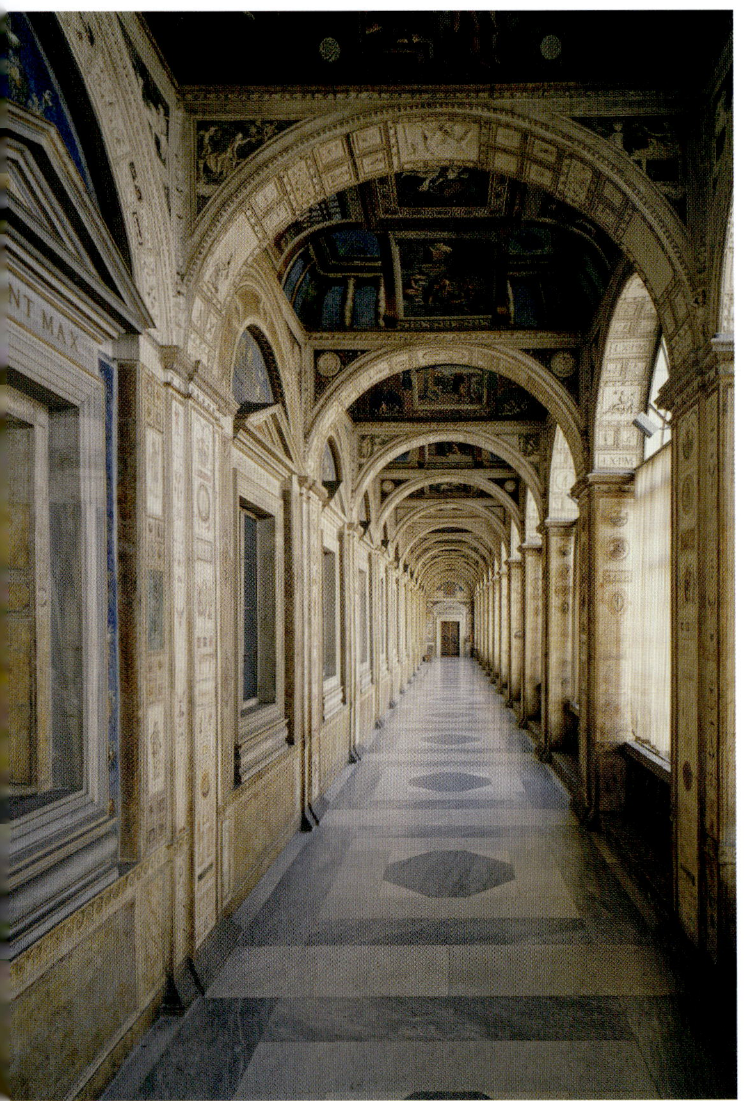

arts, letters and sciences, Leo's election as pope was enormously important for Raphael.

Having known Michelangelo from boyhood, Pope Leo might have been expected to lavish favours on him. Instead his patronage went to Raphael. Although Leo referred to Michelangelo as a brother, he is also reported to have said of the artist, 'He is terrifying, one can't get on with him.' It is no surprise, therefore, that under Leo, Raphael and his workshop enjoyed a virtual monopoly on the best artistic and architectural commissions of the day, including the painting of the Vatican's Stanza dell'Incendio di Borgo (1514–17). While Raphael may have begun with the best intention of painting the room himself, he subsequently became sidetracked and much of the work on the four frescoes, which reassert the authority of the papacy (and depict stories of earlier popes with the name Leo), was completed by studio assistants following his designs. The scene of the *Fire in the Borgo* (*see* page 116), however, with its accurate representation of the appearance and groupings of Classical monuments, appears to have been entirely prepared and in all important parts painted by Raphael.

To help him execute another commission quickly for Leo X, Raphael turned to his workshop to decorate the pope's *Loggia* (1518–19, *see* left), a covered open-air walkway with views out over Rome. Raphael restricted himself to furnishing the preparatory designs and to supervising the completion of the project, consisting of 13 vaults containing 52 biblical episodes (predominantly from the Old Testament). Known as *Raphael's Bible*, the elaborate decorations include stucco reliefs and frescoed humans and animals (grotesques) inspired by the paintings in the Emperor Nero's *Golden House* (the *Domus Aurea*, AD 65–68).

Working for a Medici Pope

Pope Leo X, son of Lorenzo de' Medici (called the Magnificent, 1449–92), was notorious for his love of banquets, dancing and theatrical and musical performances. He was also, unfortunately, a poor leader and an even poorer steward of the papal treasury, which he emptied in just two years. He allegedly declared, 'Since God has given us the papacy, let us enjoy it.' However, as a significant promoter of the

Money and Mythology

The only person other than the Pope who managed to engage Raphael to carry out large commissions was the Sienese banking tycoon Agostino Chigi (1466–1520). His pleasure villa on the banks of the Tiber (now called the Villa Farnesina), where he famously held decadent dinner parties, testifies to the scale of his ambition. Raphael's first painting for Chigi's villa was *The Triumph of Galatea* (1514, *see* page 119), a mythological scene of erotic pursuit based on a poem by Angelo Poliziano (1454–94). The nymph Galatea (her pose inspired by Leonardo's drawings and ancient prototypes) rides on a shell, assisted by dolphins, to escape the unwanted attentions of the cyclops Polyphemus, depicted in an earlier adjacent fresco by the Venetian painter Sebastiano Luciani (subsequently known as Sebastiano del Piombo, *c.* 1485–1547).

A few years later (1517–18), Raphael returned with his assistants to decorate the villa's entrance loggia (*see The Banquet of the Gods* on page 120). Raphael's subject was the secret love of Cupid and Psyche narrated in Apuleius's Latin romance *The Golden Ass* (late-second-century AD). Raphael transformed the room into an antique arbour. Garlands of leaves, fruits, flowers and avowedly sexual vegetables (painted by Giovanni da Udine) follow the divisions of the architecture and frame the stories. The two large ceiling frescoes simulate tapestries. Birds, portrayed as if flying around the vault, complete the illusion. The sensual nudes here were painted by Giulio Romano and Gianfrancesco Penni, but they or their master could have executed the numerous red chalk drawings made for some of the figures (*see* page 11). The rendering of the softness of the flesh in these drawings has prompted the suggestion that some of these are, unusually for the time in Central Italian art, studies from actual nude female models.

Raphael also designed and partially executed two chapels for Chigi: one in Santa Maria della Pace, featuring a fresco depicting four sibyls who owe much to Michelangelo (*c.* 1514, *see* page 112); and another in Santa Maria del Popolo (*c.* 1515, *see* right). For the latter, Raphael planned the architecture, the marble and bronze tombs, and the mosaic dome, which has a strong antique character. Raphael and his assistants went on to design a whole decorative scheme in an antique style for the bathroom (*stufetta*) of Cardinal Bernardo Dovizi da Bibbiena's (1470–1520) apartment in the Vatican (1516). This narrow room is filled with erotic mythological scenes.

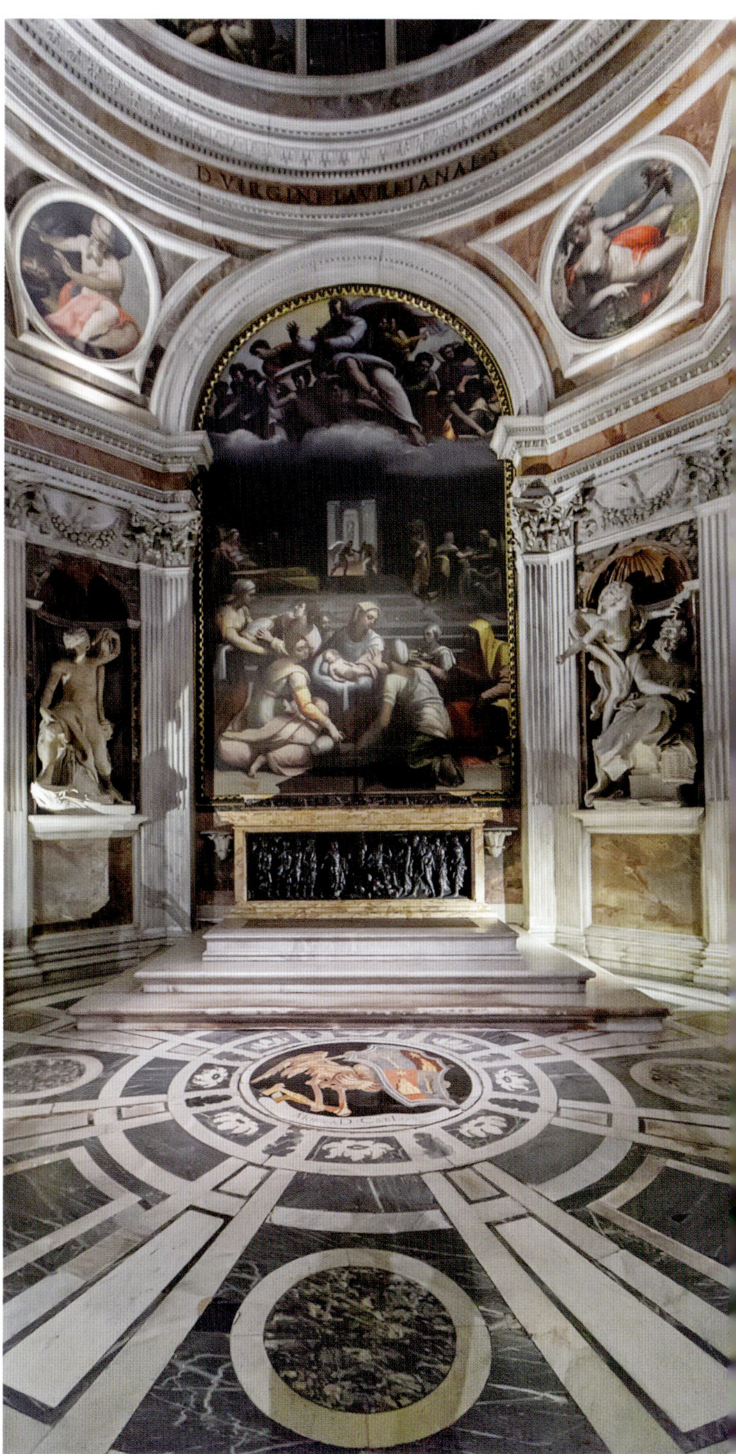

A Skilful Portraitist

Although Raphael had some experience of portrait painting before coming to Rome, much more extensive demands were made on his talents at the papal court. There is a nuanced vitality to many of Raphael's portraits, which exhibit a sense of psychological penetration new to the genre. For example, in his *Portrait of Pope Julius II* (1511–12, *see* below and page 53), Raphael depicted the pontiff not as an energetic man who had once been notorious for his temper, but as vulnerable. It is this aspect as much as the portrait's physical resemblance to Julius that explains the reaction of contemporaries when it was displayed after the Pope's death. In Vasari's words, Raphael's portrait of Julius was 'so alive and true that it made one afraid to see it as though it were in fact the living man'.

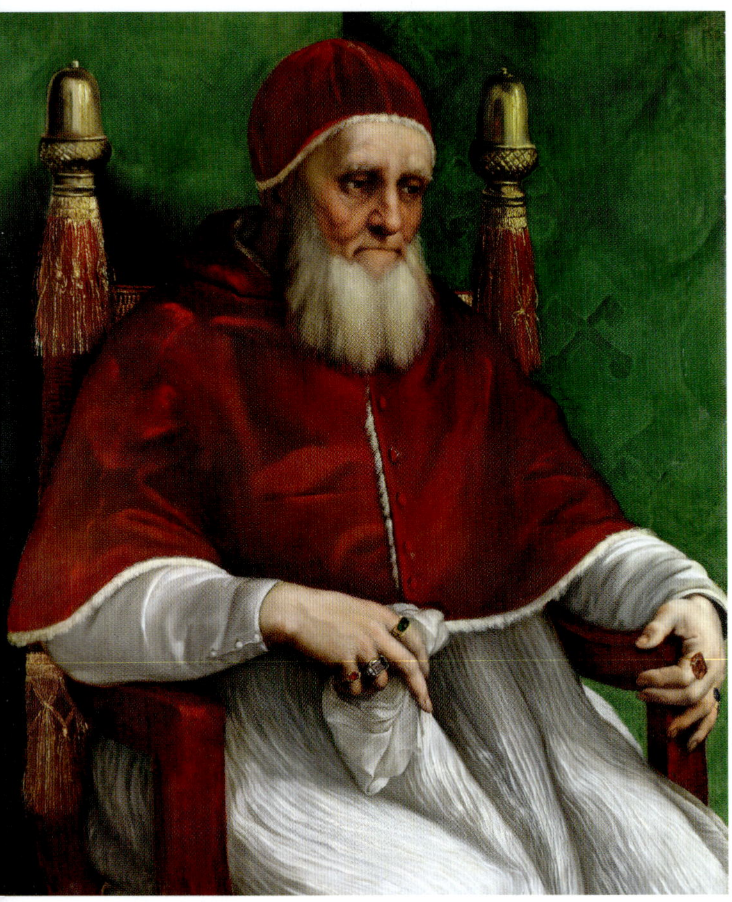

Among Raphael's most famous portraits is his likeness of his friend *Baldassare Castiglione* (1478–1529) dated to 1514–15 (*see* page 54), the diplomat and author of *The Book of the Courtier* (*Il Libro del Cortegiano*, 1528) – the ultimate handbook of courtly conduct. Castiglione is presented as elegant, his baldness disguised by his fashionable headgear and his wardrobe made up of sumptuous materials redolent of status, but the focus of the picture is the intelligent gaze of his blue eyes. The painting (influenced by Leonardo's *Mona Lisa*) conveys the concept of *sprezzatura*, a word coined by Castiglione and defined as a way of acting 'to conceal all art and make whatever is done or said appear to be without effort'.

Raphael's *Portrait of Pope Leo X with Cardinals Giulio de' Medici and Luigi de' Rossi* (*c.* 1518, *see* page 57) has been variously interpreted as a dynastic portrait (the artist dramatizes the relationship between the corpulent Pope and his relatives), a wedding gift and a spiritual message. On the table, painted with miniature-like precision, lie a book (the Hamilton Bible), which Leo needed a magnifying glass to examine, and a bell covered with Medici insignia. The fluid and precise naturalism of this image makes it a High Renaissance masterpiece. However, Raphael's most suggestive portrait is *La Fornarina* (1518–20, *see* page 59), which supposedly depicts his mistress, Margherita Luti (*c.* 1495–*c.* 1522), but the evidence is shaky. Raphael may have shown his love for this woman (who wears nothing but a gossamer gown) through painting his name in gold letters on her blue armband.

Cartoons and Tapestries

During 1515 and 1516, most of Raphael's energies were focused on the preparation of 10 full-scale coloured cartoons or designs, depicting the lives of Saint Peter and Saint Paul for tapestries to cover the lower walls of the Sistine Chapel. Raphael's tapestries constitute Pope Leo X's most ambitious artistic commission: his answer to Michelangelo's painted ceiling. Seven cartoons survive (*see* opposite and pages 81– 89), and while the hand of Raphael is evident throughout the original preparatory drawings, contributions were also made by his assistants. Raphael's cartoons are clear – the figures are large, their gestures severe and simple. The restrained colours and austere architectural settings add to the narrative stateliness of these works.

Given the large size of the cartoons, painted in a thick gouache (body-colour) with some charcoal underdrawing, it is unlikely that work was carried out simultaneously on more than one or two of them. Their supports (numerous sheets of paper) would have been fixed to a wall, where Raphael and his assistants could work with the aid of ladders or scaffolding. Once completed, the cartoons were sent to the workshop of the tapestry-maker Pieter van Aelst (c. 1495–c. 1560) in Brussels. They were cut into vertical strips to enable the weavers to place the cartoons directly under low-warp looms. It was probably when the cartoons reached Brussels that they were pricked for transfer, to make a duplicate set of cartoons. Confronted with designs in a very unfamiliar style, the task of translating Raphael's

cartoons into tapestries (woven with silk and with gold and silver thread) must have been a demanding one. Raphael was also faced with the problem of designing for a very different art form and in mirror image to the finished tapestries, because the pictures were reversed during the weaving process – some of the figures had to be painted as if left-handed!

On 26 December 1519, seven of the tapestries were displayed in the Sistine Chapel. All 10 had arrived by the time of Pope Leo's death on 1 December 1521. Purposefully emphasizing the papal majesty of Leo X, the impact of these sumptuous works was recorded by the Pope's Master of Ceremonies, Paris de Grassis (c. 1470–1528), who stated: 'Everyone was astounded at the sight of those magnificent tapestries, which by unanimous acclaim, belong to those works of art whose beauty have no rival in all the Universe.'

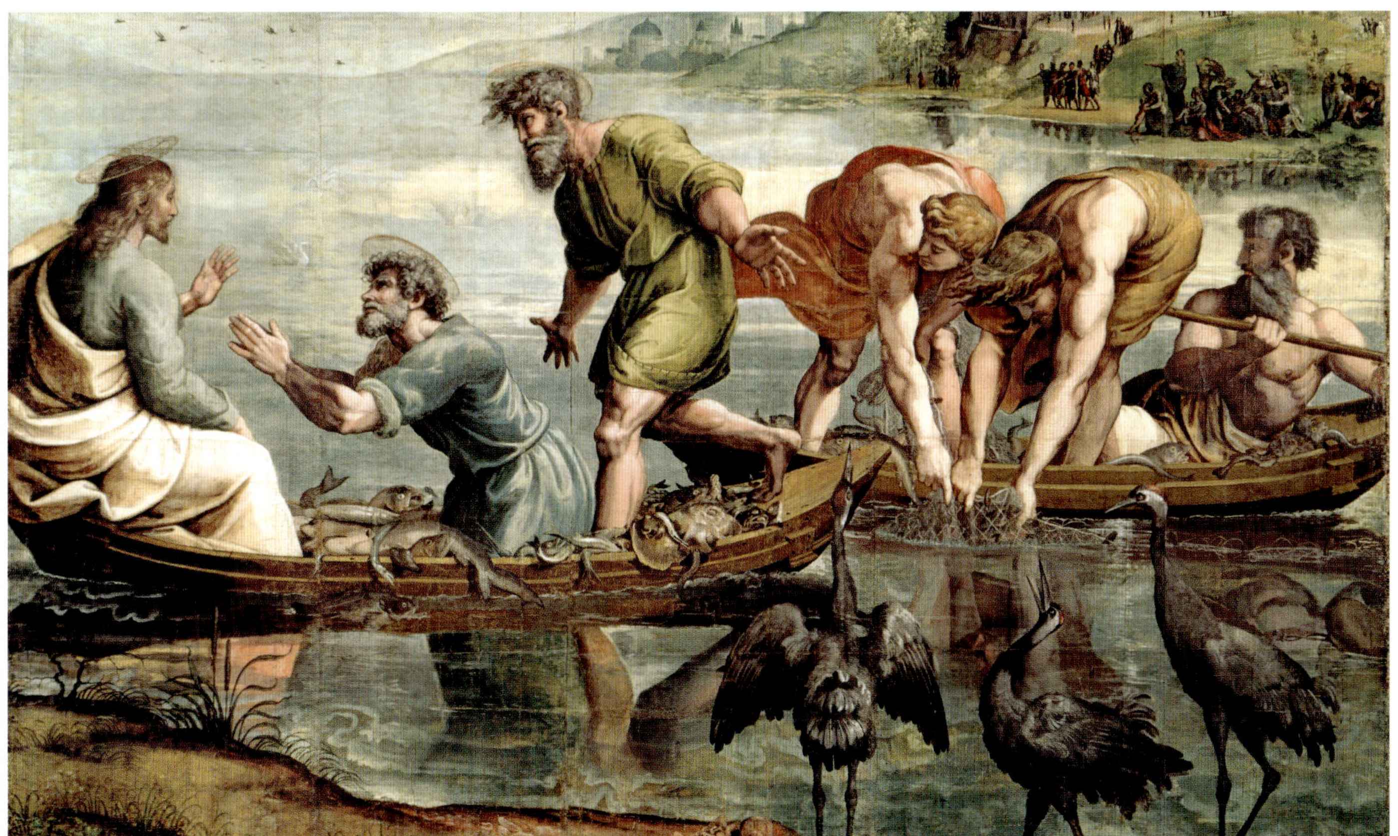

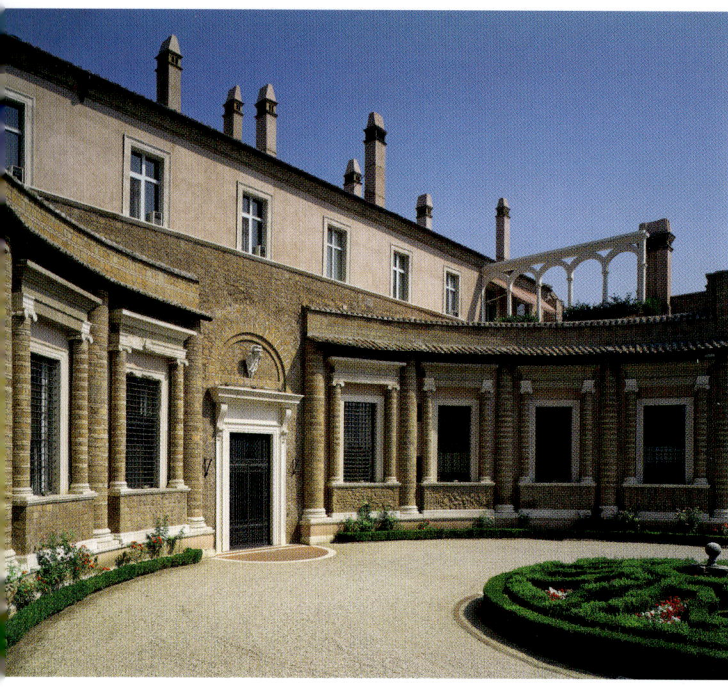

From Painter to Architect and Archaeologist

It was only with Bramante's death in April 1514 that Raphael's career as an architect began, as Leo X promoted him to Bramante's office as chief architect of St Peter's. Deeply involved in all aspects of an architect's work, Raphael nonetheless relied on the assistance of draughtsmen with more practical experience of building. Much of what was built at St Peter's under his supervision was later demolished, but surviving project drawings give some idea of his intentions (which included modifying Bramante's plan for the façade). A written criticism of Raphael's design by his assistant and successor, Antonio da Sangallo the Younger (1484–1546), reveals that there were concerns that the enormous main nave would 'seem like an alley'.

In addition to designing the small church of Sant'Eligio degli Orefici for the Goldsmiths' Guild in Rome (c. 1515), Raphael worked on the Palazzo Branconio dell'Aquila (destroyed) in the city in 1518. Marking an epoch in palace façades, Raphael gave the building the appearance of a triumphal arch, employing painted representations of ancient

stories, stucco figures and an irregular pattern of niches. However, his greatest (though unfinished) work as an architect was the villa just outside Rome, now known as the Villa Madama (see left), for Leo X's cousin Giulio de' Medici (1478–1534), who later became Pope Clement VII. By 1518, Raphael had thought out the design, which was strongly influenced by his study of Vitruvius (c. 85–c. 20 BC) and his desire to recreate an ancient Roman house, as described in the letters of Pliny the Younger (AD c. 61–c. 113), with separate living quarters for summer and winter, a theatre, baths, a fish pond and terrace gardens.

Raphael's enthusiasm for the idea of restoring to papal Rome the glory of imperial Rome, and his commitment to gaining a greater understanding of antiquity, culminated in his appointment in 1517 as papal superintendent of antiquities, and his plan to draw up a complete reconstruction (based on excavation and careful reading of Classical texts) of Ancient Rome. Raphael hoped to find, measure and sketch all the surviving examples of ancient monuments in the city and, where possible, preserve them. (Leo X decreed no workers be allowed to use any stones with inscriptions or carvings for building, without Raphael's permission.) Although the project never got past the earliest stages, Raphael's activity as an archaeologist was pioneering.

The Final Flourish

Judged by Vasari to be 'the most famous, the most beautiful and most divine' of the artist's works, The Transfiguration (1516–20, see opposite and page 92) was Raphael's last painting. The altarpiece was commissioned by Cardinal Giulio de' Medici for the cathedral of Narbonne in southern France, alongside a painting of The Raising of Lazarus (1517–19) by Sebastiano del Piombo, for whom Michelangelo provided drawings in an effort to outshine Raphael. Raphael took this direct competition very seriously, executing the painting entirely in his own hands. His painstaking preparation and pursuit of perfection are revealed in several existing drawings, including some so-called 'auxiliary cartoons', a type of drawing that he used at this late stage in his career for the exploration and refinement of important details, notably the heads and hands of the most significant figures in the complex figure group of the apostles (see page 93) in the painting's lower half.

The altarpiece speaks volumes about Raphael's life-long concern with rendering pictorially the relationship between the terrestrial and the celestial, and it proves that he was determined to find ways of presenting the supernatural as a plausible visual experience.

The painting was essentially complete by the time of Raphael's death and the contemporary response to the work was extraordinary. It was displayed in the Vatican, to be seen for the first and only time with its rival, Sebastiano's altarpiece, before it was installed on the high altar of the church of San Pietro in Montorio in Rome. Meanwhile, Sebastiano's painting was dispatched to Narbonne. The jealous Sebastiano wrote to Michelangelo describing the figures in Raphael's picture as looking 'as though they had been hung up in smoke, or were made of iron', but he had failed to trounce his opponent in the altarpiece contest.

Passion and Death

According to Vasari, Raphael's untimely death on Good Friday, 6 April 1520 – his thirty-seventh birthday – from a fever purportedly contracted after sexual over-indulgence with his mistress, plunged the entire papal court into grief. Making a not-so-subtle connection between the artist and Christ, Raphael's painting of *The Transfiguration* was placed at the head of his body as he lay in state in his studio, and the Mantuan envoy wrote to his patroness Isabella d'Este (1474–1539), saying that cracks had appeared in the walls of the Vatican on the very day Raphael died, an echo of the tremors that were felt the moment Christ died. A grand funeral cortege of one hundred torchbearers was organized to bury Raphael in the Pantheon, a sacred space formerly reserved for canons of the Catholic Church. The scholar and writer Pietro Bembo (1470–1547) composed the inscription on the painter's marble sarcophagus: 'Here lies that famous Raphael by whom Nature feared to be conquered while he lived and when he was dying feared herself to die.'

At the time of Raphael's death, the scaffolding was being constructed for the fourth and final room to be frescoed in the papal suite, the Sala di Costantino (1520–24). The commission stipulated the portrayal of four episodes from the life of the first Christian emperor, Constantine the Great (AD *c.* 280–337): his *Vision of the Cross* (*see* page 122); his

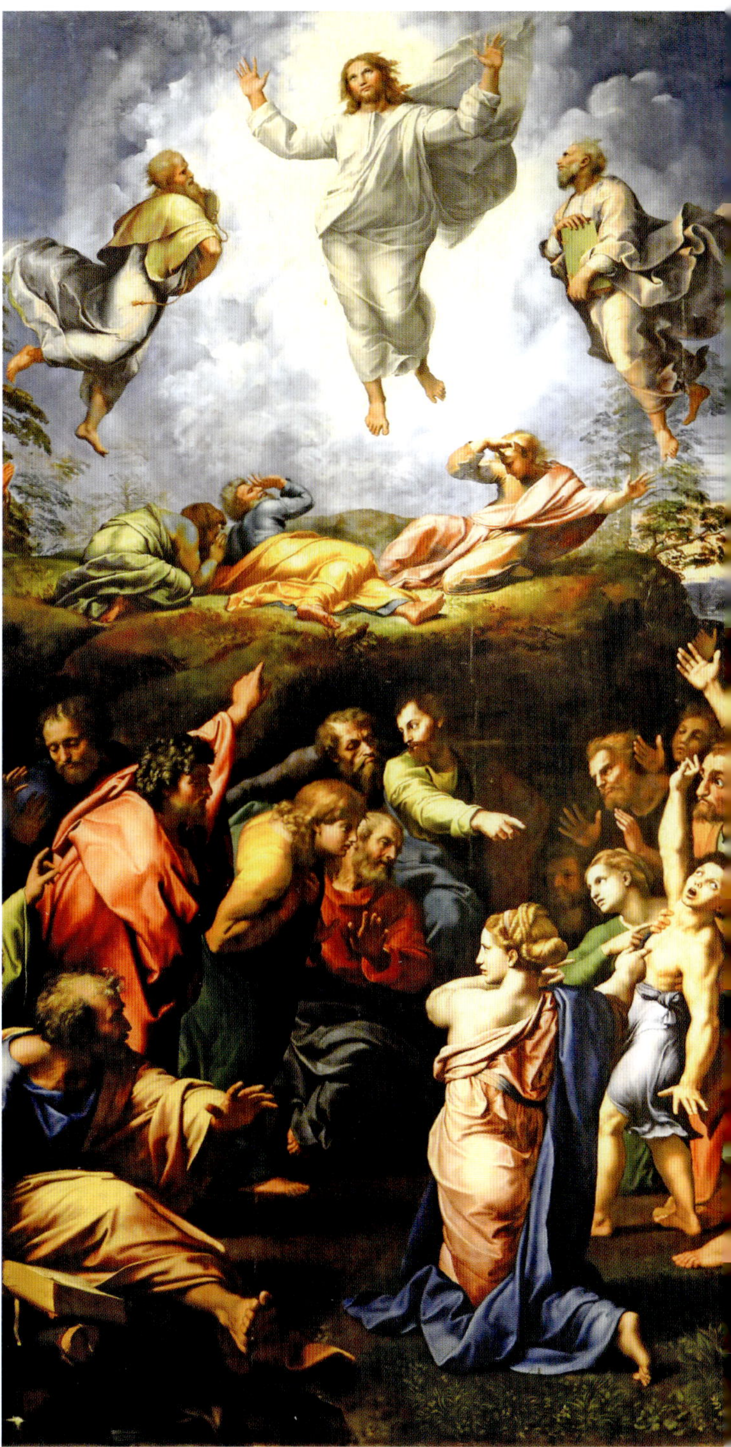

victory over Maxentius (*see* below and page 123, *The Battle of the Milvian Bridge*); his baptism (*see* page 124); and his donation of Rome to Pope Sylvester (*see* page 125). The frescoes were painted by Giulio Romano and Gianfrancesco Penni, who were guided, at least in part, by Raphael's cartoons. Both were named their master's artistic heirs and inheritors of his workshop, commissions and designs for unfinished projects.

Raphael died at the peak of his powers, having also reached the dizzy social heights and been lauded with honours, including the titles Groom of the Chamber of the Pope and Knight of the Papal Order of the Golden Spur. There was even talk of his being made a cardinal. However, as far as the legend of lustful Raphael goes, it seems likely that the artist was worn out by work, not love.

Changing Tastes

Reception of an artist is never stable across centuries. Raphael was adored and admired in his lifetime, and his innovations have been plundered by generations of artists, from Correggio (Antonio Allegri, 1489–1534) to Peter Paul Rubens (1577–1640), Diego Velázquez (1599–1660) to Eugène Delacroix (1798–1863), and from Pierre-Auguste Renoir (1841–1919) to Pablo Picasso (1881–1973). Up until the early nineteenth century, Raphael was studied as the model of classical perfection. Every young artist had to imitate his mathematically pure and balanced compositions. However, with Romanticism's revolt against the academic tradition, Raphael's past canonical status and the sense of perfection for which he was renowned worked against him, and his reputation went

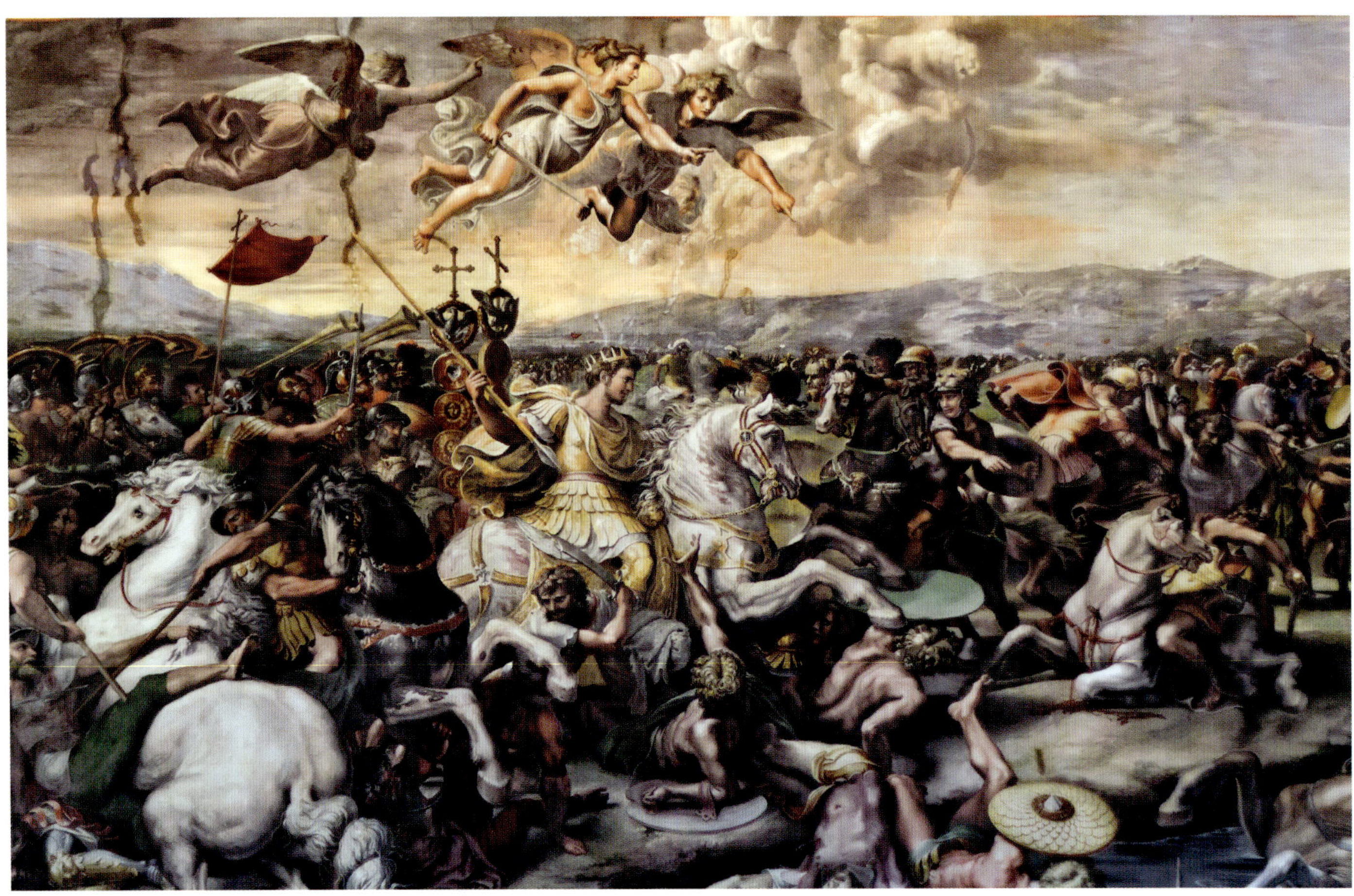

into decline. Coupled with the negative assessment of his colouring that had prevailed from the late seventeenth century (one French art critic lamented that the artist's colour was not eye-catching), Raphael seemed to many not so much a paragon as boringly sweet and mannered.

Measured against the intense lives and disturbingly immediate works of Leonardo and Michelangelo, Raphael can look cosy and remote to twenty-first-century viewers. With his smoothly beautiful compositions and his well-mannered personality, he does not conform to the modern ideal of the artist as someone who struggles in brooding isolation, leading an unconventional life, touched by a kind of creative madness. Yet the taste for Raphael has returned. Recent renewed appreciation for him as an antiquarian and courtier has also rekindled fascination for the vivacity of his drawings, his ceaseless assimilation of the styles of others, his wide vocabulary of techniques and his skill in achieving subtle emotive tension in his figures. Today, Raphael can be said to be back.

The Prince of Painters

Arguably, no Renaissance artist so successfully – and repeatedly – invented and reinvented himself as did Raphael. A prolific painter, distinguished architect, the head of a highly skilled team and the creator of what would today be termed an internationally recognized visual brand, Raphael was also a man noted for his fertile imagination, charm, confidence and ambition. He translated the more unusual inventions of Leonardo and Michelangelo into a pictorial language that could be more widely understood. As Picasso observed, 'Leonardo promises us heaven, but Raphael gives it to us.'

During his brief yet brilliant career, from his start as a talented teenager in provincial Umbria until his death when he was the most celebrated painter in Rome, this efficient and accomplished artist developed a seductive, powerful personal style and came to embody the spirit of the Italian Renaissance. His patrons, among the most powerful men in Europe, paid far more for his paintings than they did for those by most of his eminent contemporaries. Given Vasari's stated admiration for the 'gracious' Raphael, he deserves the final word: 'While we may term other works paintings, those of Raphael are living things; the flesh palpitates, the breath comes and goes, every organ lives, life pulsates everywhere.'

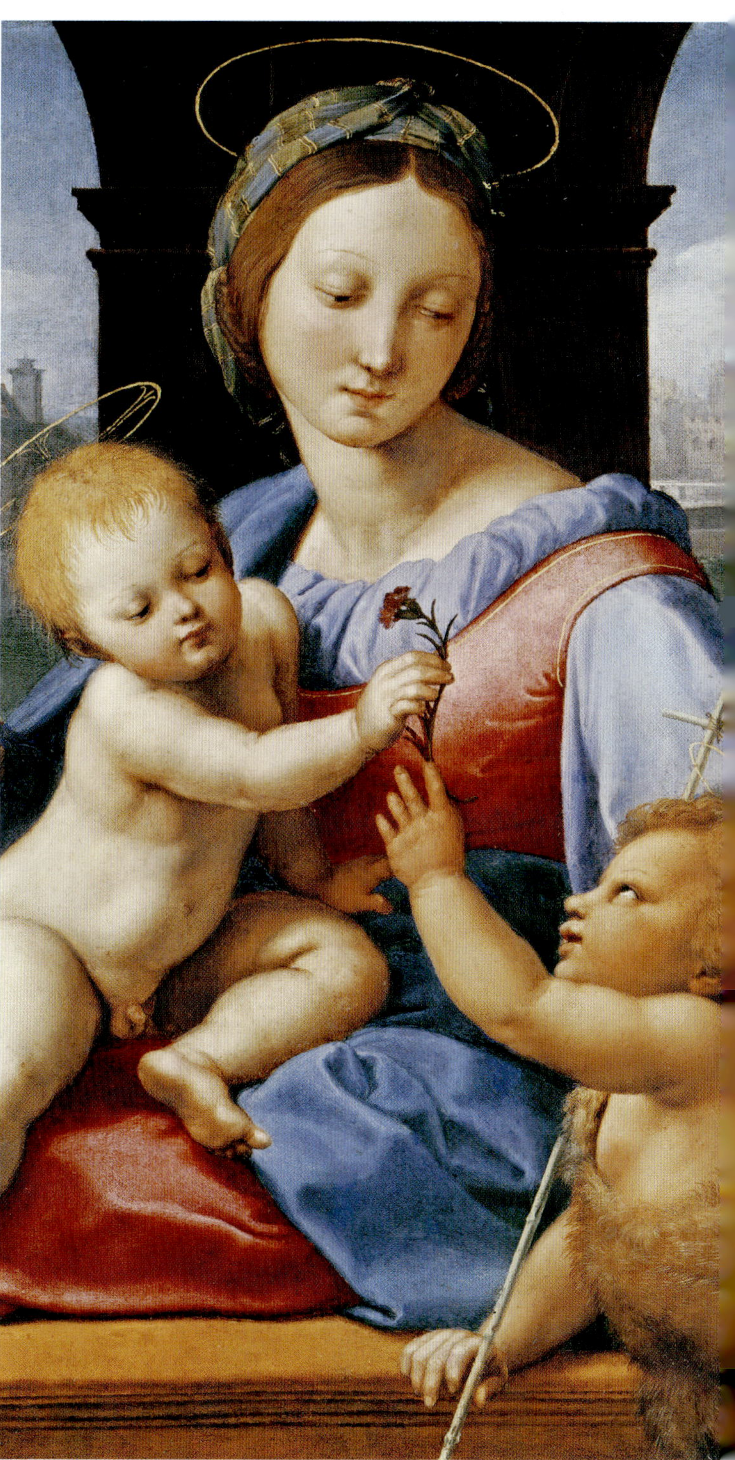

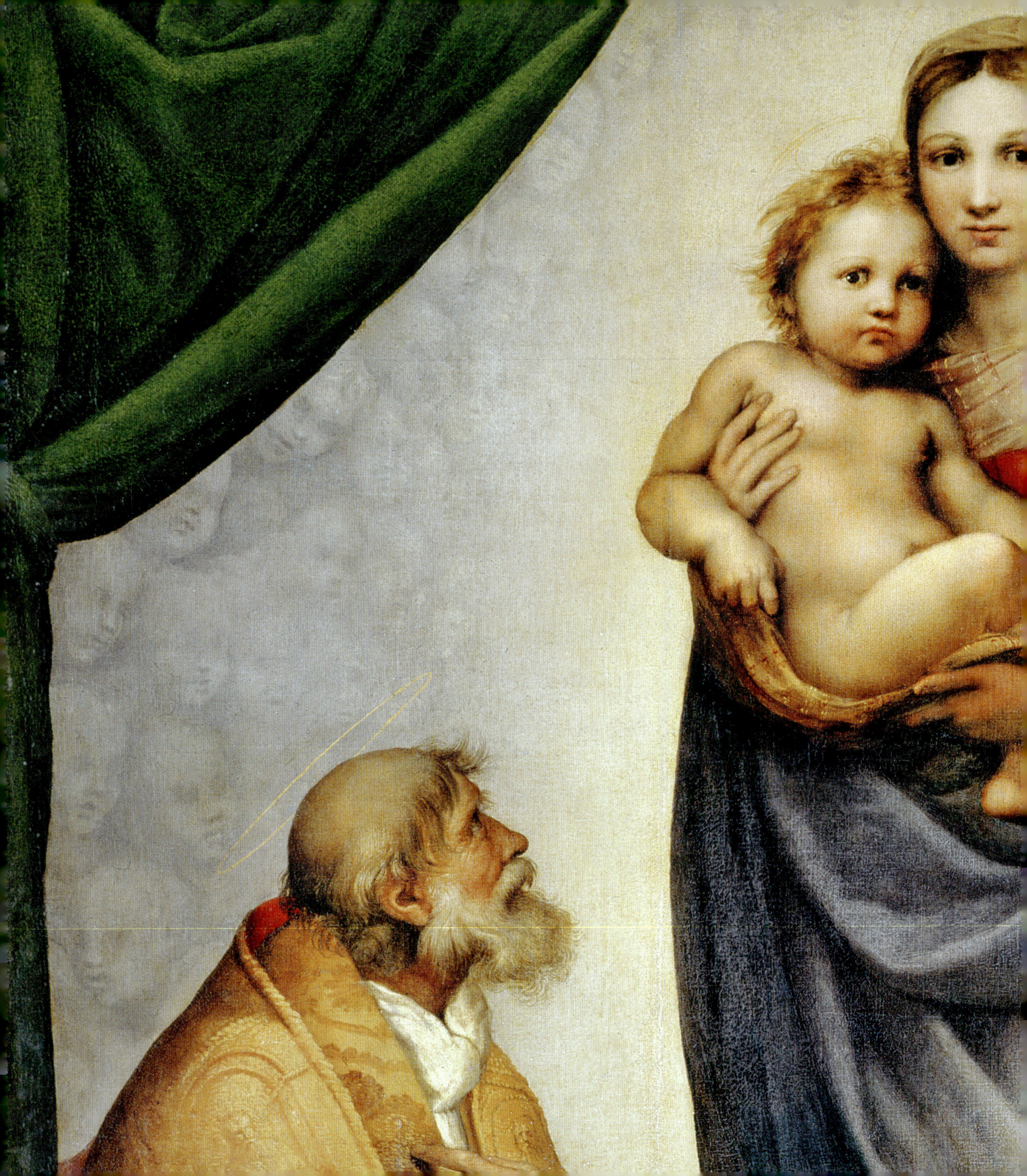

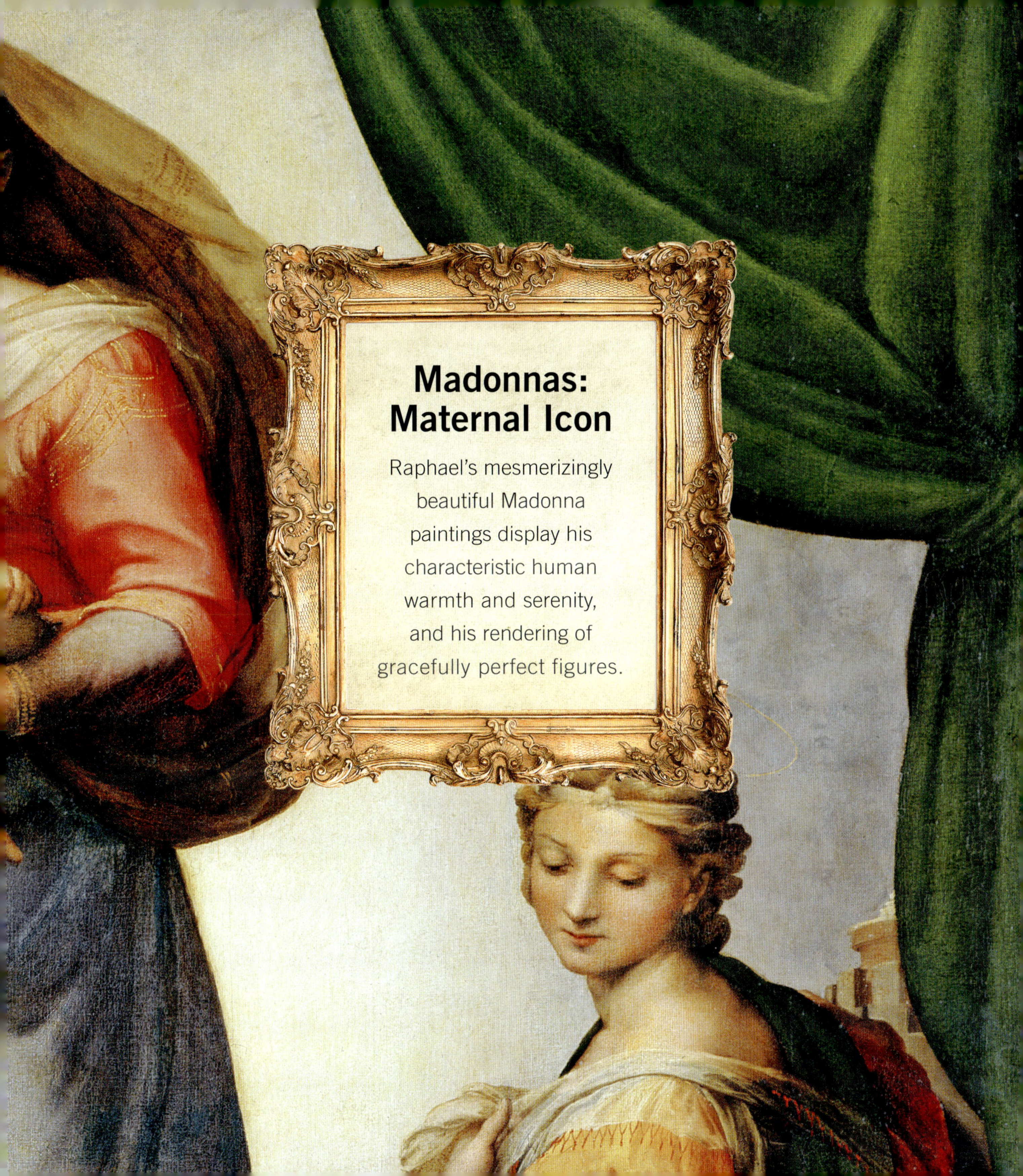

Madonnas:
Maternal Icon

Raphael's mesmerizingly
beautiful Madonna
paintings display his
characteristic human
warmth and serenity,
and his rendering of
gracefully perfect figures.

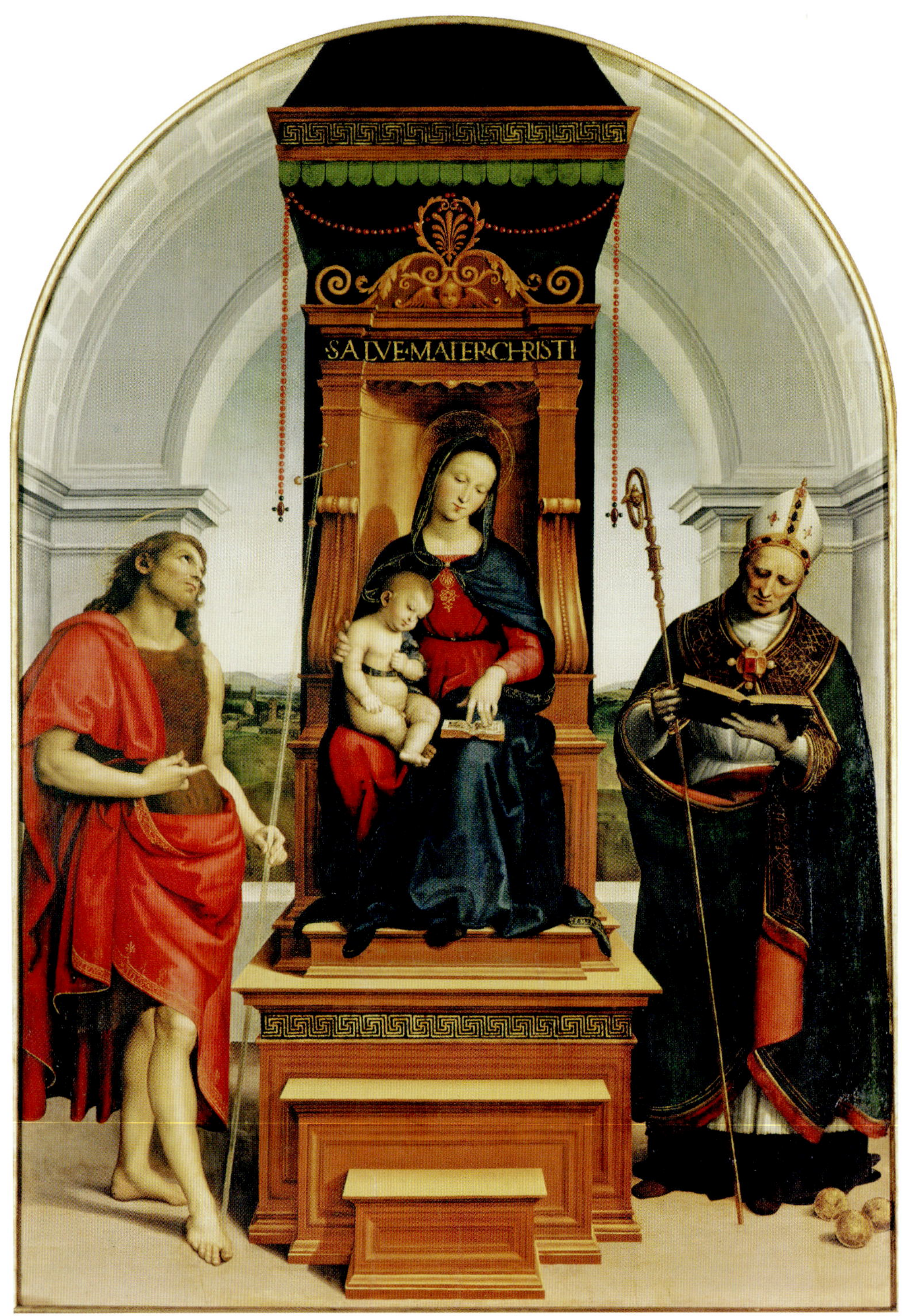

The Madonna and Child with Saint John the Baptist and Saint Nicholas of Bari (The Ansidei Madonna), 1505
Oil on poplar, 216.8 x 147.6 cm (85⅔ x 58 in) • National Gallery, London

This altarpiece was painted for the Ansidei family chapel in the Perugian church of San Fiorenzo. The arrangement of the figures (including a chubby Christ Child and handsome John the Baptist) is an example of a *sacra conversazione* (holy conversation).

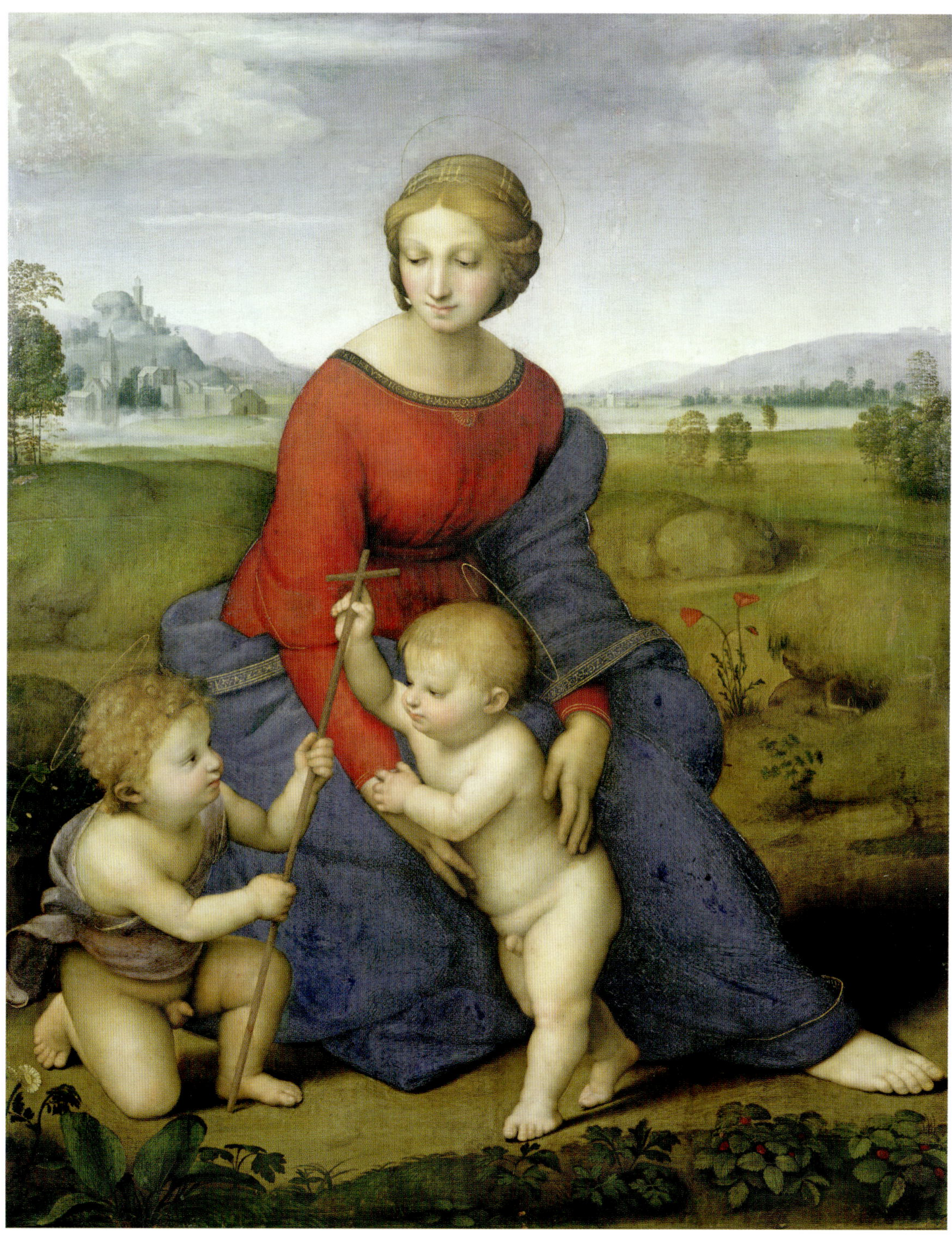

Madonna del Prato (Madonna of the Meadow), 1505–06
Oil on wood, 113 x 88 cm (44½ x 35 in)
• Kunsthistorisches Museum, Vienna

Raphael's study of Leonardo is manifest in the poses and natural expressions of the convincingly monumental figures, the soft flesh of the children and the pyramidal design of the group.

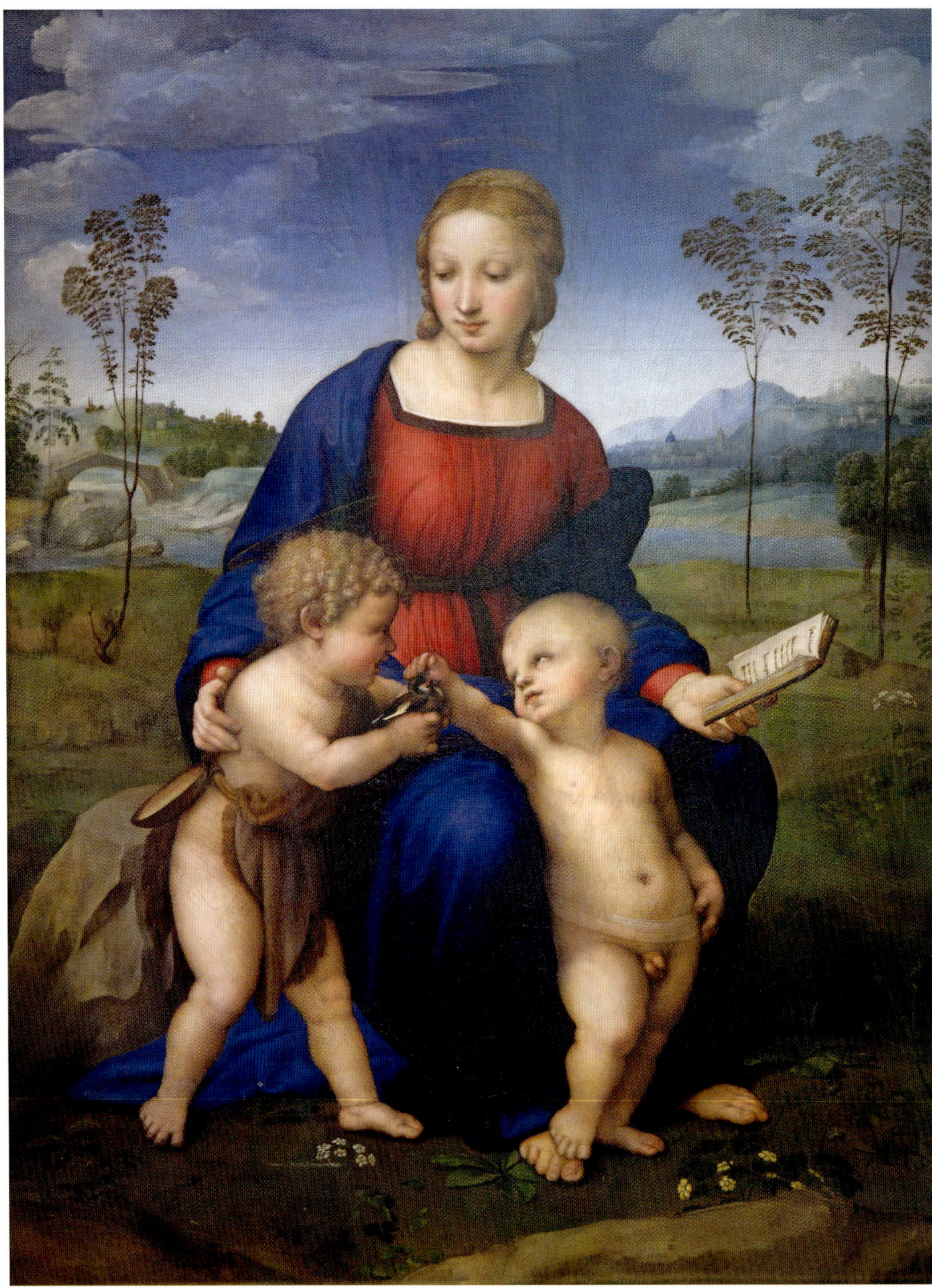

**Mary, Christ and the Young John the Baptist
(Madonna of the Goldfinch),** *c.* **1505–06**
Oil on wood, 107 x 77.2 cm (42 x 30⅖ in) • Galleria degli Uffizi, Florence

Painted for Lorenzo Nasi (a Florentine merchant), this picture was shattered into 17 pieces when Nasi's house collapsed in 1547. A 10-year restoration project was completed in 2008. Again, Raphael borrowed Leonardo's pyramid composition to balance the figures. Saint John holds a goldfinch, symbolizing the crucifixion.

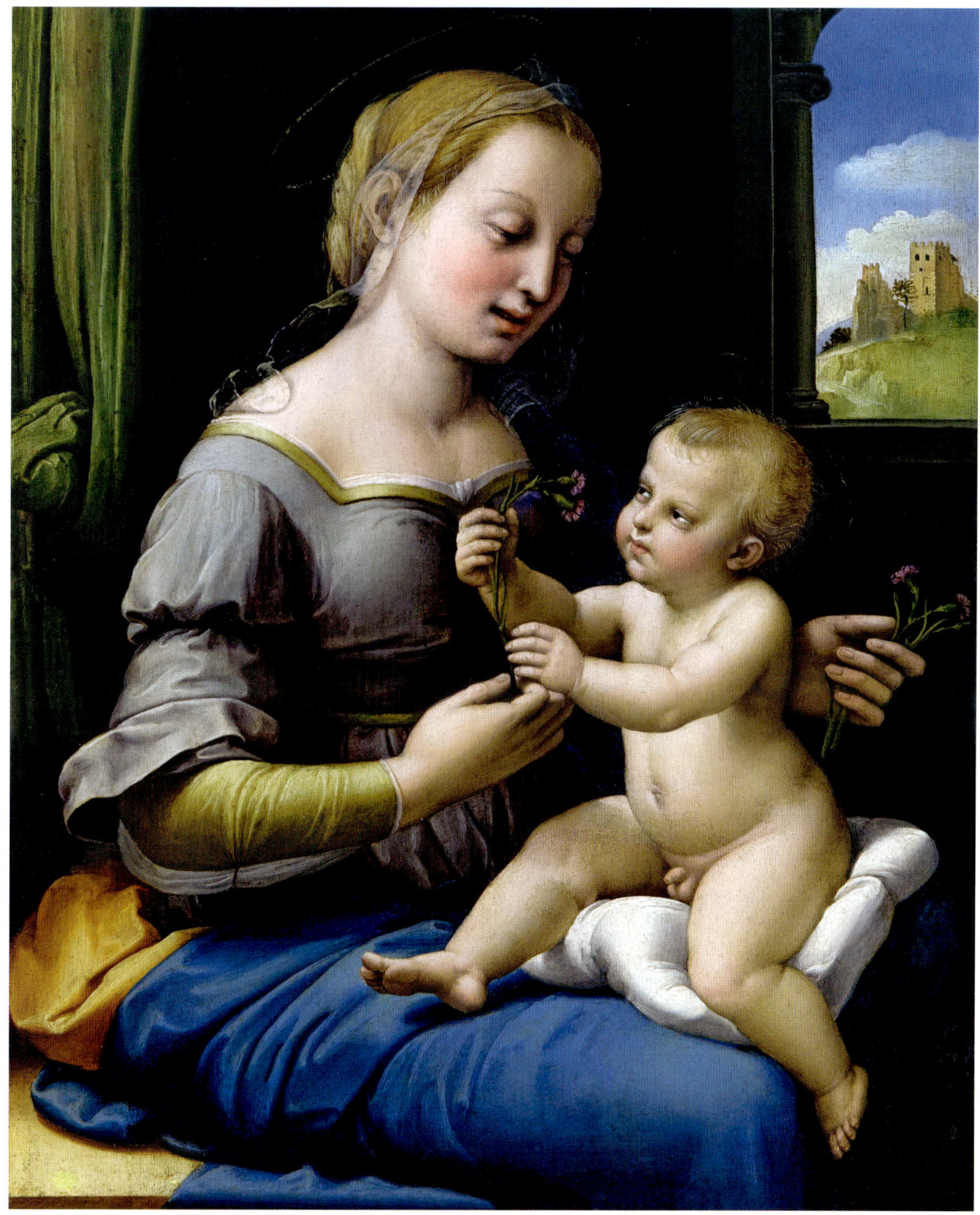

Madonna of the Pinks, _c._ 1506–07
Oil on yew, 27.9 x 22.4 cm (11 x 8⅘ in) • National Gallery, London

Possibly made for a nun in Perugia and designed to be held in the hand for prayer, Raphael here paid homage to a work by Leonardo. The figures exchange carnations, symbolic of love.

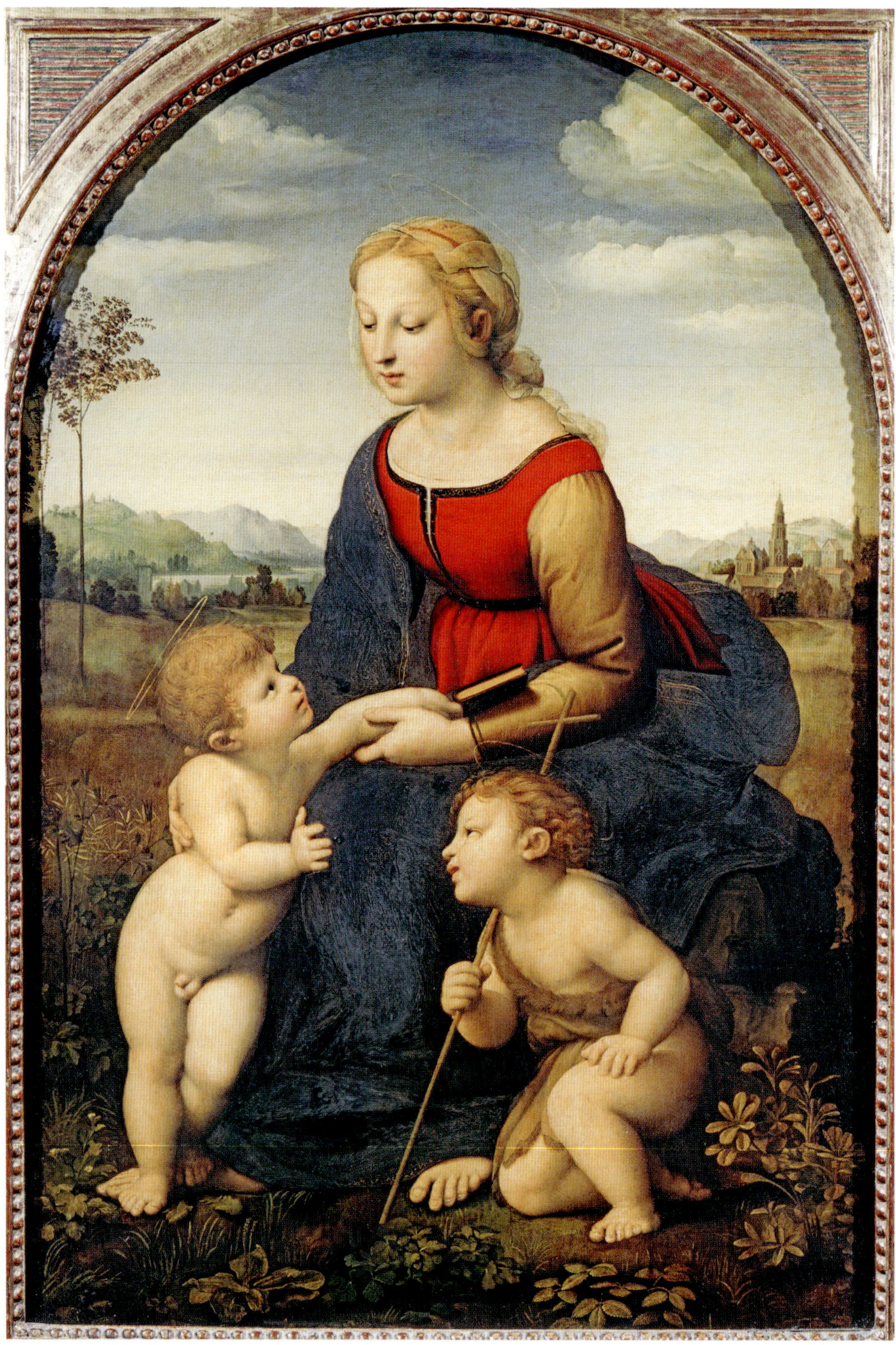

**The Virgin and Child with Saint John the Baptist
(La Belle Jardinière), 1507**
Oil on panel, 122 x 80 cm (48 x 31½ in) • Musée du Louvre, Paris

Raphael referred to the art of Leonardo when painting the gestures connecting the figures. His original drawings show John the Baptist crowned by grapevine leaves, alluding to the god of wine (and the communion wine).

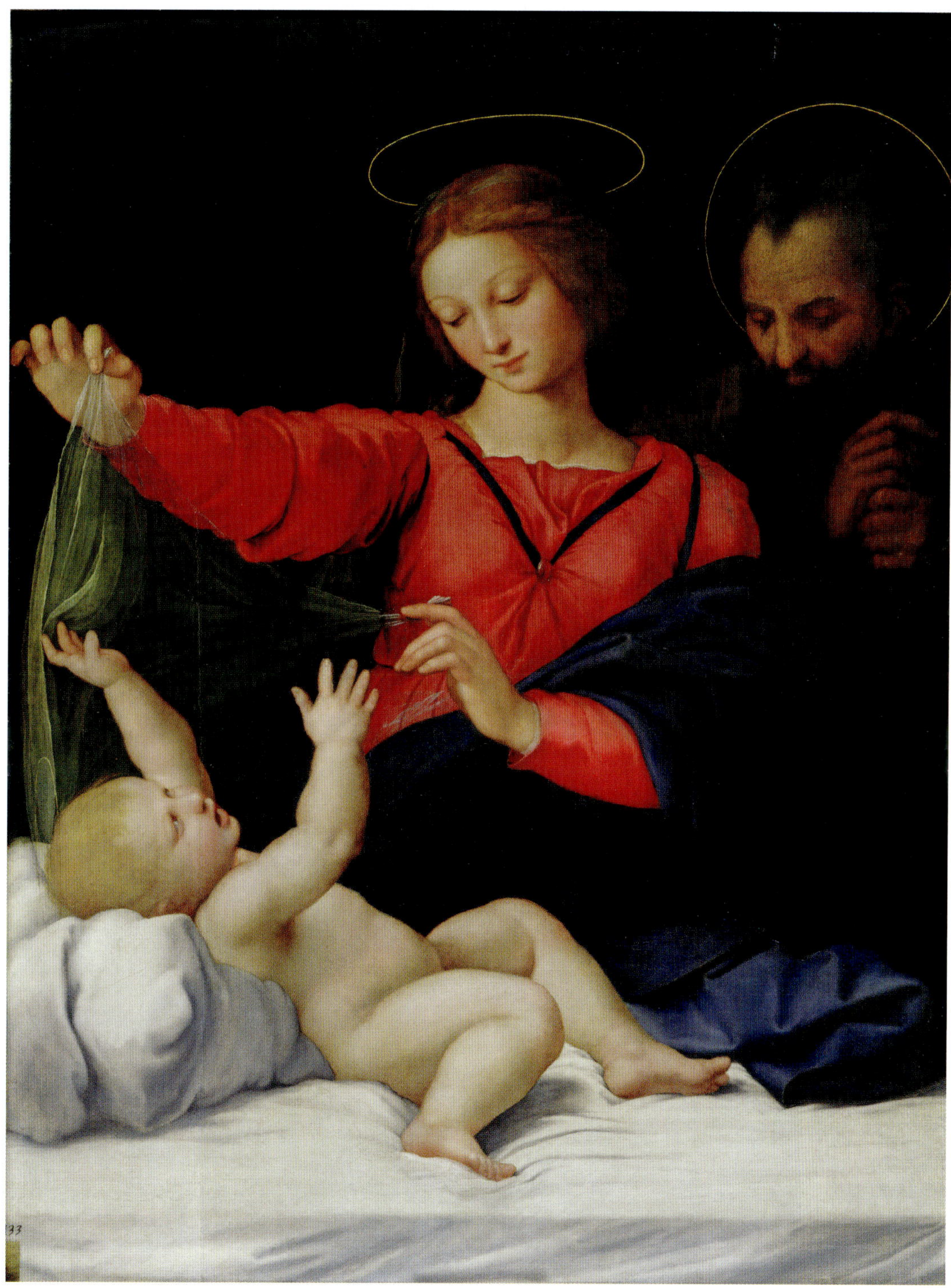

Madonna of Loreto (Madonna del Velo), 1509
Oil on panel, 120 x 90 cm (47.2 x 35⅔ in) • Musée Condé, Chantilly

Commissioned by Pope Julius II, this intimate and touching image of the Holy Family reflects the Renaissance fascination with Christ's humanity. The infant Christ Child, reclining on pillows, playfully extends his hands towards the Madonna's veil.

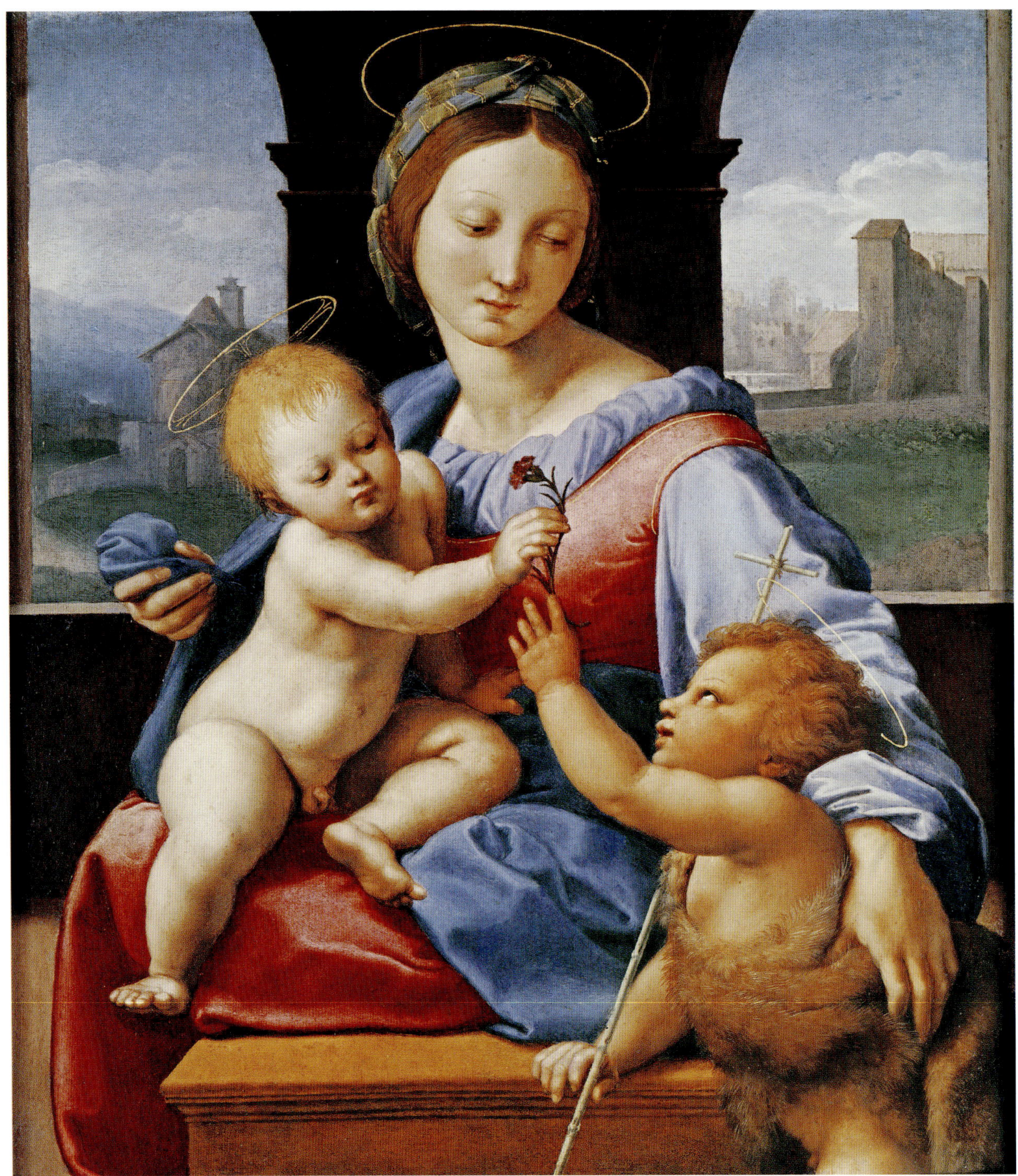

The Aldobrandini Madonna, *c.* 1509–10
Oil on wood, 38.9 x 32.9 cm (15⅓ x 13 in) • National Gallery, London

The small scale and exquisite finish of this work imply a discriminating patron (and private devotional context). The Madonna and Child gaze down at John the Baptist, who gives the Christ Child a carnation, symbolizing his crucifixion and divine love.

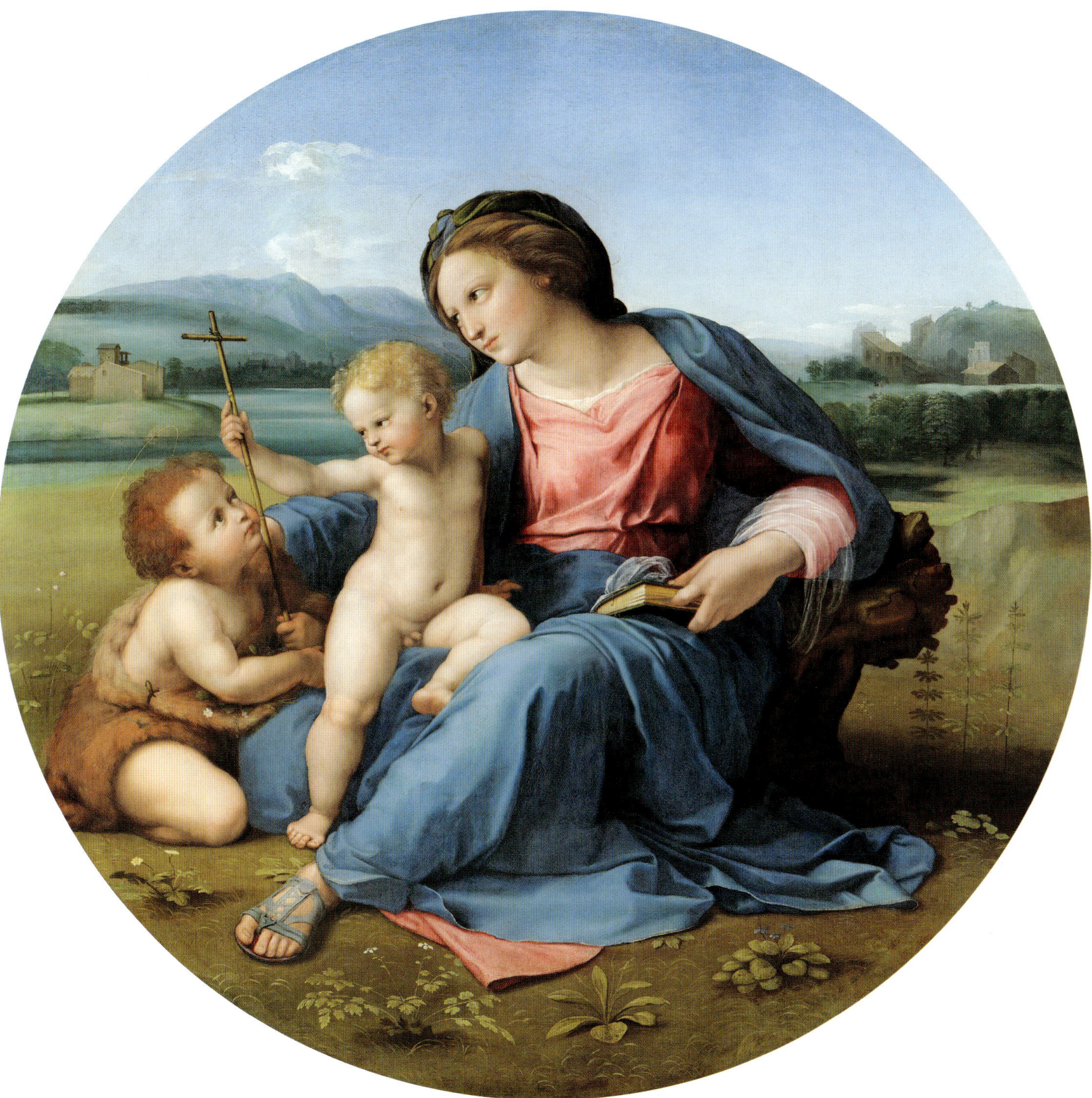

The Alba Madonna, *c.* 1510
Oil on panel transferred to canvas, diameter 94.5 cm (37¼ in)
• National Gallery of Art, Washington, DC

Raphael exploited the circular (*tondo*) style popular in Florence at the time and emphasized the diagonal movement of the Madonna and Child (employing Michelangelo's figure style). The delicate pastel colours reveal the depth and brilliance of the landscape background.

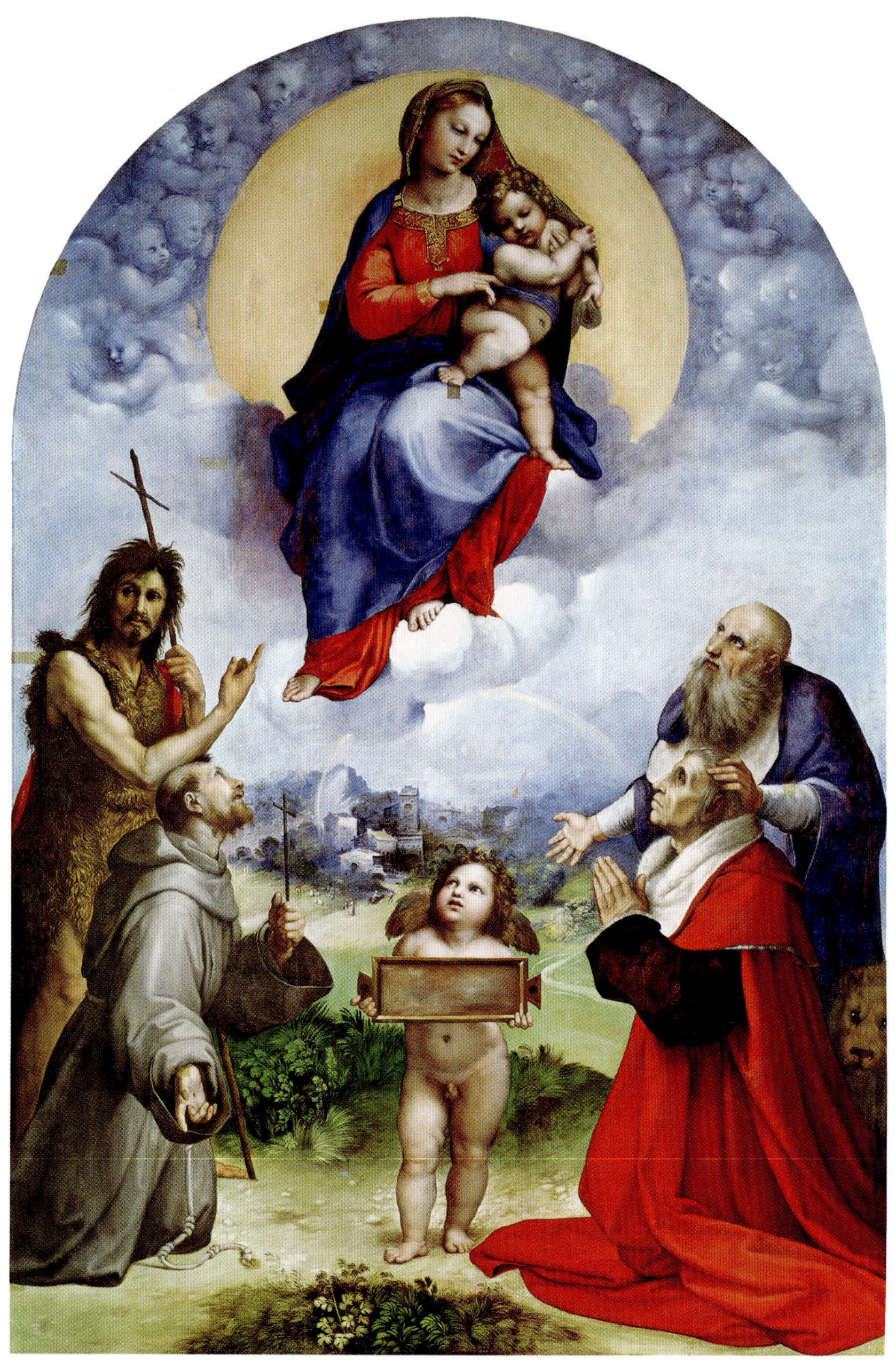

Madonna di Foligno, *c.* **1511–12**
Oil on wood transferred to canvas, 320 x 194 cm (126 x 76⅖ in)
• Pinacoteca Vaticana, Rome

This altarpiece was commissioned by Sigismondo de' Conti (1432–1512), who is depicted next to
Saint Jerome (right) and opposite Saint Francis and John the Baptist. The Madonna and Child hover
above in clouds of cherubim.

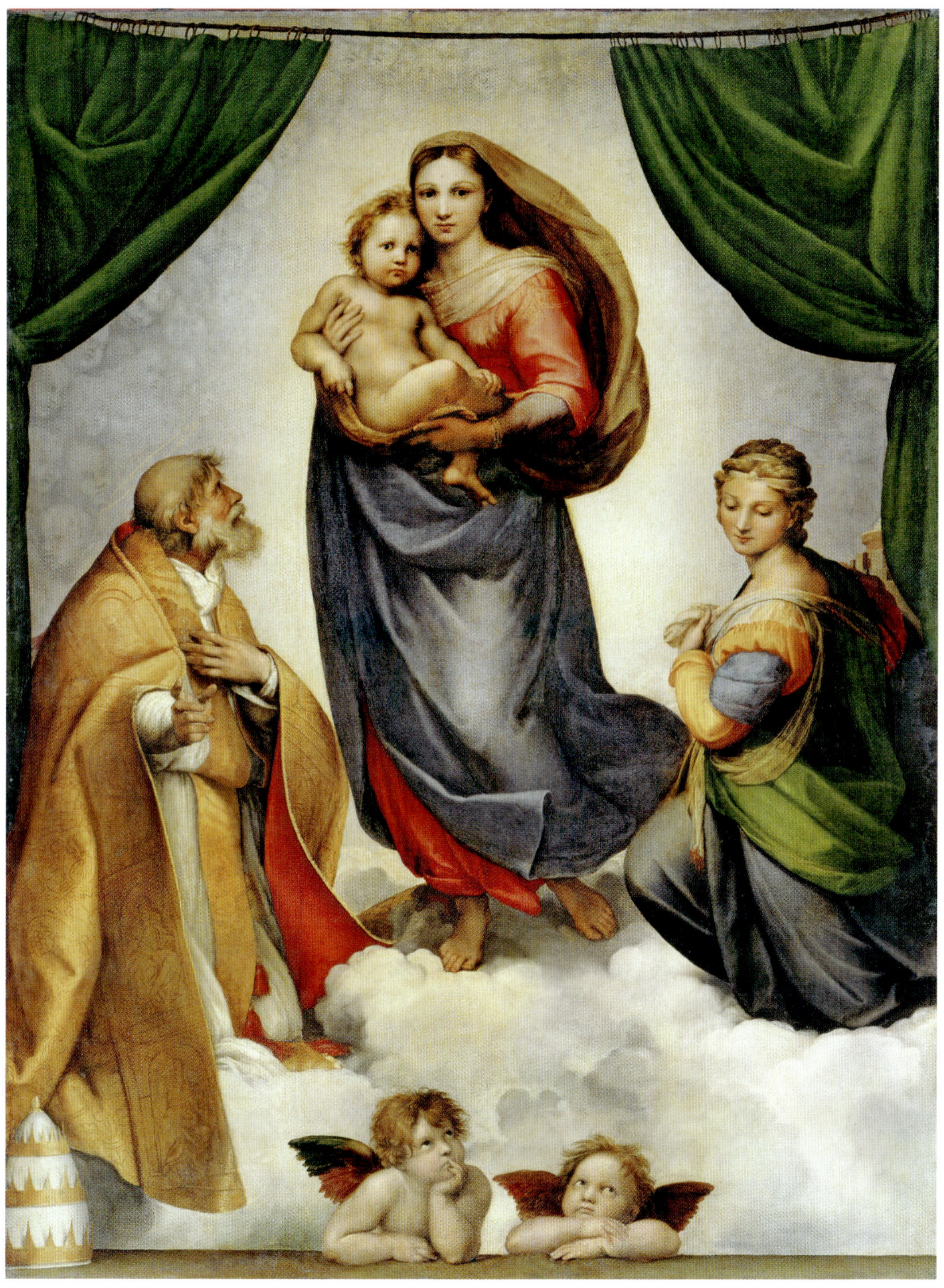

The Sistine Madonna, *c.* 1512–13
Oil on canvas, 265 x 196 cm (104⅓ x 77¼ in)
• Gemäldegalerie Alte Meister, Dresden

Relating the earthly to the divine via pose, gesture and glance, Raphael's canvas features a weightless while at the same time strongly corporeal Madonna and Child, with saints Sixtus (honouring Pope Julius II's late uncle) and Barbara.

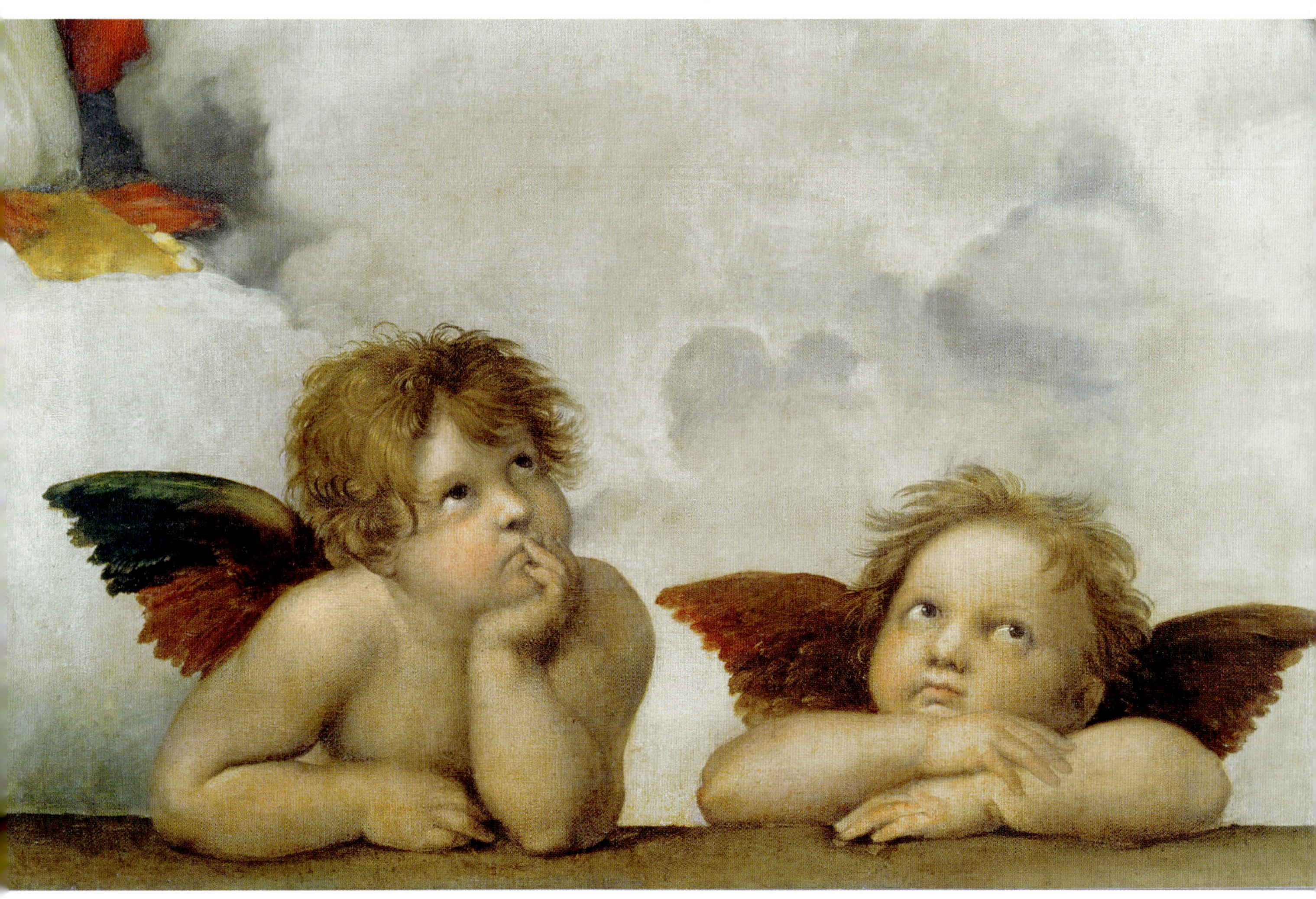

Cherubs, detail from The Sistine Madonna, *c.* 1512–13
Oil on canvas • Gemäldegalerie Alte Meister, Dresden

This altarpiece has been made famous by the two less-than-reverent cherubs (depicted with light brushstrokes), who roll their eyes and lean sulkily on a balustrade at the bottom of the composition.

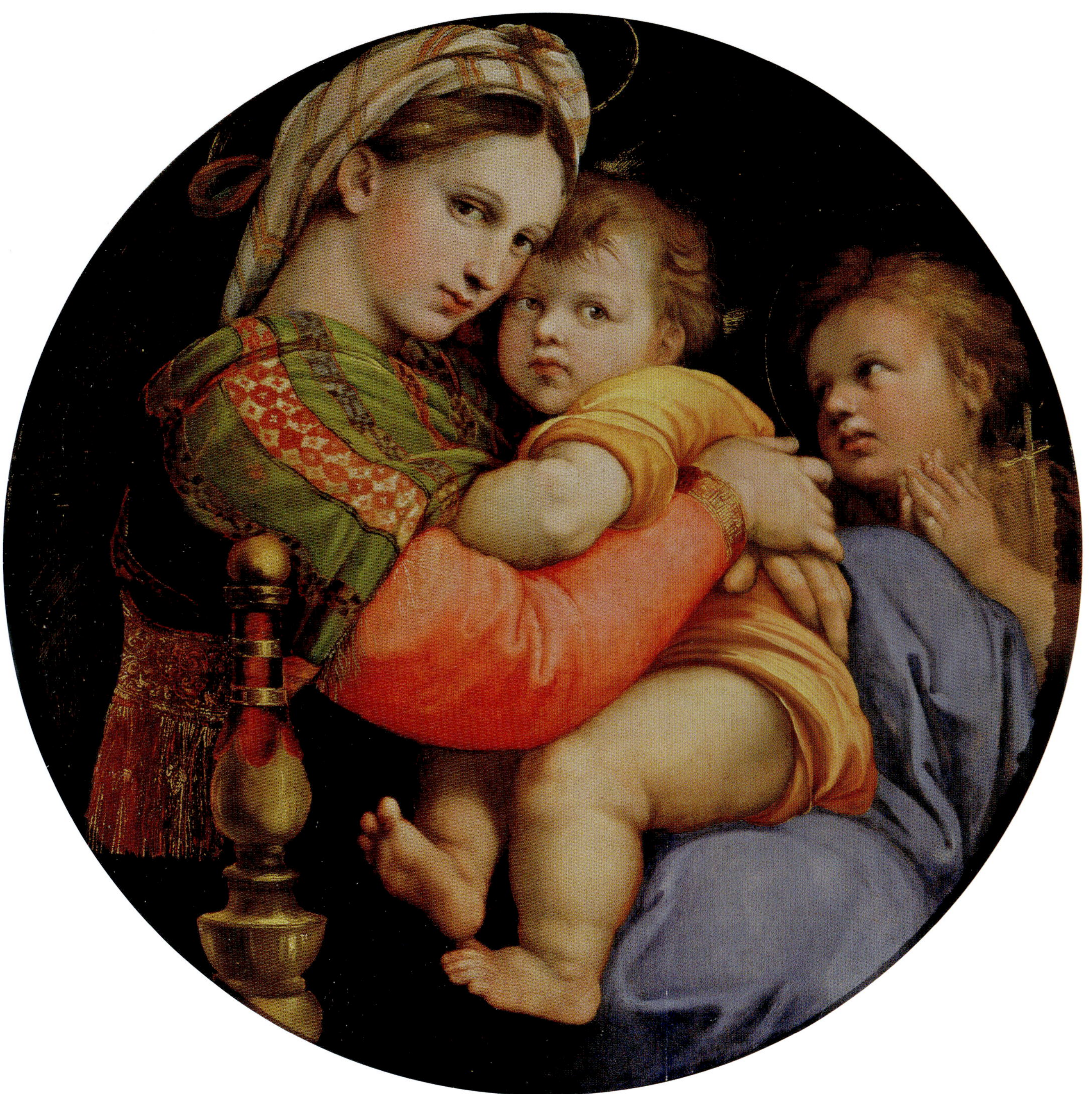

Madonna della Sedia, *c.* 1513–14
Oil on panel, 71 x 71 cm (28 x 28 in)
• Galleria Palatina, Palazzo Pitti, Florence

According to legend, this picture (whose title refers to the chair in which Mary sits) was painted on the bottom of a barrel. The figures interact tenderly with each other. The warm colours suggest the influence of Venetian artists.

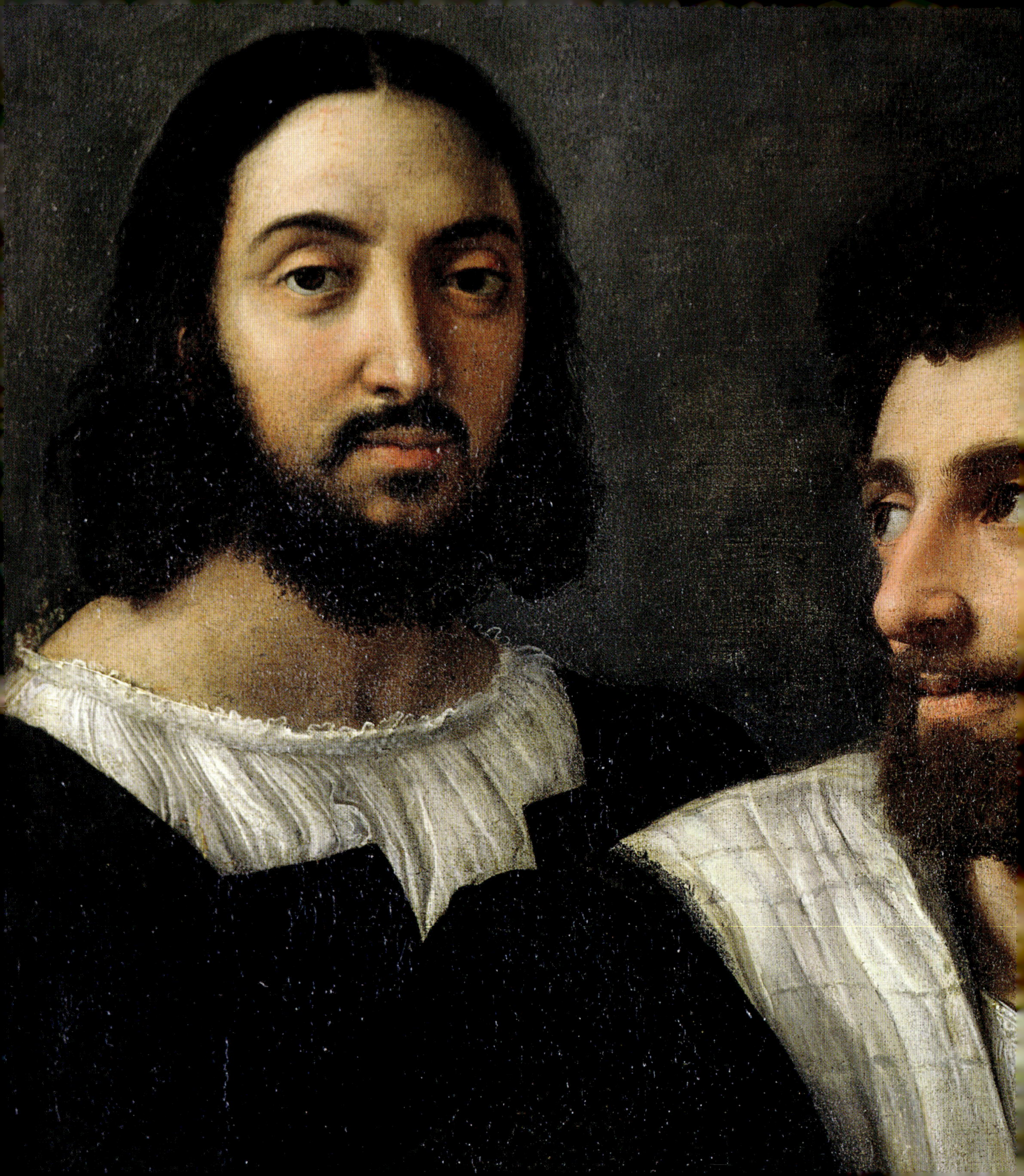

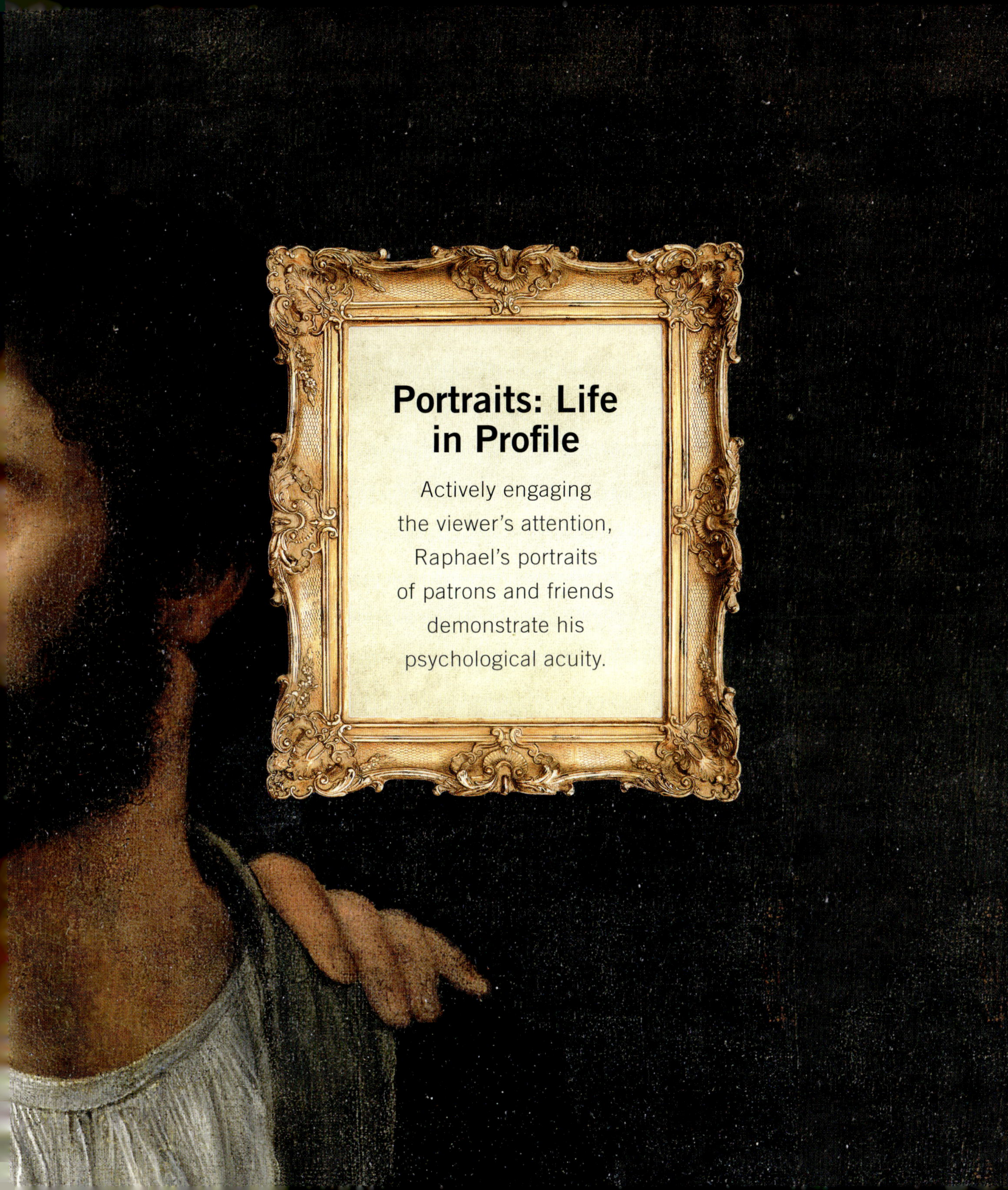

Portraits: Life
in Profile

Actively engaging
the viewer's attention,
Raphael's portraits
of patrons and friends
demonstrate his
psychological acuity.

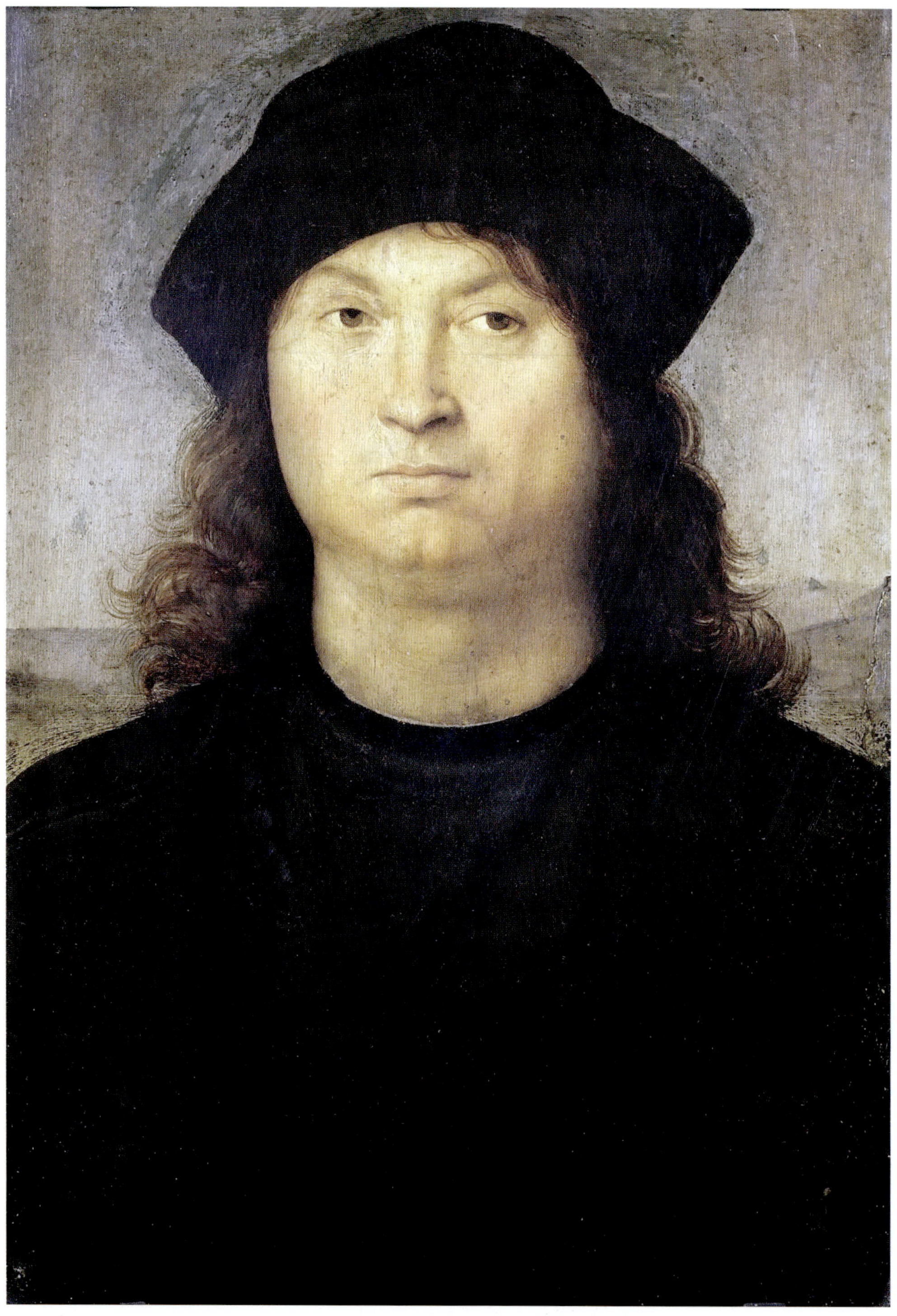

Portrait of a Man, *c.* 1502

Oil on wood, 45 x 31 cm (17¾ x 12¼ in) • Galleria Borghese, Rome

Previously attributed to Perugino, this portrait by Raphael may depict a duke (based on the shape of the sitter's hat). The man's severe appearance is balanced with idealized features such as his flowing hair.

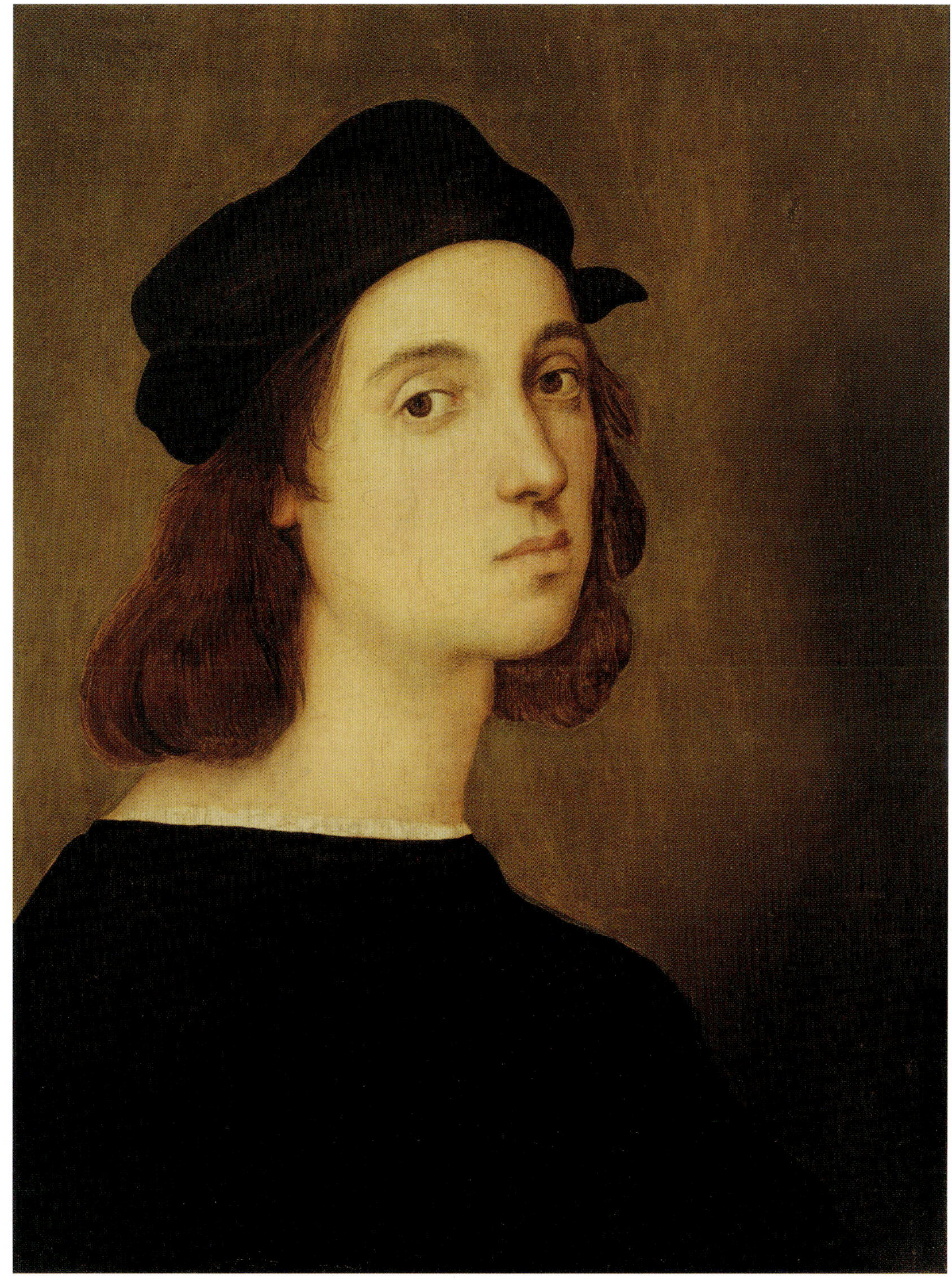

Self-Portrait, 1504–06

Oil on board, 47.5 x 33 cm (18¾ x 13 in) • Galleria degli Uffizi, Florence

This work is considered to be one of Raphael's earliest self-portraits. He is modestly dressed in black with a simple cap and has slightly melancholic features and mournful brown doe eyes.

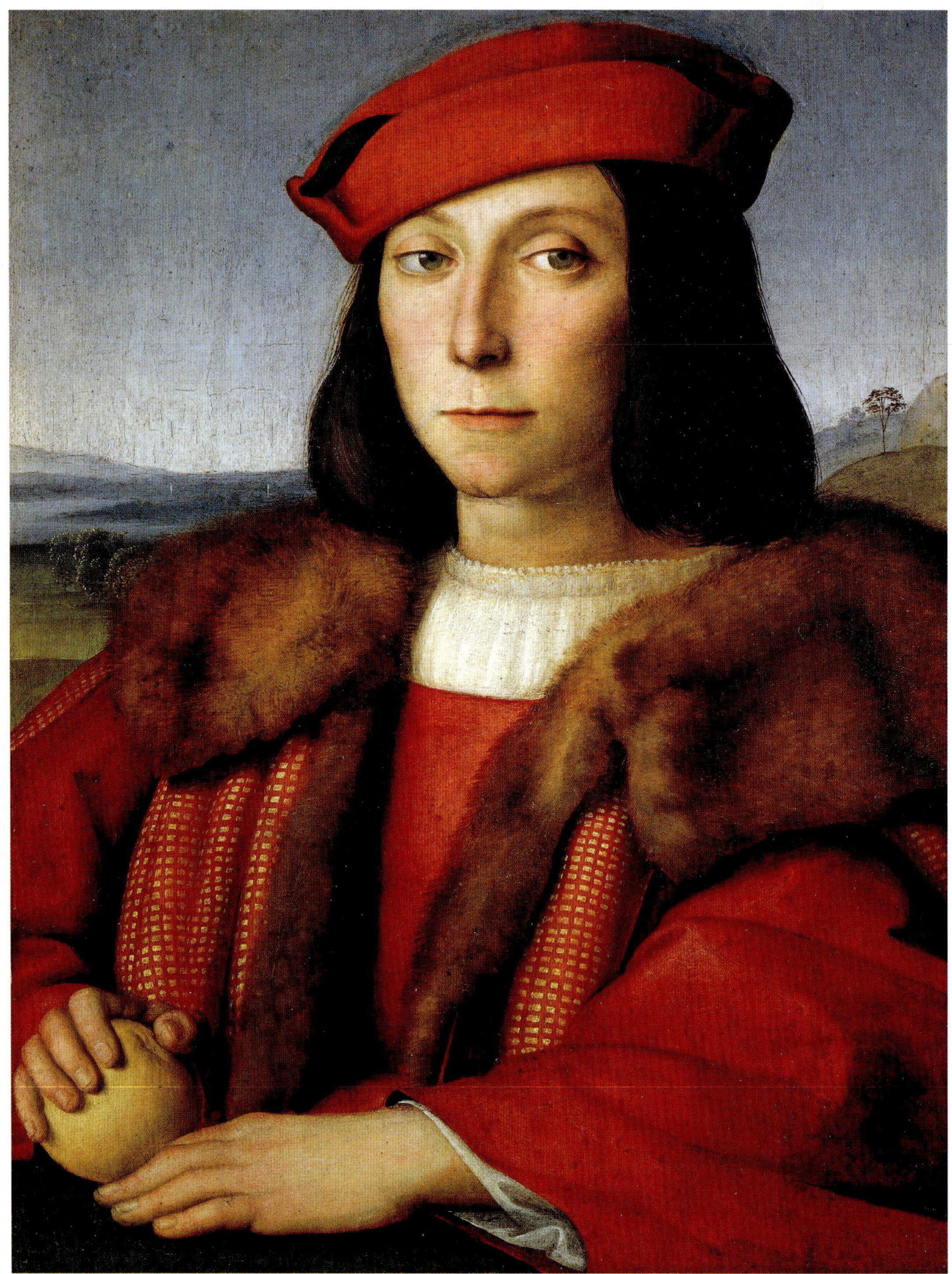

Young Man with an Apple, *c.* 1505
Oil on wood, 47 x 35 cm (18½ x 14 in) • Galleria degli Uffizi, Florence

This portrait, possibly of Francesco Maria I Della Rovere, Duke of Urbino (1490–1538), takes its resonant colour, softly modulated lighting, clear composition and tree-dotted panorama from a 1494 portrait by Perugino.

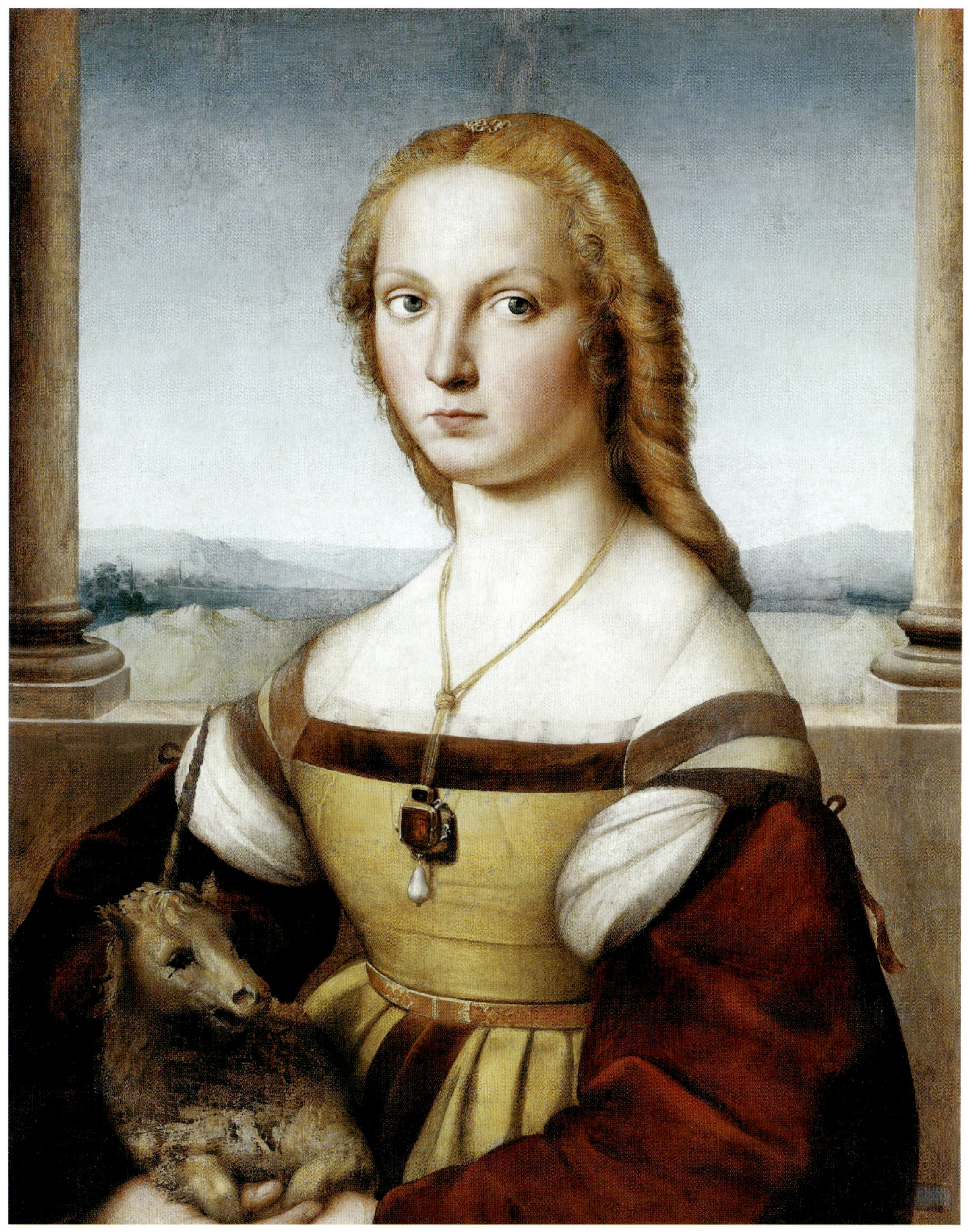

Lady with a Unicorn, c. 1505–06
Oil on panel transferred to canvas, 65 x 61 cm (26 x 24 in)
• Galleria Borghese, Rome

Raphael initially painted this blonde, blue-eyed woman holding a dog instead of a unicorn, a symbol of chastity or virginity. She is depicted in front of the low wall of a balcony or loggia.

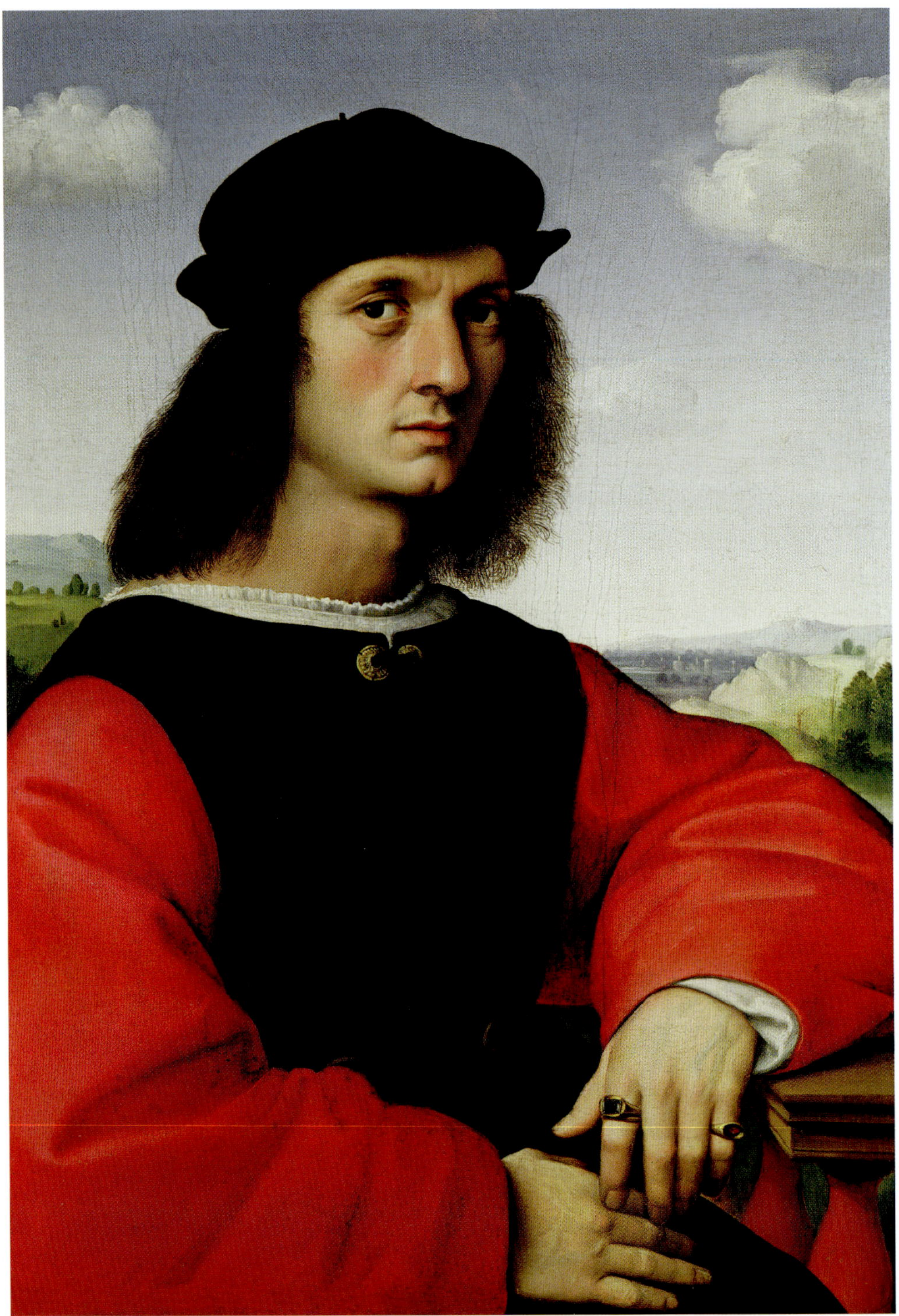

Portrait of Agnolo Doni, 1506

Oil on panel, 63.5 x 45 cm (25 x 17¾ in)
• Galleria Palatina, Palazzo Pitti, Florence

Probably no marriage has been more superbly commemorated than Agnolo Doni's to Maddalena Strozzi. Leaning his arm against a parapet, the bridegroom's cleft chin, frown of concentration and hands are portrayed in impressive detail.

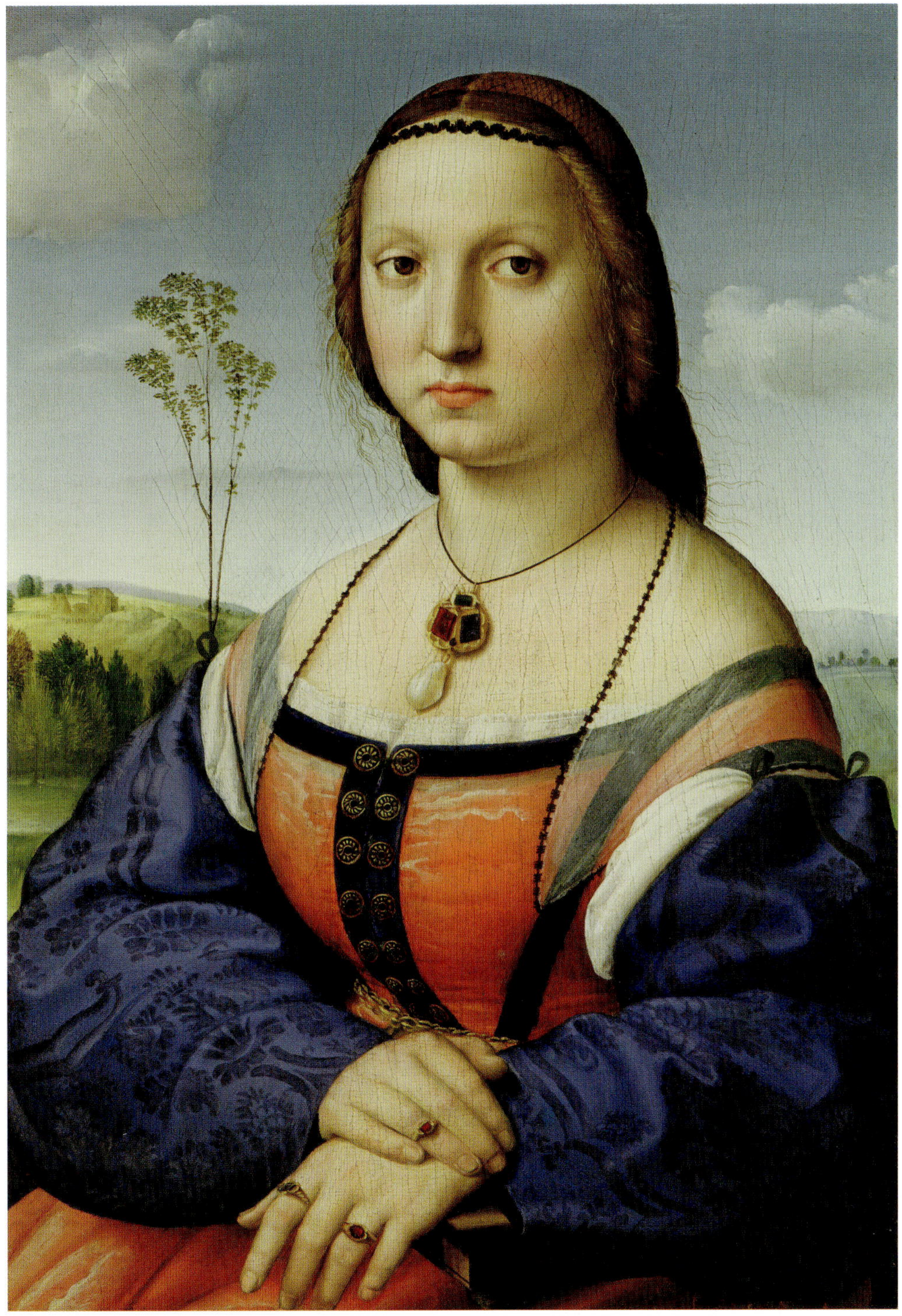

Portrait of Maddalena Doni, 1506
Oil on panel, 63.5 x 45 cm (25 x 17¾ in)
• Galleria Palatina, Palazzo Pitti, Florence

This portrait is in effect a richly coloured variant of Leonardo's *Mona Lisa*. Maddalena was in her teens when Raphael painted her. Her jewellery (including a pear-shaped pearl as big as an eye) is spectacular.

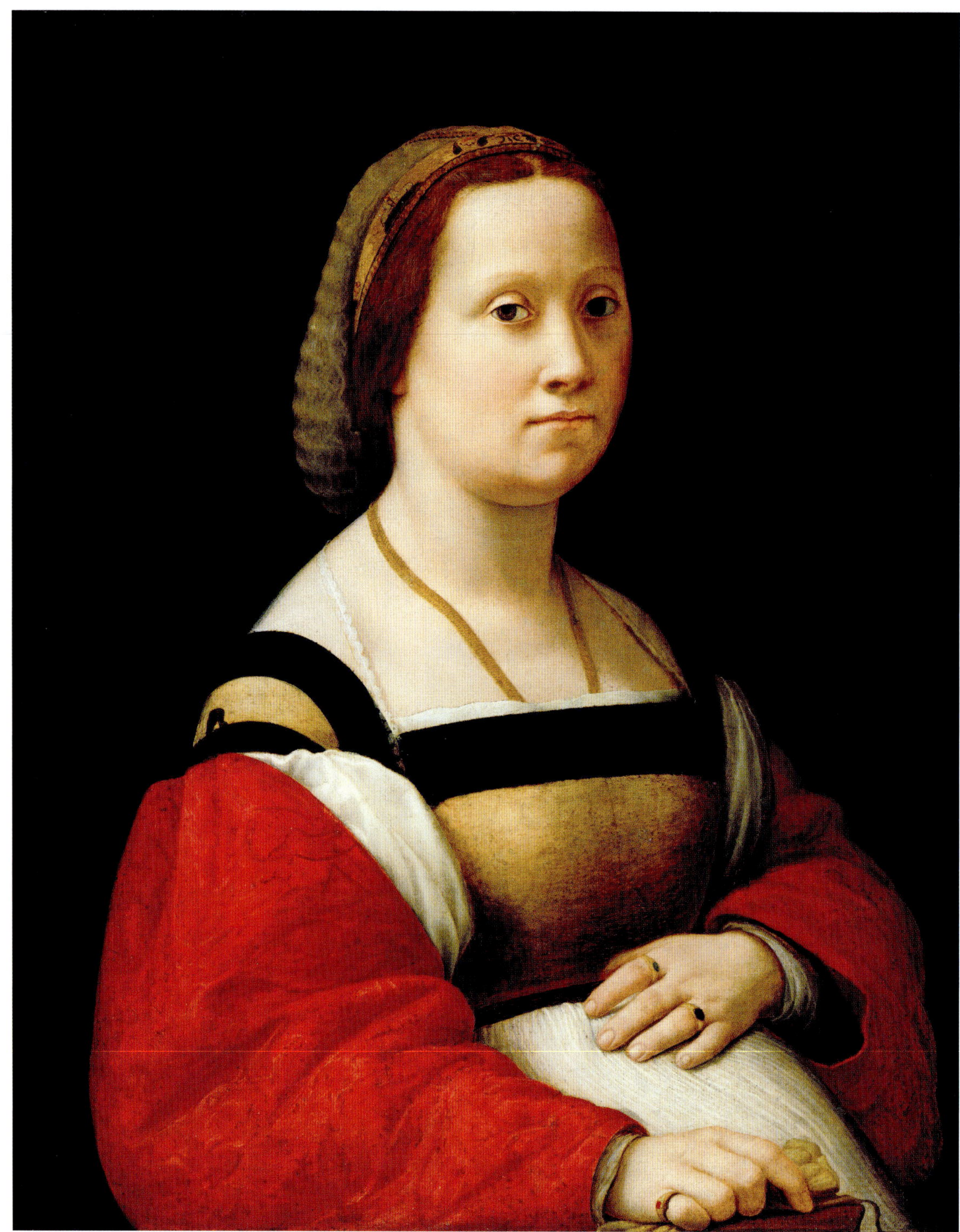

La Donna Gravida, _c._ 1505–06
Oil on panel, 66 x 52 cm (26 x 20 in)
• Galleria Palatina, Palazzo Pitti, Florence

There are not many Renaissance portraits of pregnant women, but Raphael sensitively depicted this mother-to-be with her left hand resting protectively on her stomach. She gazes directly at the viewer.

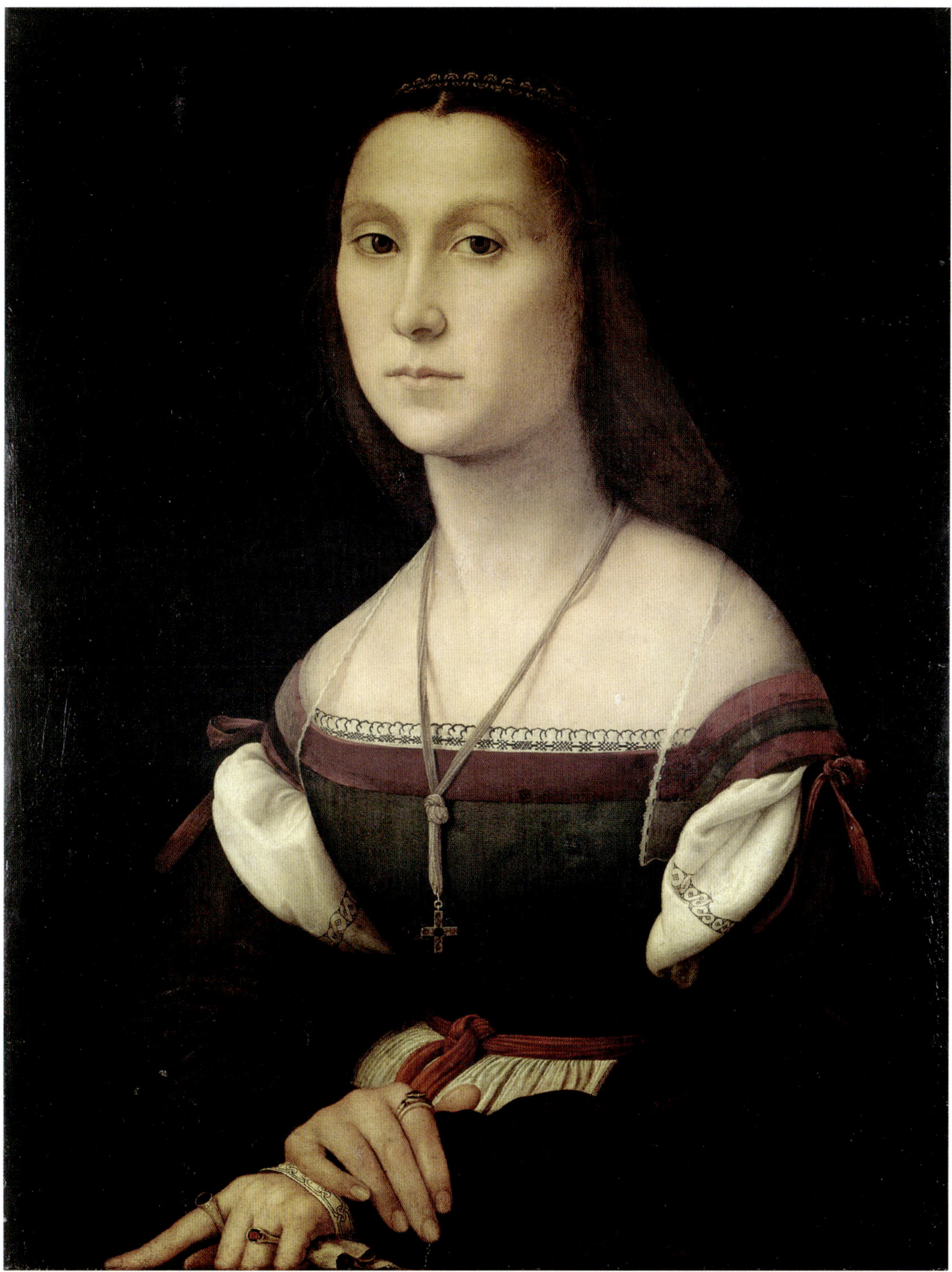

Portrait of a Woman (La Muta), *c.* **1507**
Oil on wood, 64 x 48 cm (25¼ x 19 in)
• Galleria Nazionale delle Marche, Urbino

Known as *La Muta*, the silent one, this unknown noblewoman extends her index finger and presses it against a ledge that has become the painting's frame. She wears three rings, but her gold necklace is a later addition.

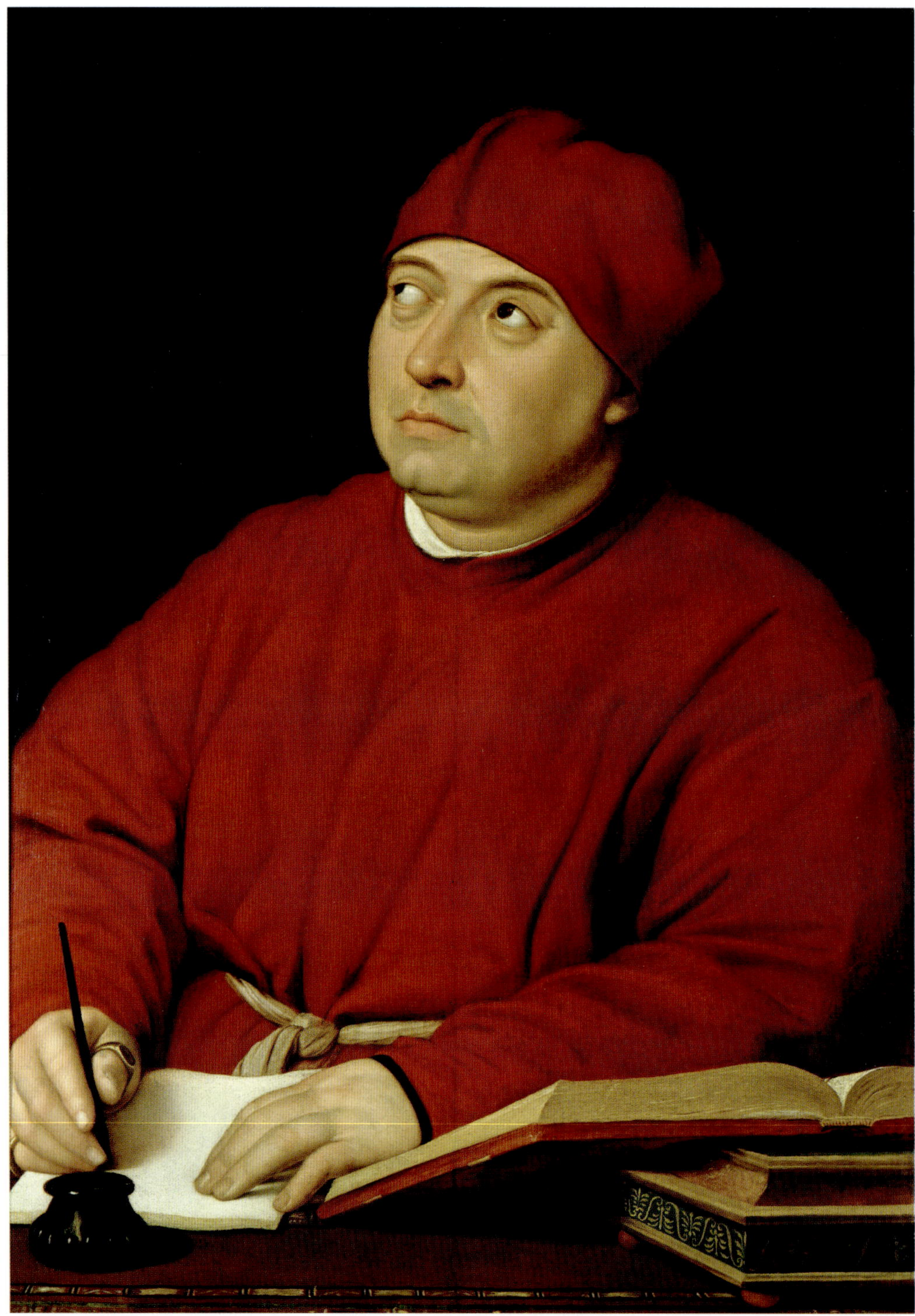

Portrait of Tommaso Inghirami, 1509
Oil on wood, 91 x 61 cm (36 x 24 in)
• Galleria Palatina, Palazzo Pitti, Florence

Tommaso Inghirami (1470–1516) was a Renaissance celebrity, esteemed for his erudition and theatrical abilities, but Raphael (who knew him well) portrayed him in his role as Vatican librarian. His eyes pronouncedly misaligned, Inghirami's gaze is tactfully presented as an expression of inspiration.

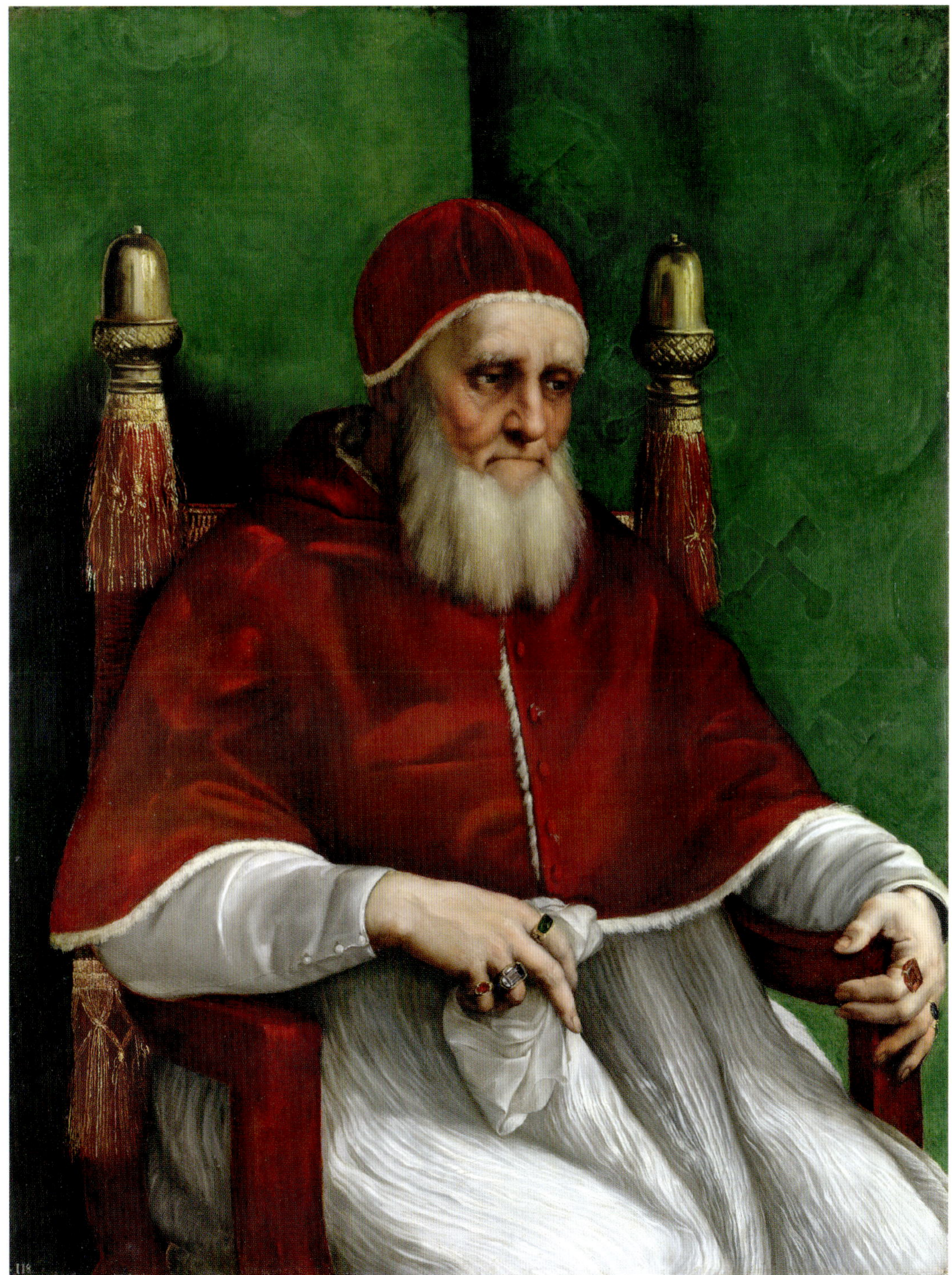

Portrait of Pope Julius II, 1511–12
Oil on poplar, 108.7 x 81cm (43 x 32 in) • National Gallery, London

Pope Julius is shown lost in thought, clutching a silk handkerchief. The acorns on his chair refer to his family name – Della Rovere (*rovere* is Italian for oak). Raphael skilfully manipulated the paint to depict wrinkled skin and ruched fabric.

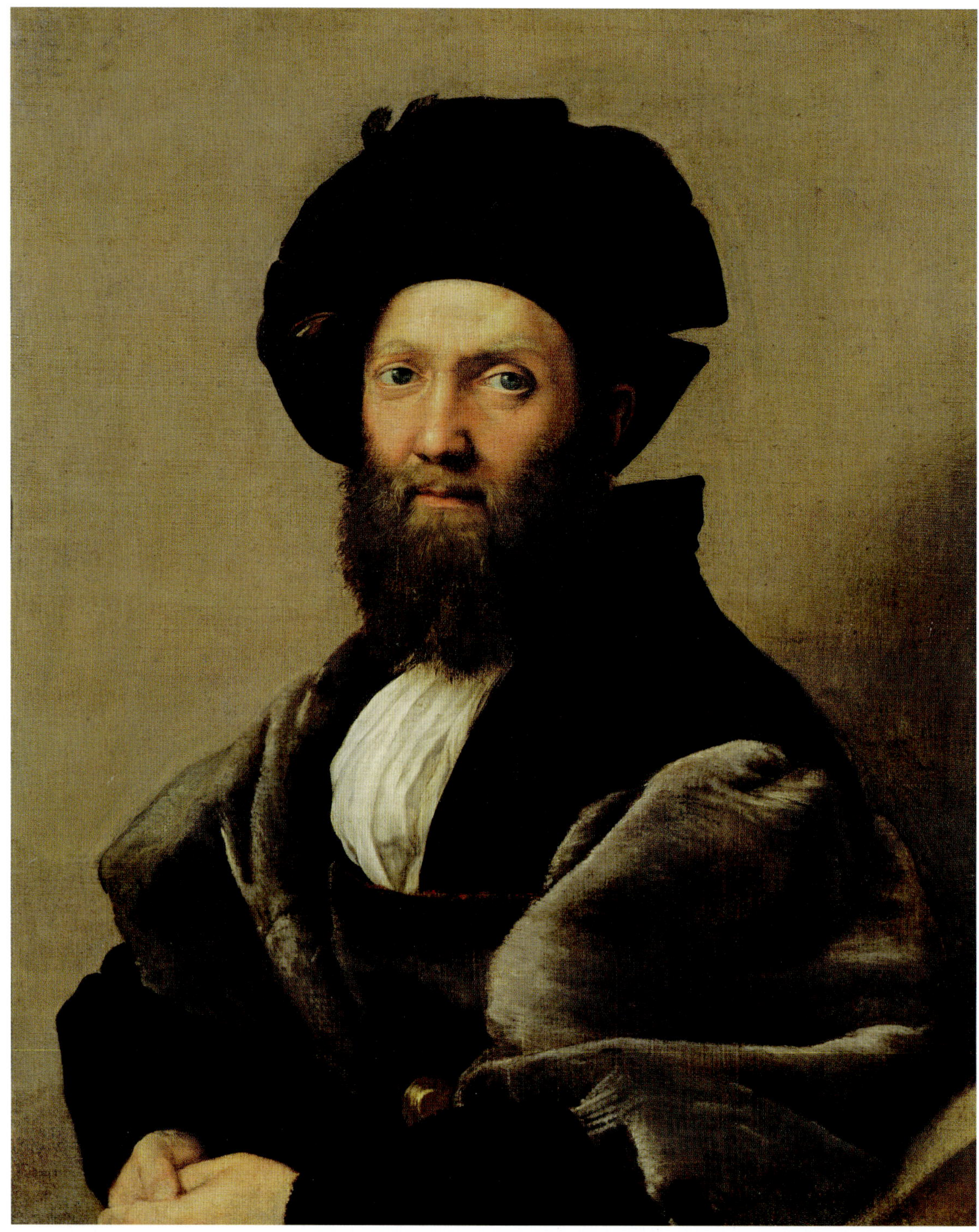

Portrait of Baldassare Castiglione, 1514–15
Oil on canvas, 82 x 67 cm (32⅓ x 26⅔ in) • Musée du Louvre, Paris

The impression of Castiglione's compelling physical presence is enhanced by Raphael's tight framing of his body and cropping of his hands. Castiglione is depicted in a sober monochrome palette, applied very thinly on the canvas.

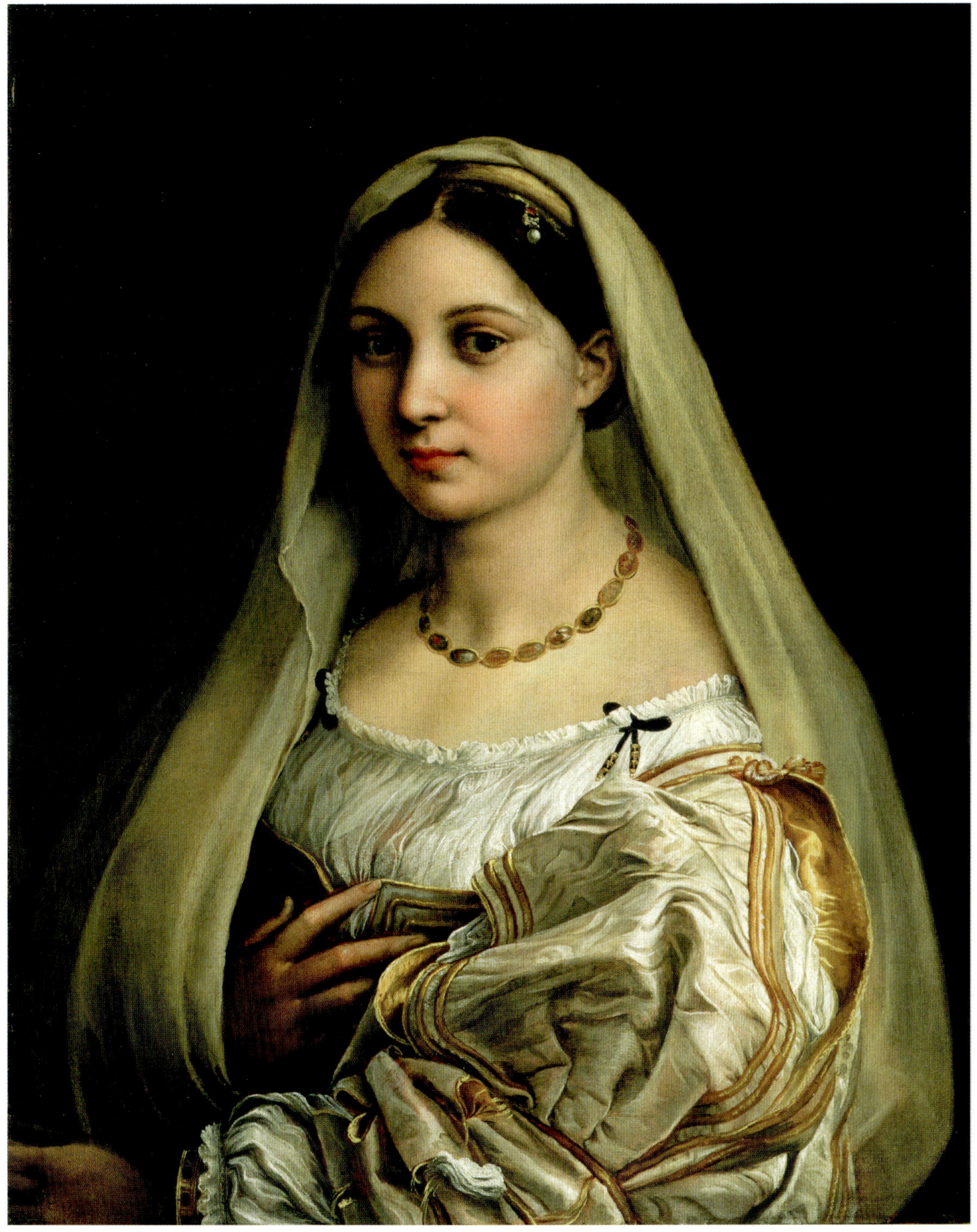

La Donna Velata, 1515
Oil on canvas, 82 x 60.5 cm (32⅓ x 23⅖ in)
• Galleria Palatina, Palazzo Pitti, Florence

The opulently dressed sitter of *La Donna Velata* (the veiled woman) is unknown. She may have been Raphael's mistress but the gesture of her hand pointing to her heart suggests this is a matrimonial portrait.

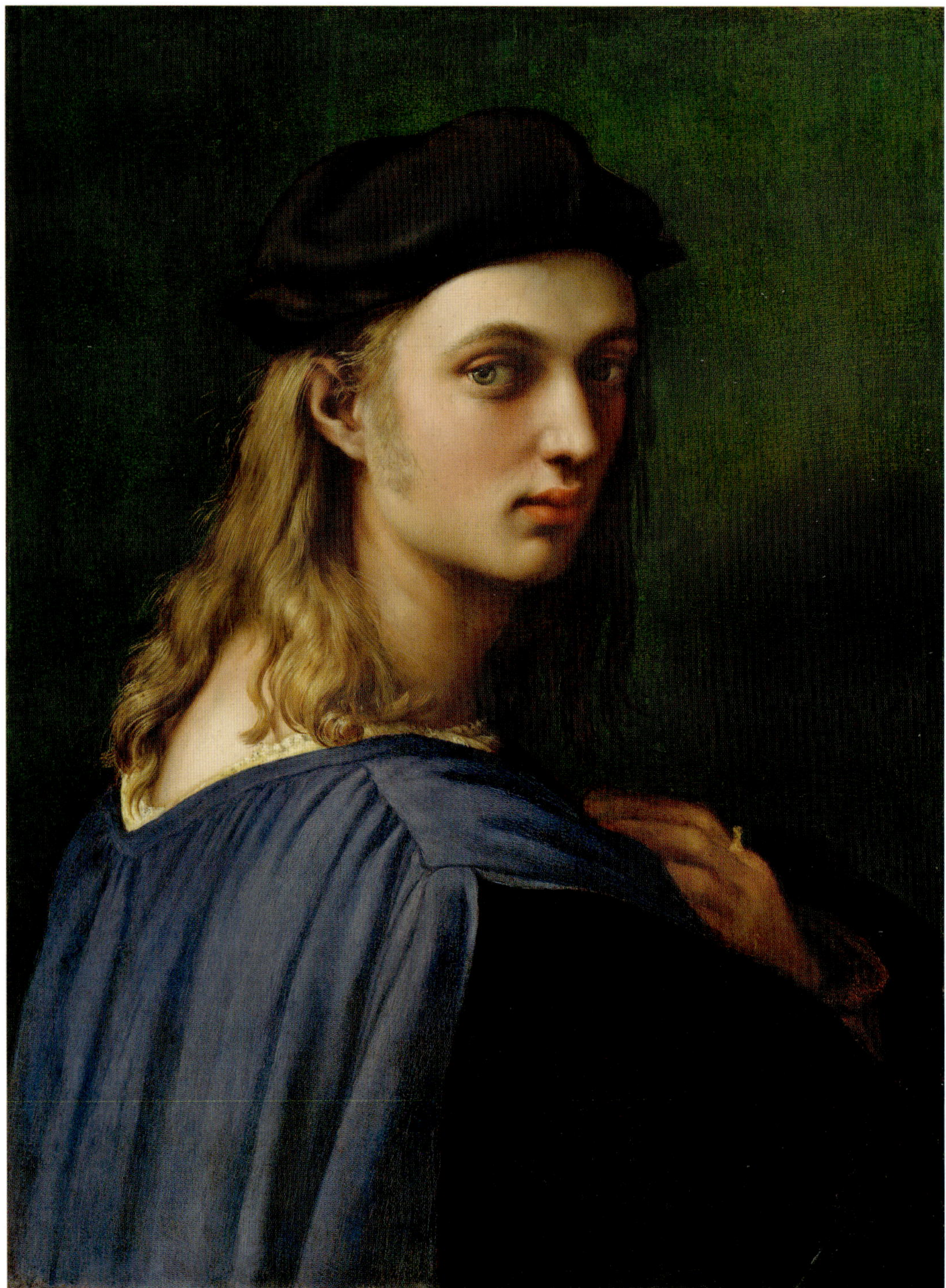

Portrait of Bindo Altoviti, *c.* **1515**
Oil on panel, 59.7 x 43.8 cm (23½ x 17¼ in)
• National Gallery of Art, Washington, DC

This portrait was commissioned by the sitter, the 'beautiful banker' and art patron, Bindo Altoviti (1491–1557). In this palpably erotic image, Raphael depicts his friend looking back seductively over his shoulder, his smooth, pale skin framed by curls.

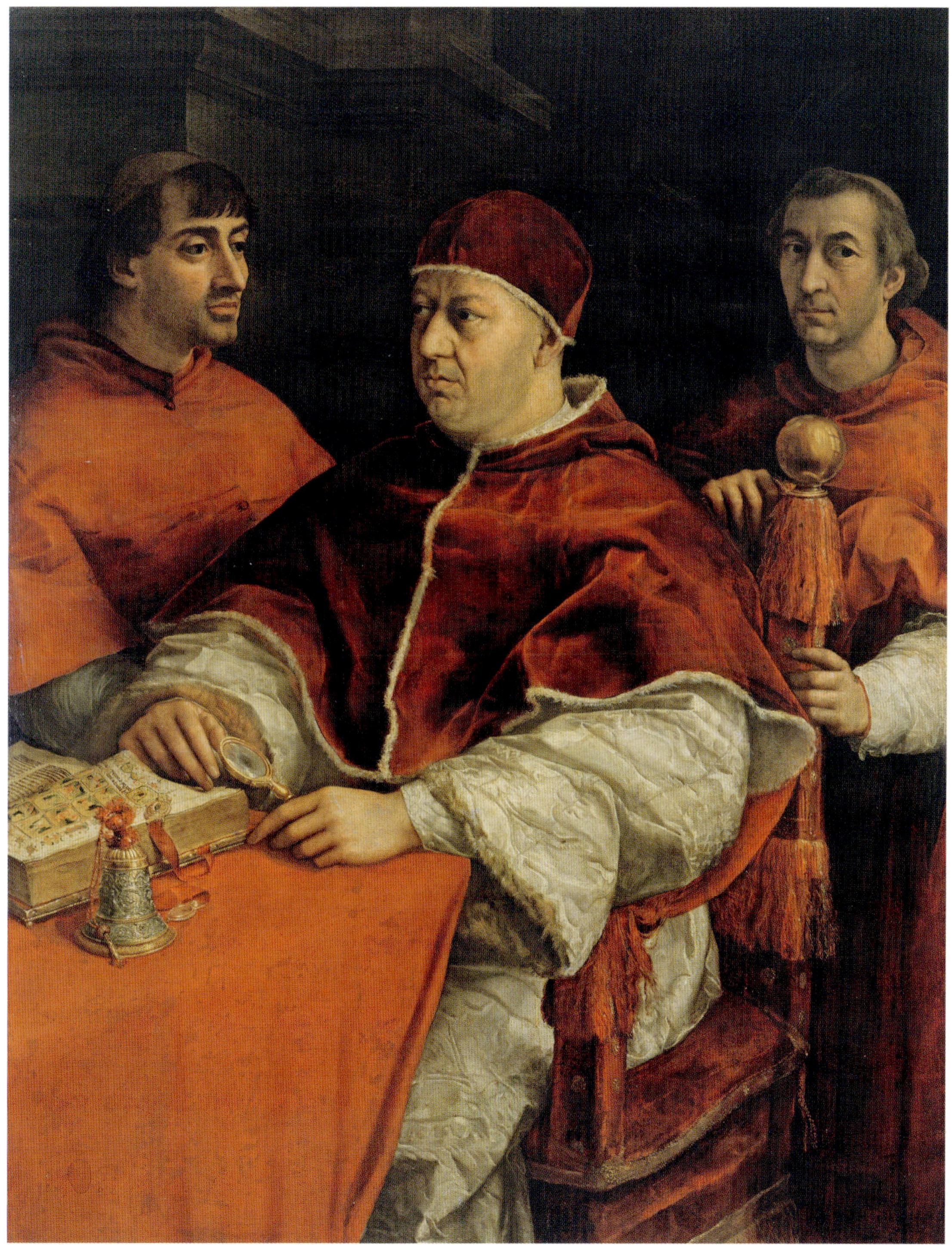

Portrait of Pope Leo X with Cardinals Giulio de' Medici and Luigi de' Rossi, c. 1518

Oil on wood, 154 x 119 cm (60⅔ x 47 in) • Galleria degli Uffizi, Florence

A key feature in this sumptuous portrait is the sensual feel of the contrasting textures of velvet and silk in the Pope's attire (indicating his penchant for excess). This complex, realistic painting is full of intricate details.

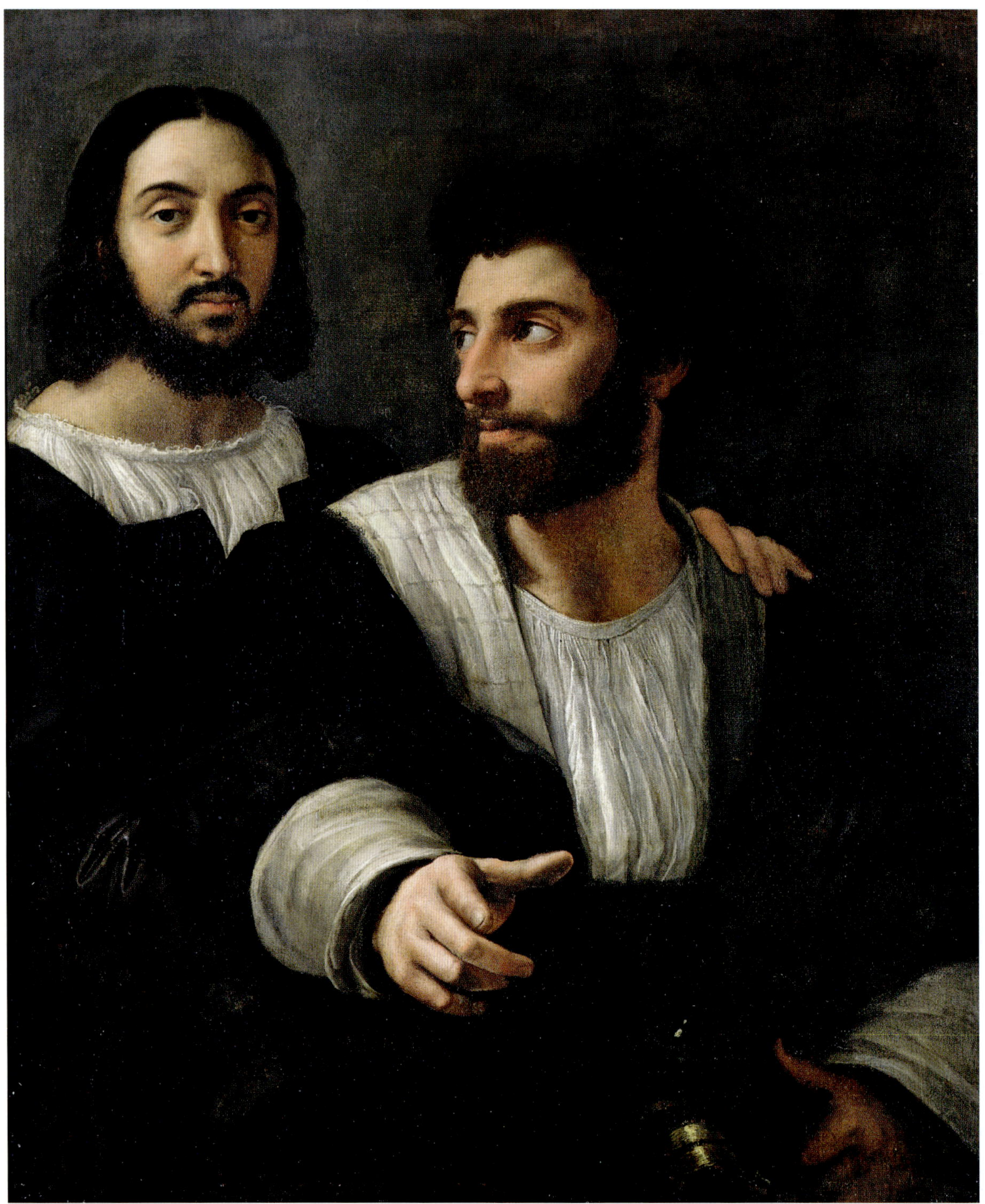

Self-Portrait with a Friend (Double Portrait), 1518–20
Oil on canvas, 99 x 83 cm (39 x 32⅓ in) • Musée du Louvre, Paris

Raphael painted himself with a serene Christ-like appearance, his hand resting on the shoulder of his close friend. The latter was traditionally identified as the artist's fencing master because of the sword at his hip.

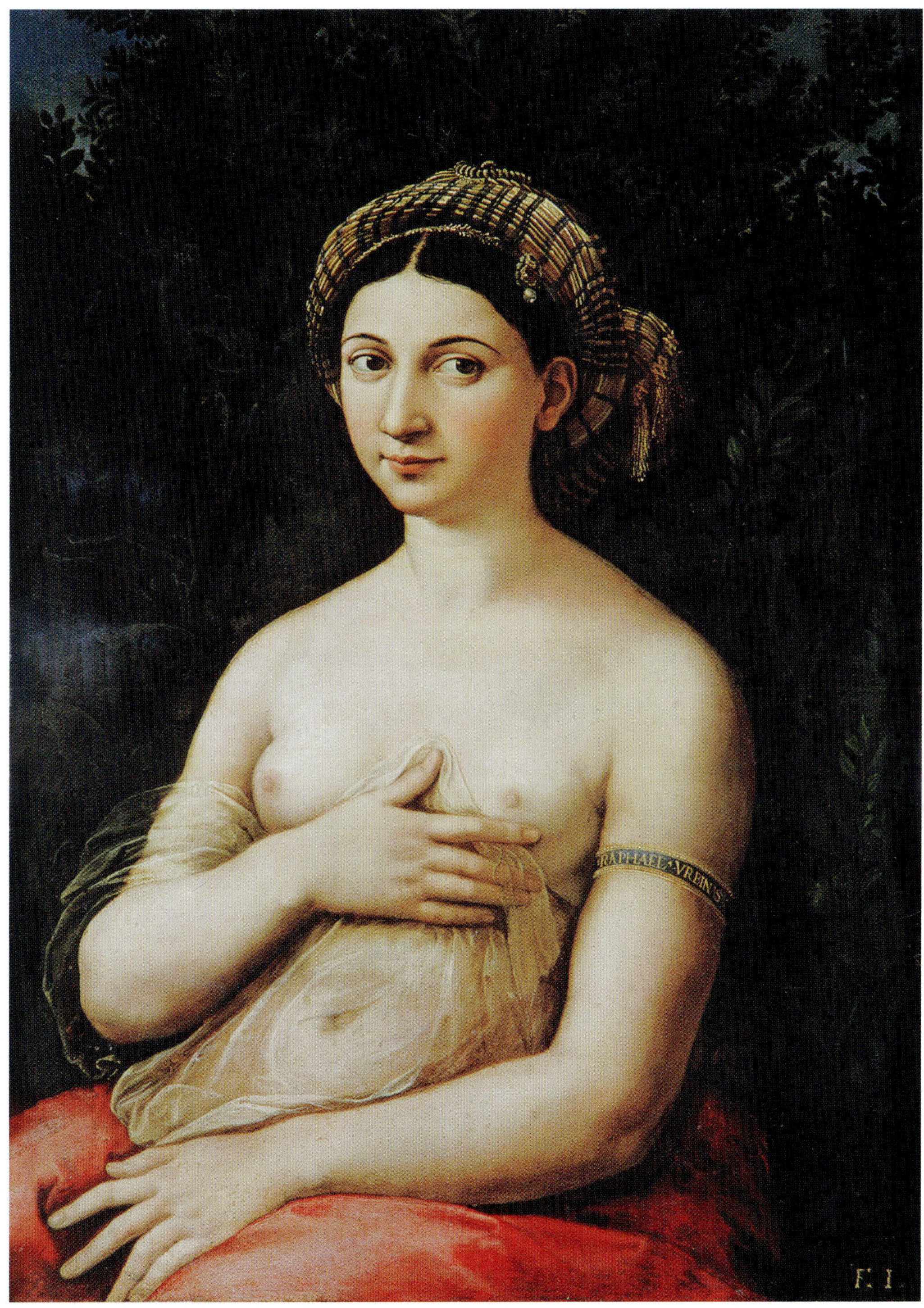

La Fornarina, 1518–20
Oil on wood, 85 x 60 cm (33½ x 23⅔ in)
• Galleria Nazionale d'Arte Antica, Palazzo Barberini, Rome

La Fornarina (the baker's girl) is believed to depict Raphael's mistress. The woman, with individualized features, is seated in the pose of a Classical sculpture of Venus, her breasts bare. She is adorned with a contemporary transparent veil and jewel.

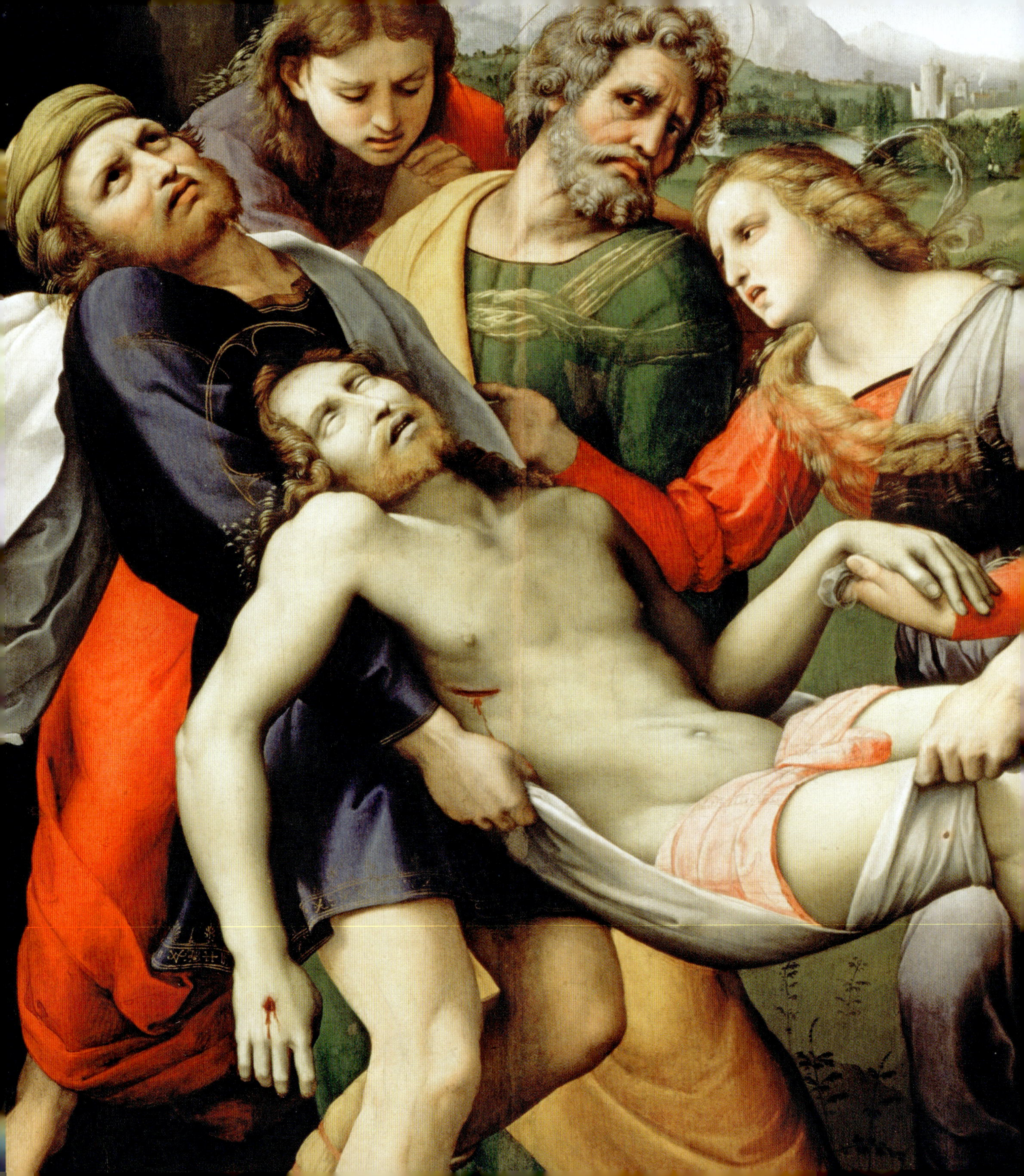

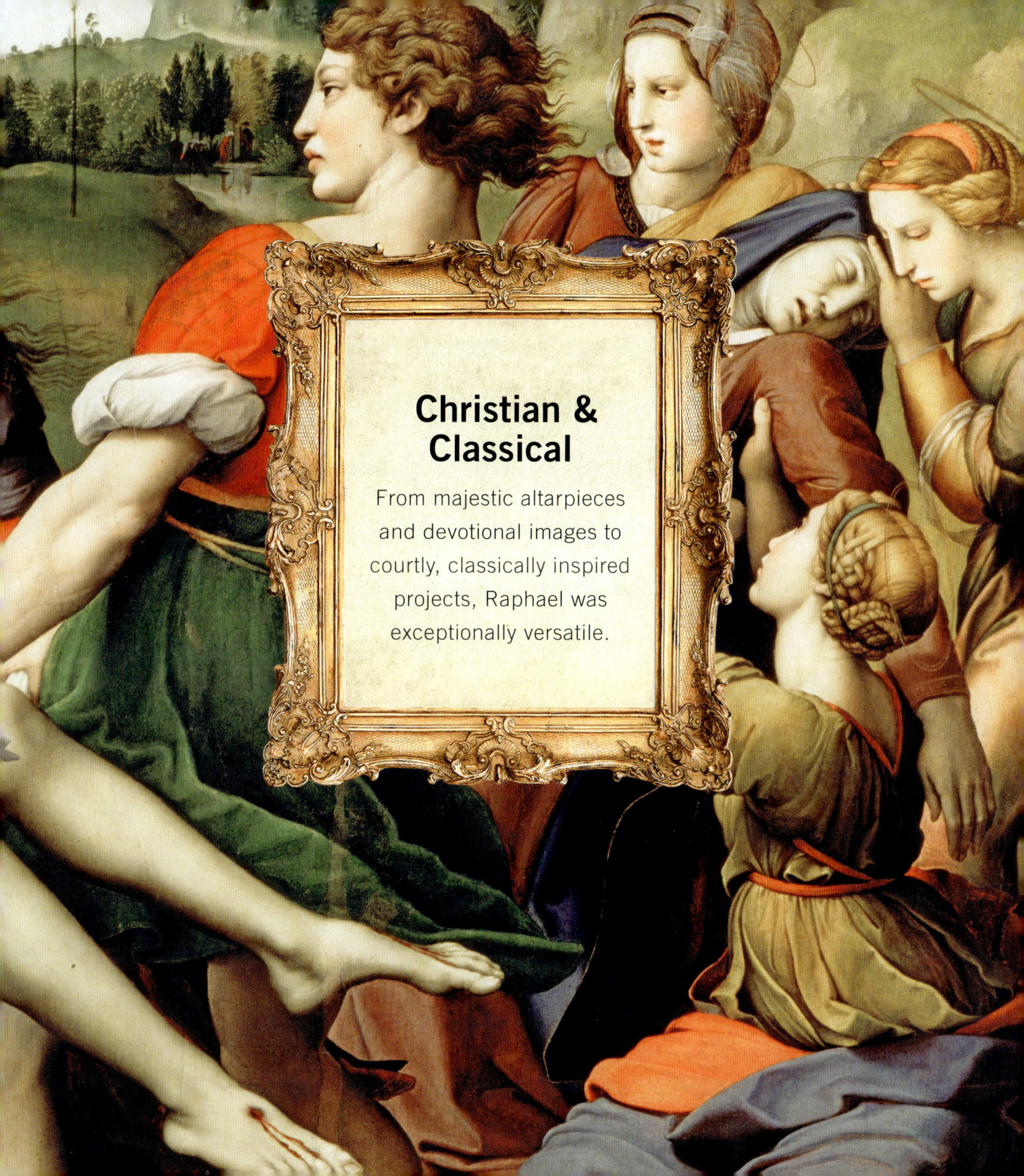

Christian &
Classical

From majestic altarpieces
and devotional images to
courtly, classically inspired
projects, Raphael was
exceptionally versatile.

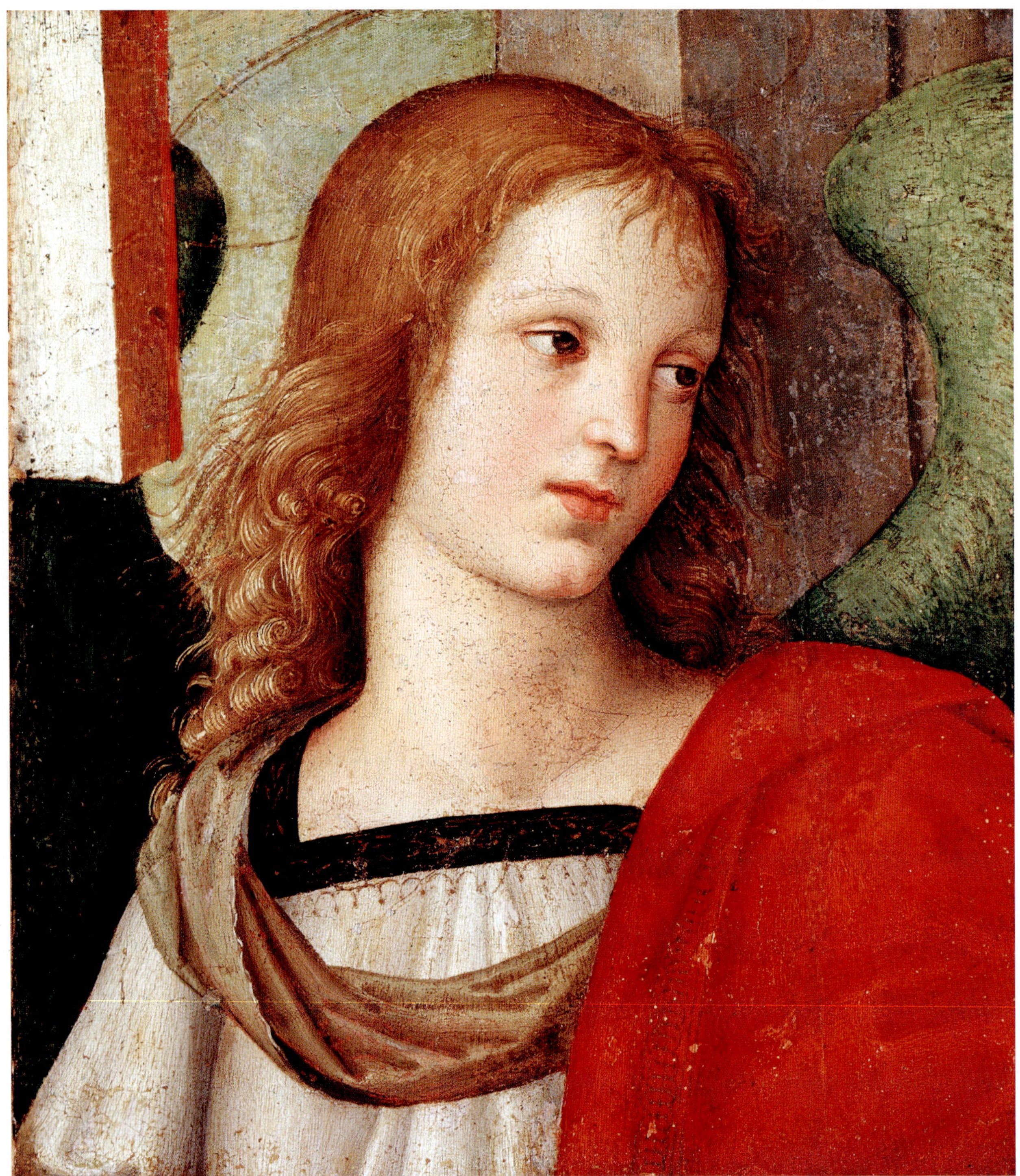

Angel (fragment from Coronation of Saint Nicholas of Tolentino, or Baronci Altarpiece), 1501
Oil on wood, 31 x 27 cm (12¼ x 10⅔ in)
• Pinacoteca Tosio Martinengo, Brescia

Only fragments of Raphael's first altarpiece survive. Originally, Nicholas of Tolentino stood in the centre, a demon under his feet, flanked by angels. The Madonna, Saint Augustine and God the Father suspended a crown above Nicholas's head.

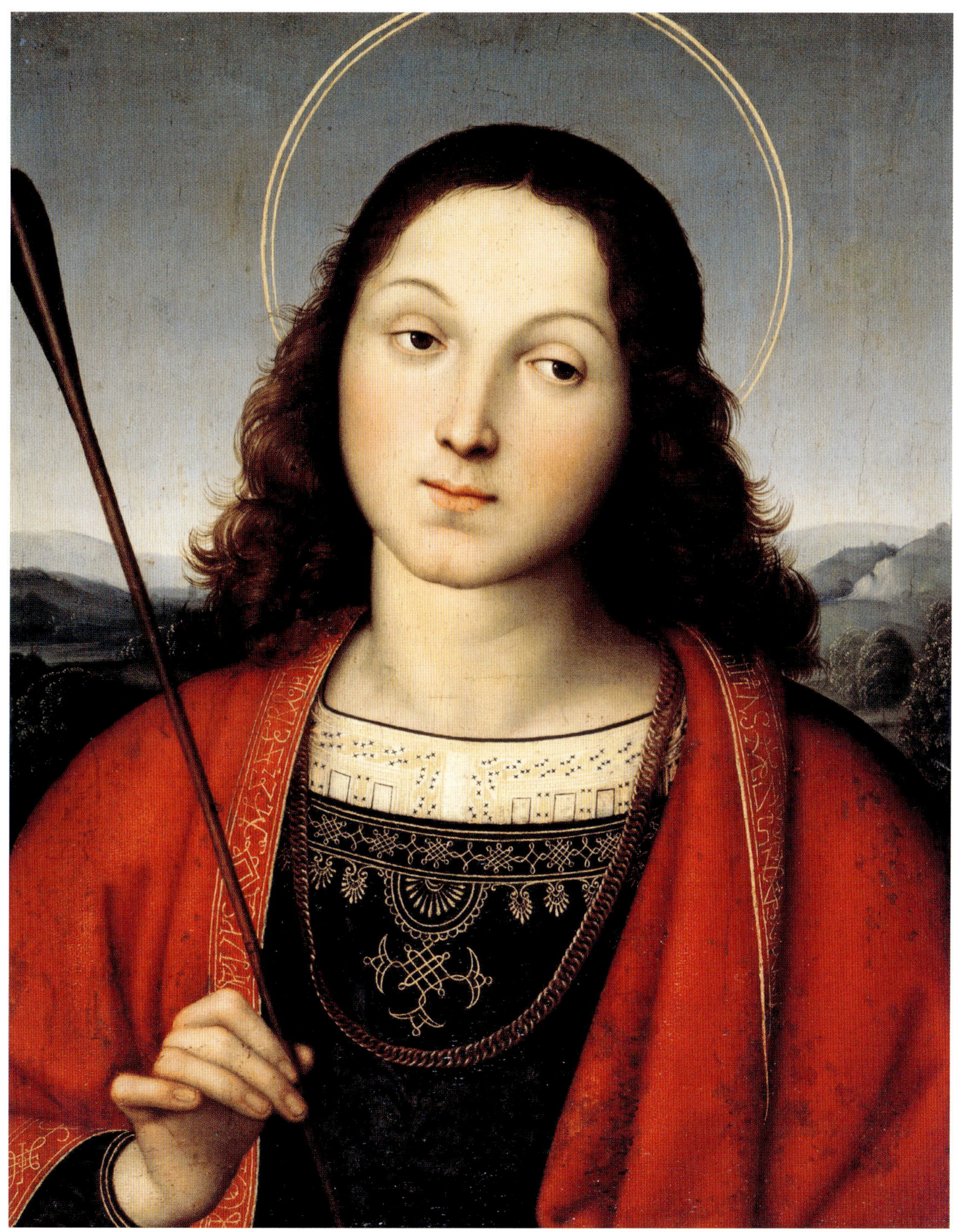

Saint Sebastian, *c.* **1501–02**
Oil on wood, 43 x 34 cm (17 x 13⅖ in) • Accademia Carrara, Bergamo

A serene-looking Sebastian (his pose reminiscent of Perugino's figures) is shown half-length and richly dressed in embroidered robes and a gold chain. He holds a single arrow (the symbol of his martyrdom), his little finger delicately crooked.

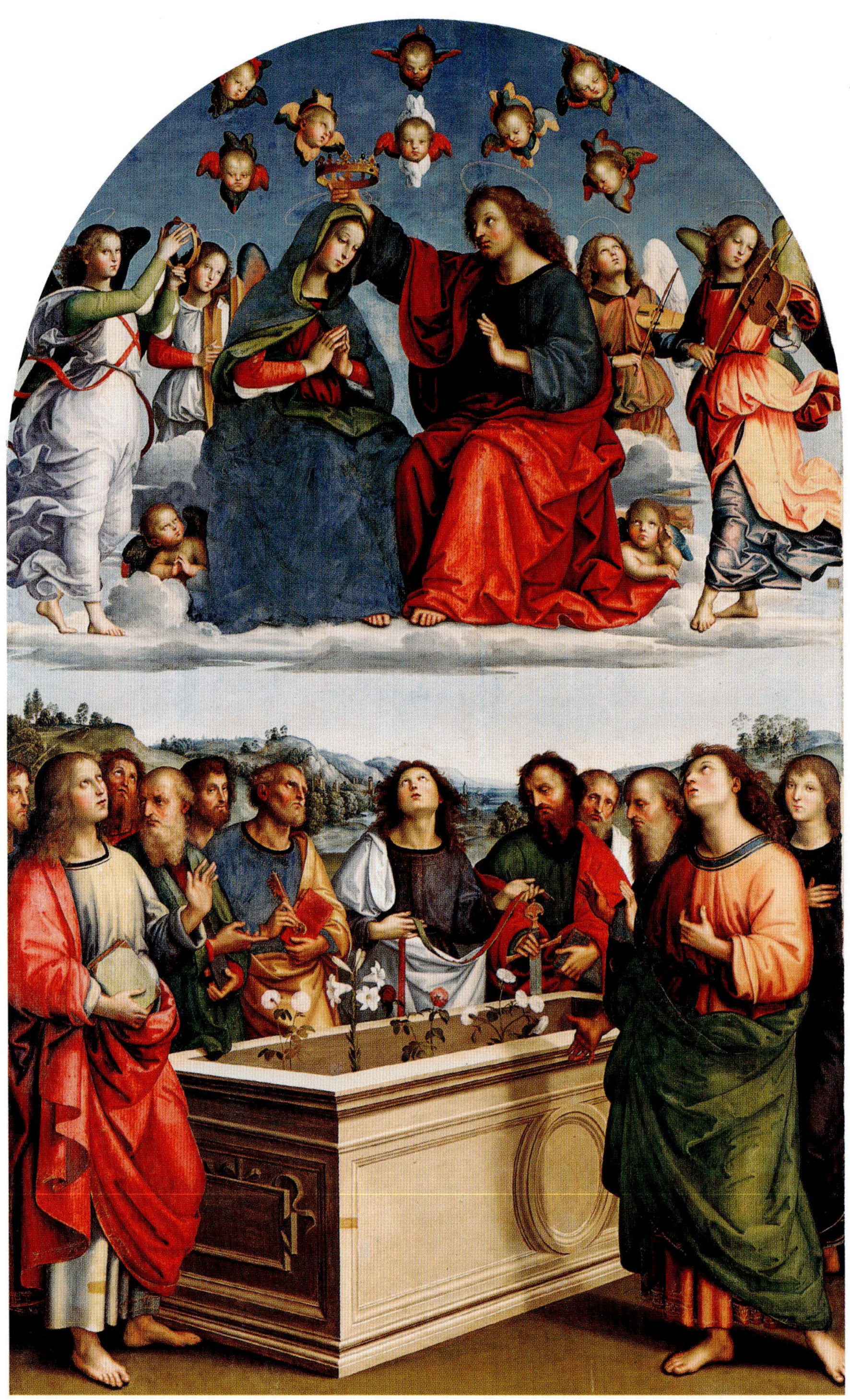

Coronation of the Virgin (Oddi Altarpiece), 1502–04
Oil on wood transferred to canvas, 267 x 163 cm (105 x 64¼ in)
• Pinacoteca Vaticana, Rome

Painted for the Oddi family chapel in Perugia, this altarpiece shows the depth of Raphael's immersion in Perugino's style. The celestial and earthly realms (Christ crowning the Virgin above and Saint Thomas and the other apostles below) are carefully differentiated.

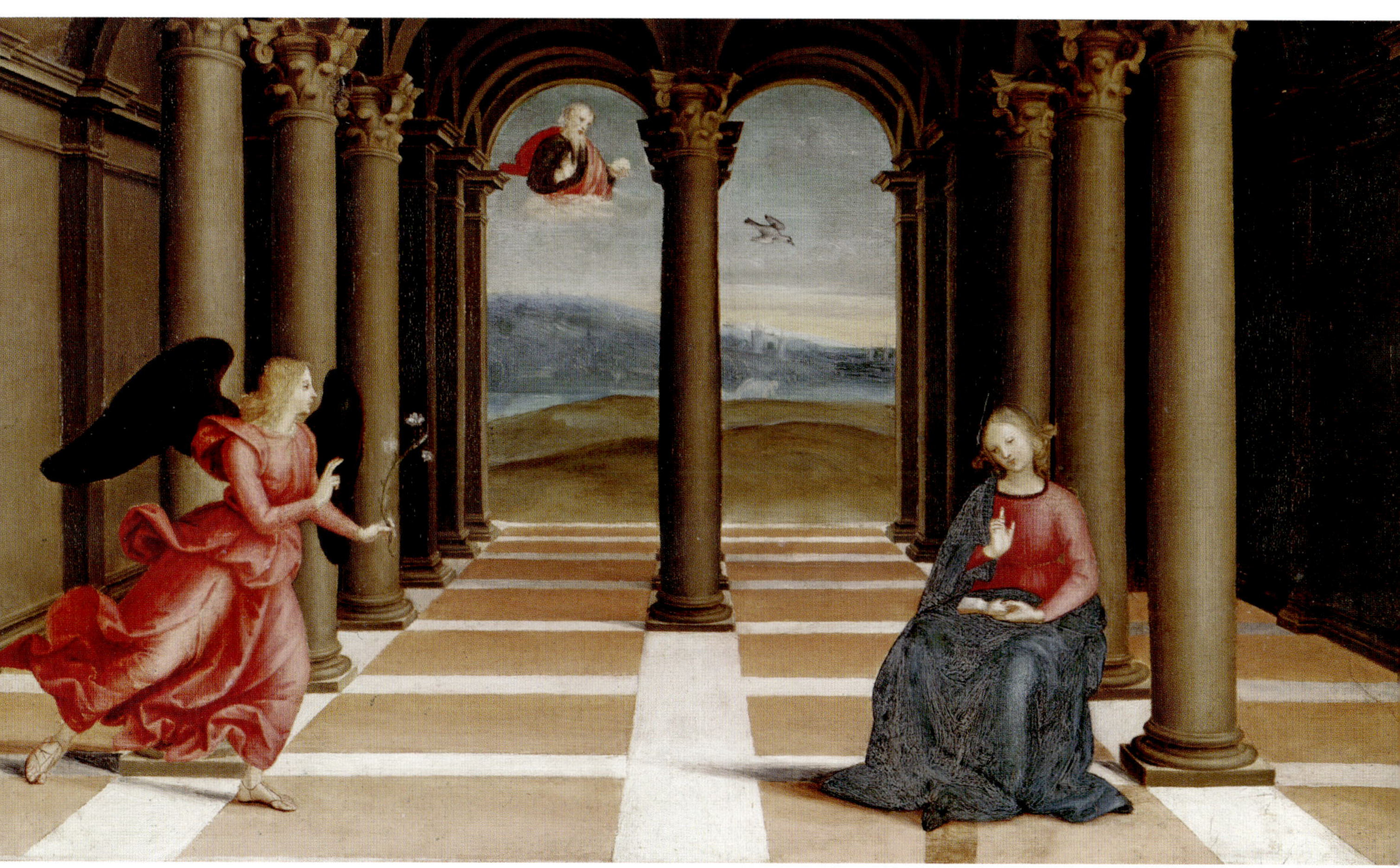

The Annunciation (Oddi Altarpiece predella), 1502–04
Oil on wood transferred to canvas, 27 x 50 cm (10⅔ x 20 in)
• Pinacoteca Vaticana, Rome

Raphael made full cartoons for this predella (the long horizontal structure at the base of the altarpiece). This scene is notable for the angel with his delicately articulated form and lightly rippling drapery, and the open and wide landscape.

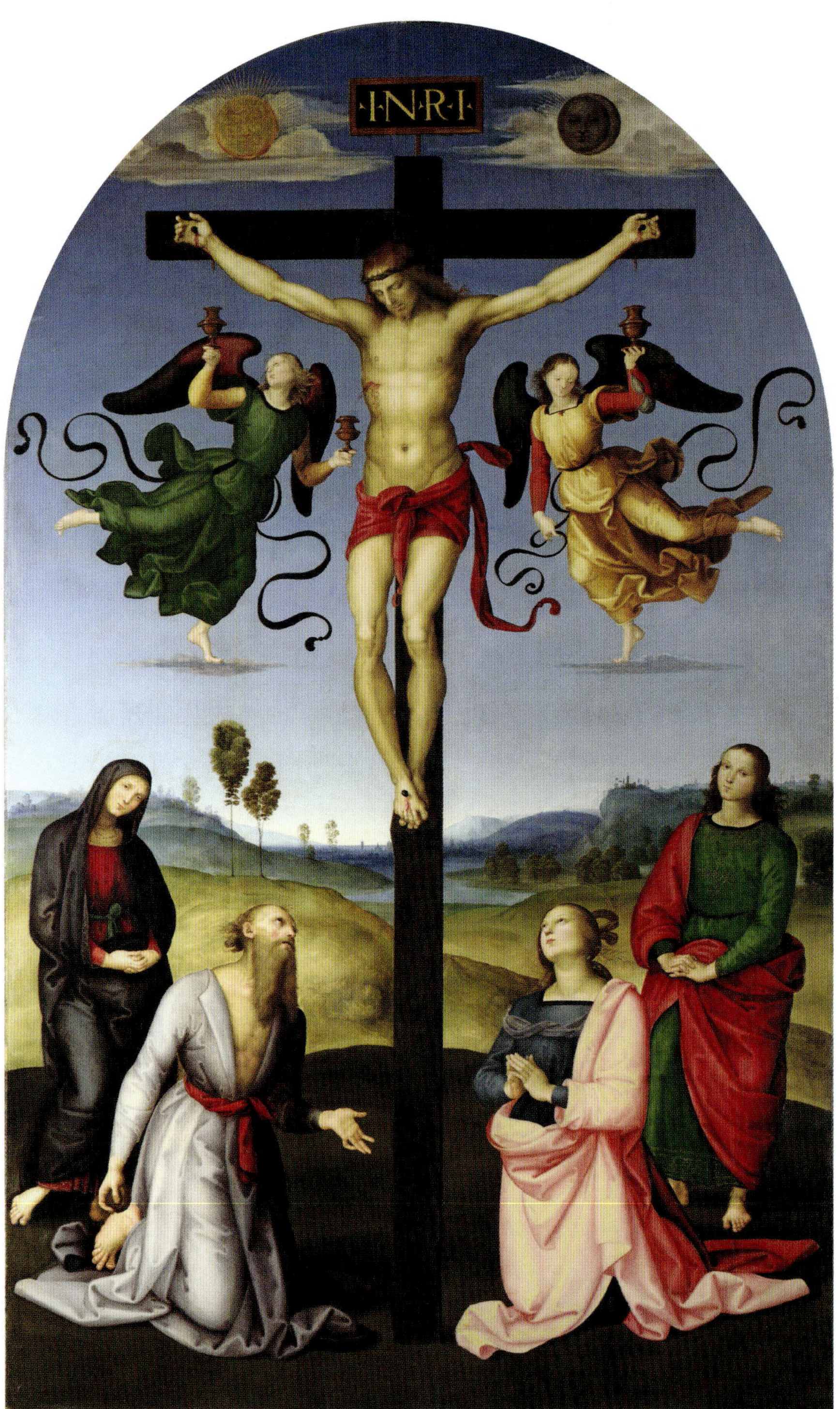

The Mond Crucifixion, 1503
Oil on poplar, 283.3 x 167.3 cm (111½ x 66 in)
• National Gallery, London

This painting includes the earliest of Raphael's signatures (written on the bottom of the cross). It owes a great debt to Perugino, apparent in the idealized faces of the figures (with almond eyes and small mouths).

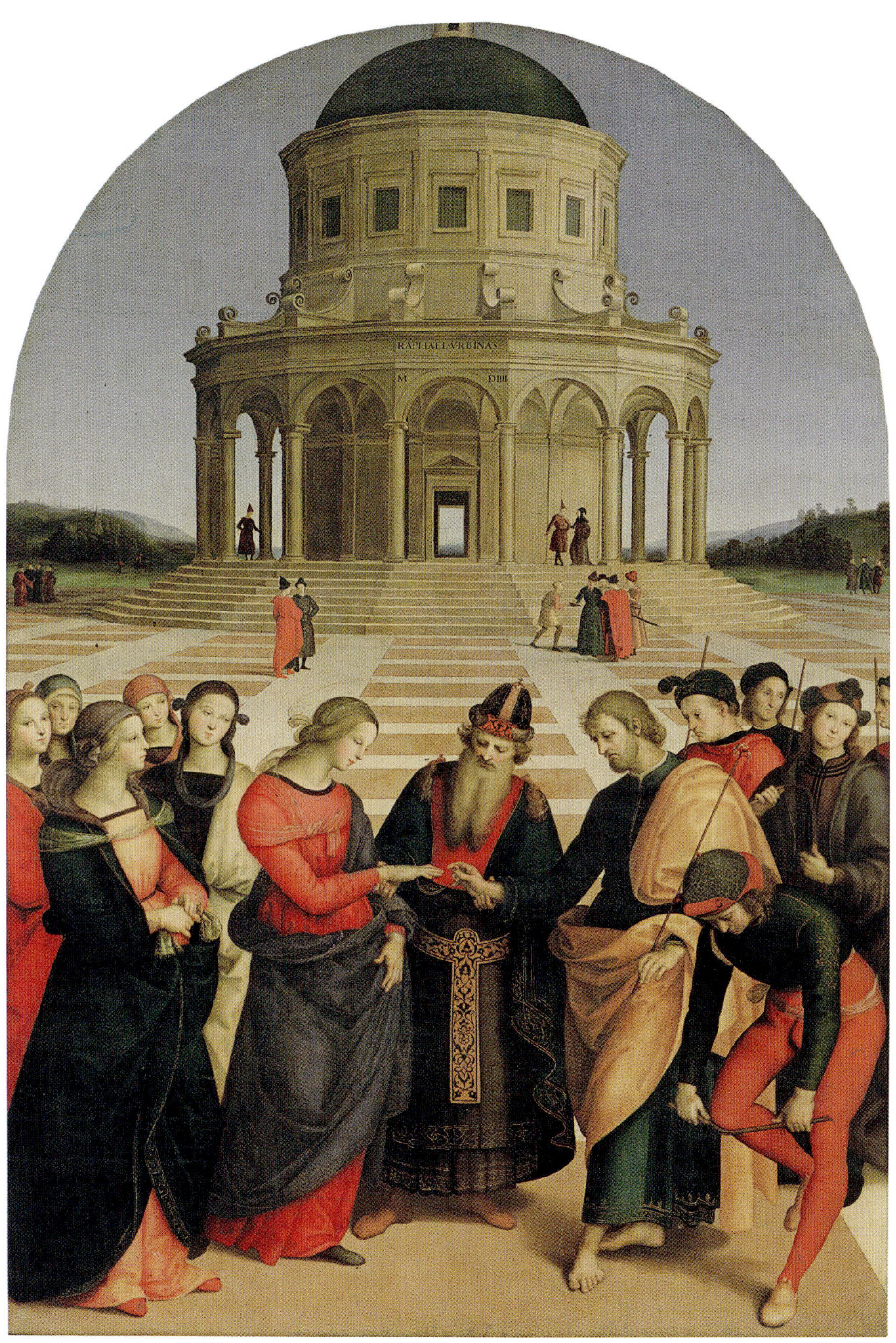

Betrothal of the Virgin (Lo Sposalizio), 1504
Oil on panel, 170 x 118 cm (67 x 46½ in)
• Pinacoteca di Brera, Milan

This altarpiece suggests that Raphael may have had access to drawings from Perugino's workshop. However, Raphael added a more nuanced narrative and a greater sense of space to Perugino's original idea.

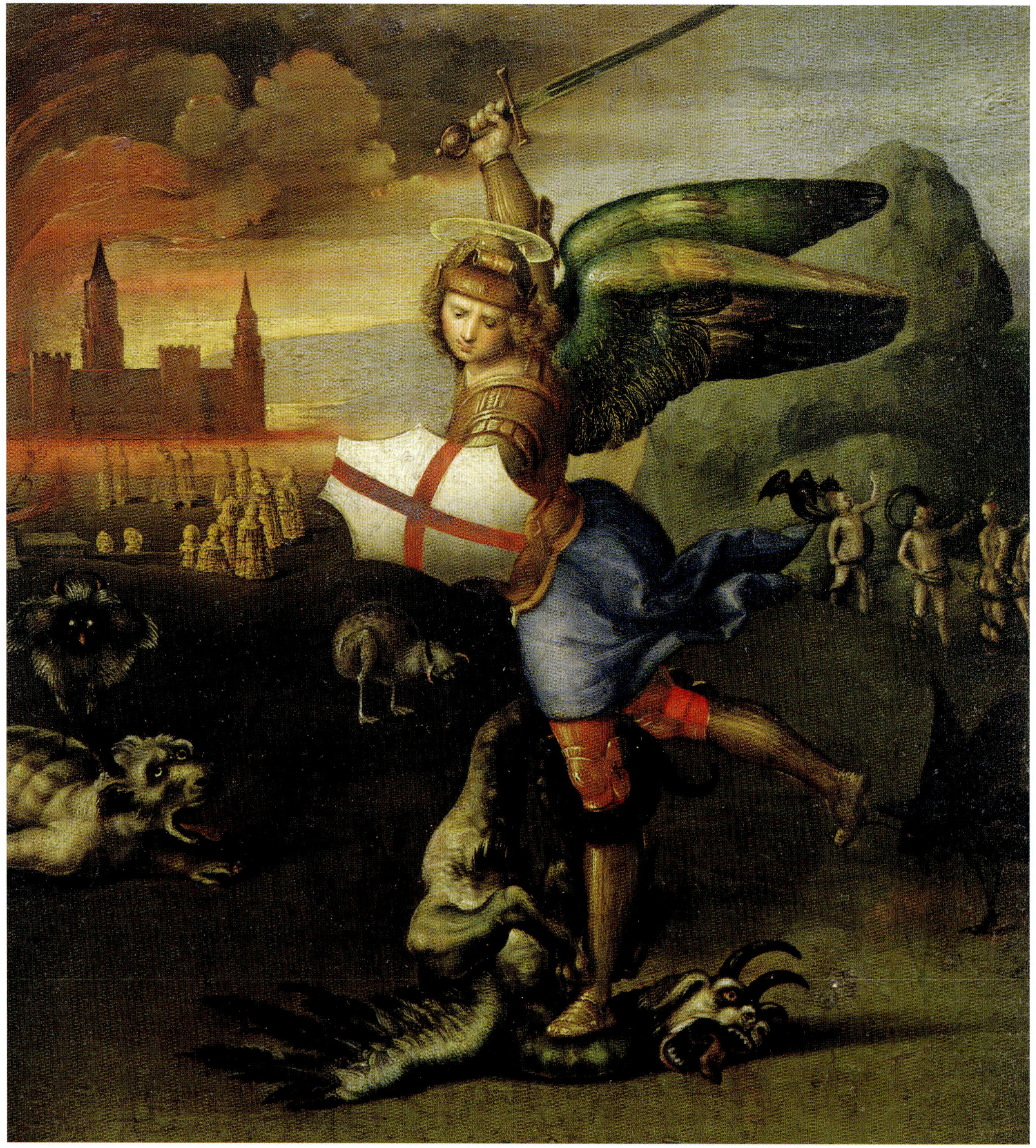

St Michael, 1504–05
Oil on wood, 30 x 26 cm (11⅓ x 10¼ in) • Musée du Louvre, Paris

Executed for the Duke of Urbino, this work depicts Saint Michael about to kill the dragon (embodying evil). The additional figures recall Dante's (1265–1321) vision of hell and the punishment of hypocrites and thieves in the *Divine Comedy* (1320).

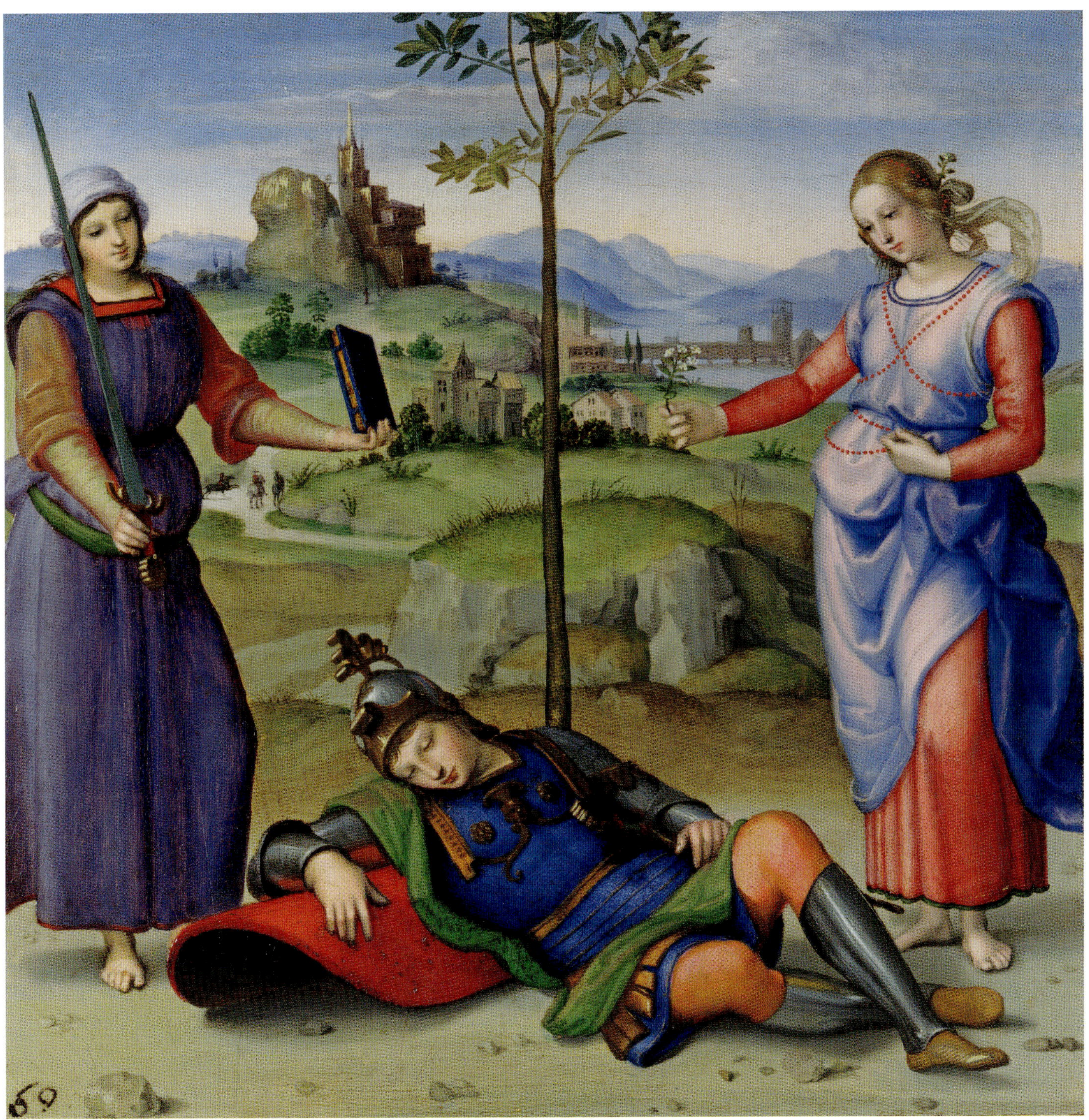

An Allegory (Vision of a Knight), *c.* **1504**
Oil on poplar, 17.1 x 17.3 cm (6¾ x 6⅔ in) • National Gallery, London

The slumbering knight Scipio is flanked by Minerva, who presents him with a sword and book, and Venus, who holds out a flower. Will he choose to follow the path of virtue and wisdom or beauty, idleness and pleasure?

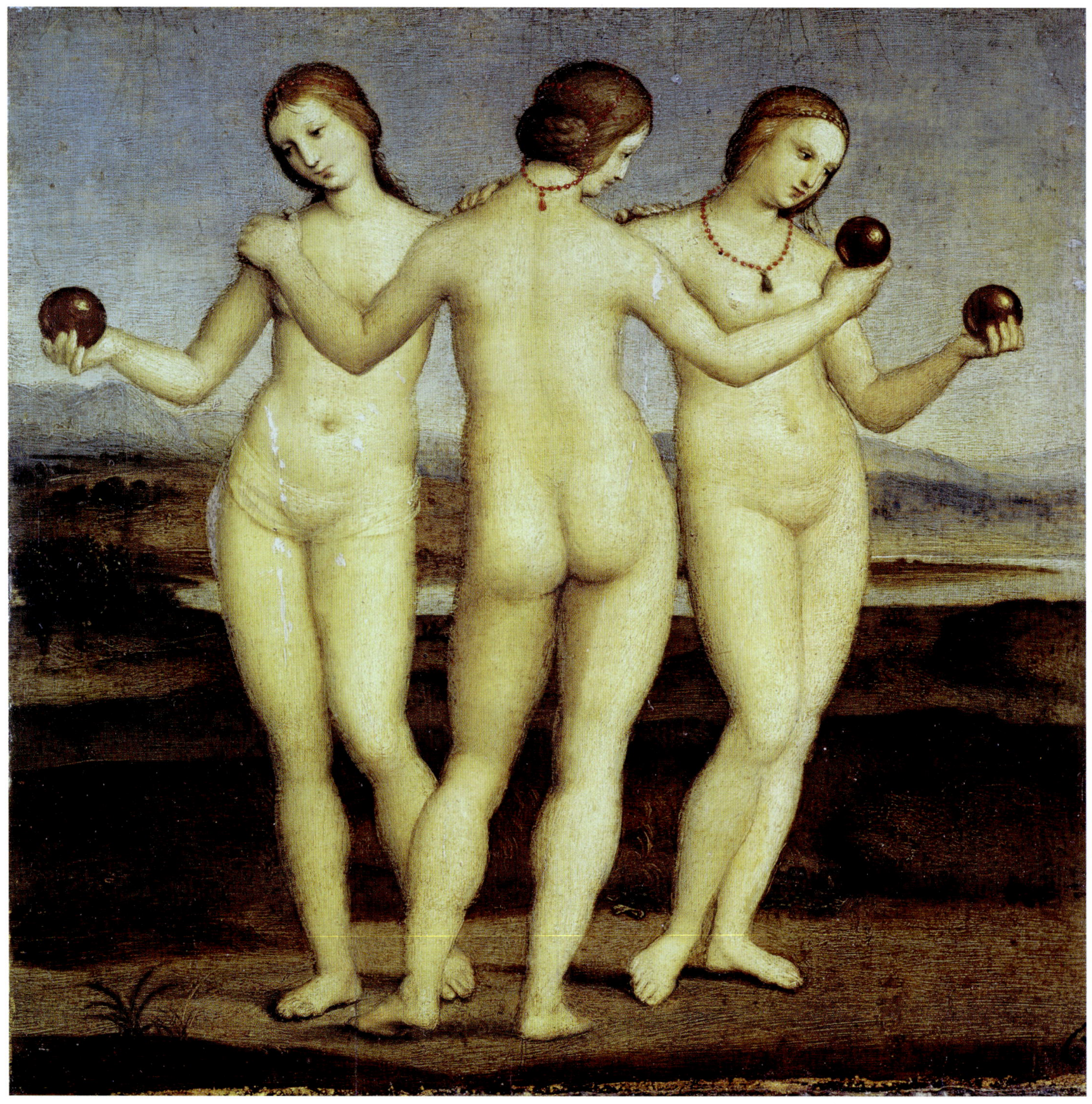

Three Graces, 1504–05
Oil on panel, 17.1 x 17.1 cm (6¾ x 6¾ in) • Musée Condé, Chantilly

Possibly intended to form a pair with *An Allegory (Vision of a Knight)*, this image depicts the Three Graces, the handmaidens of Venus and personifications of beauty. Raphael may have been inspired by a Classical sculpture group.

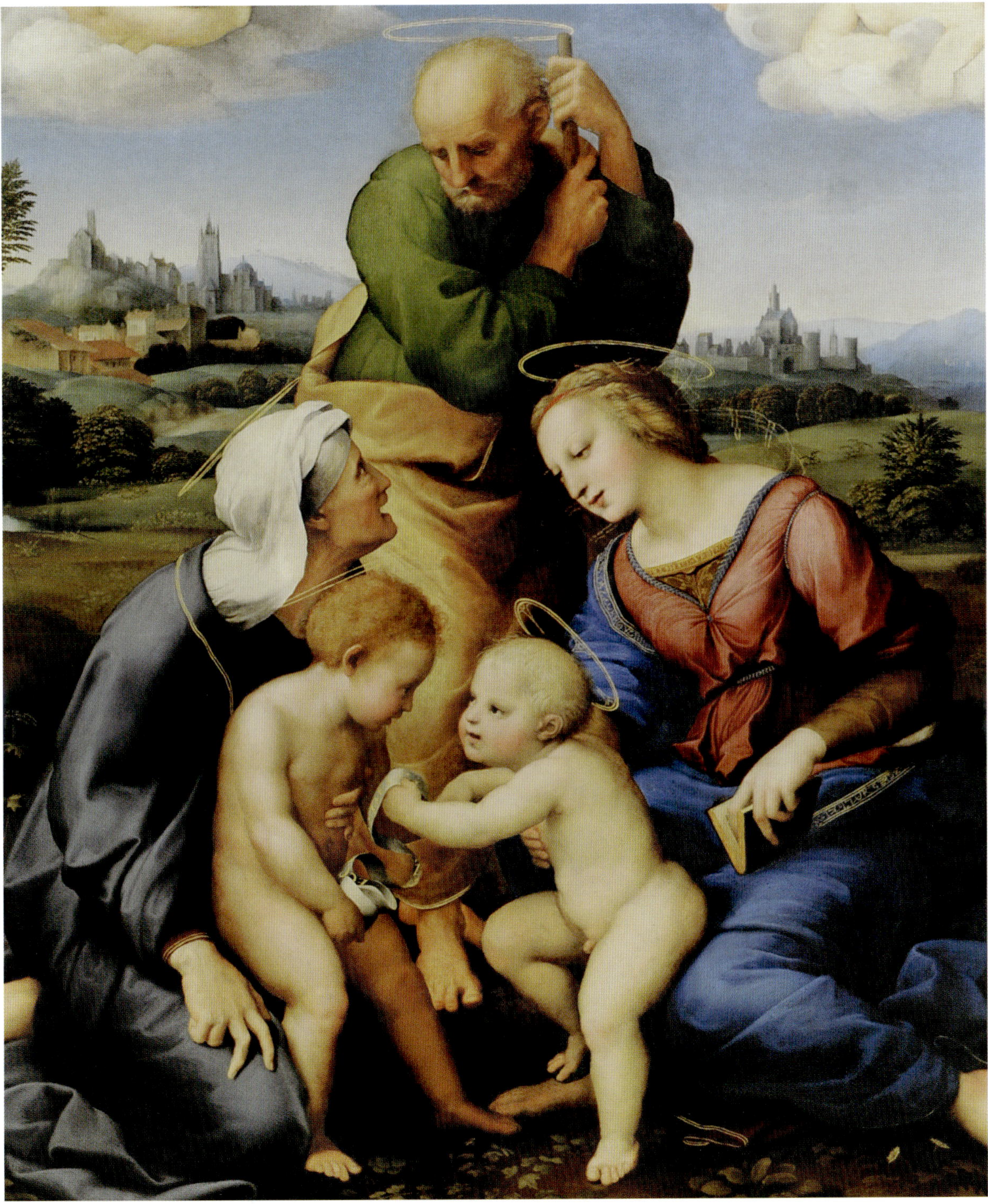

The Canigiani Holy Family, c. 1506
Oil on wood, 131 x 107 cm (51⅔ x 42 in) • Alte Pinakothek, Munich

This large-format devotional image was painted for the Florentine merchant Domenico Canigiani. The figures have been placed in a Leonardo-style pyramidal arrangement and the interplay of their glances bolsters the composition.

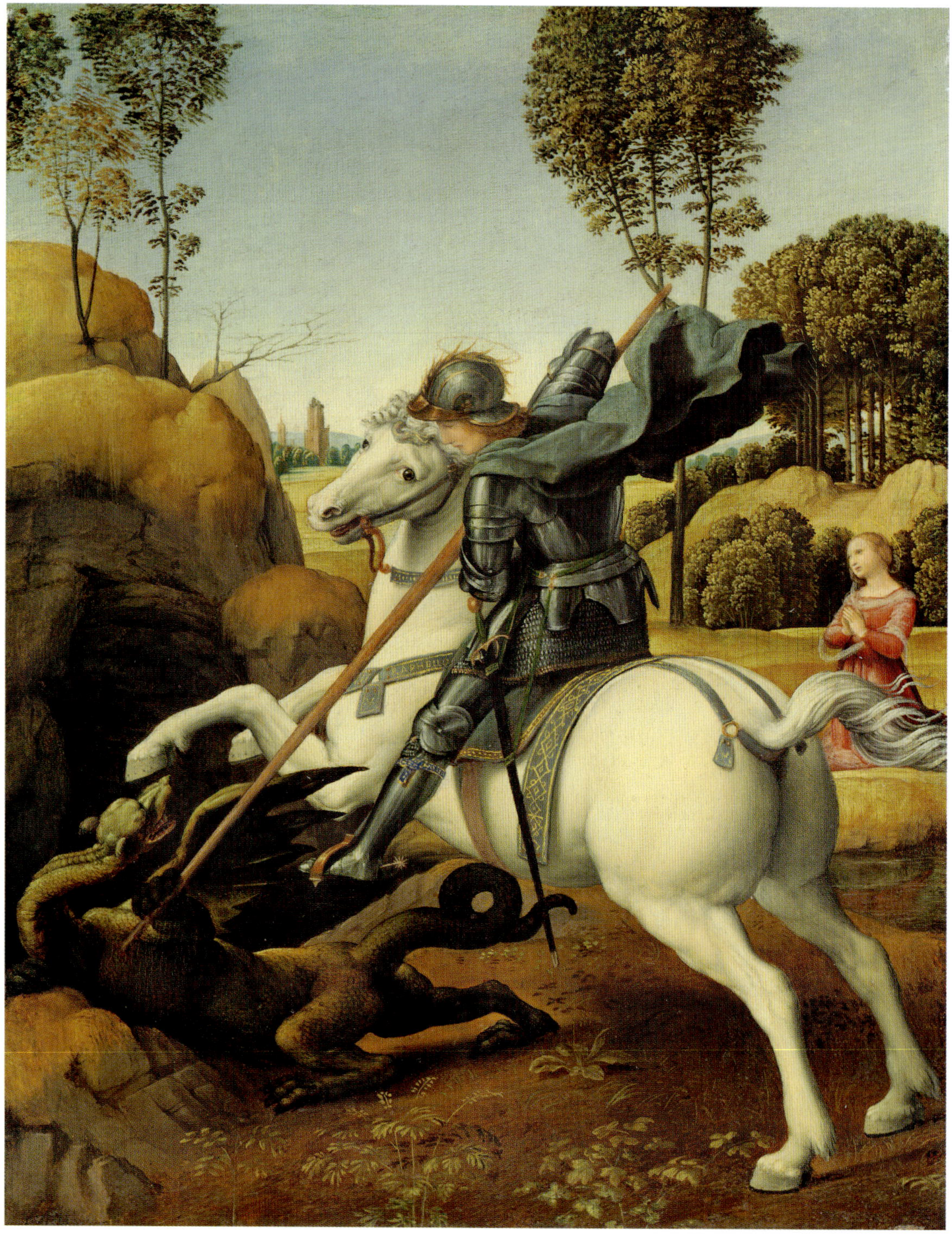

Saint George and the Dragon, c. 1506
Oil on wood, 28.5 x 21.5 cm (11¼ x 8½ in)
• National Gallery of Art, Washington, DC

This miniature panel, painted for the court of Urbino, shows an episode from *The Golden Legend* (*c.* 1260), in which the Christian soldier George saves the daughter of a pagan king by slaying a dragon.

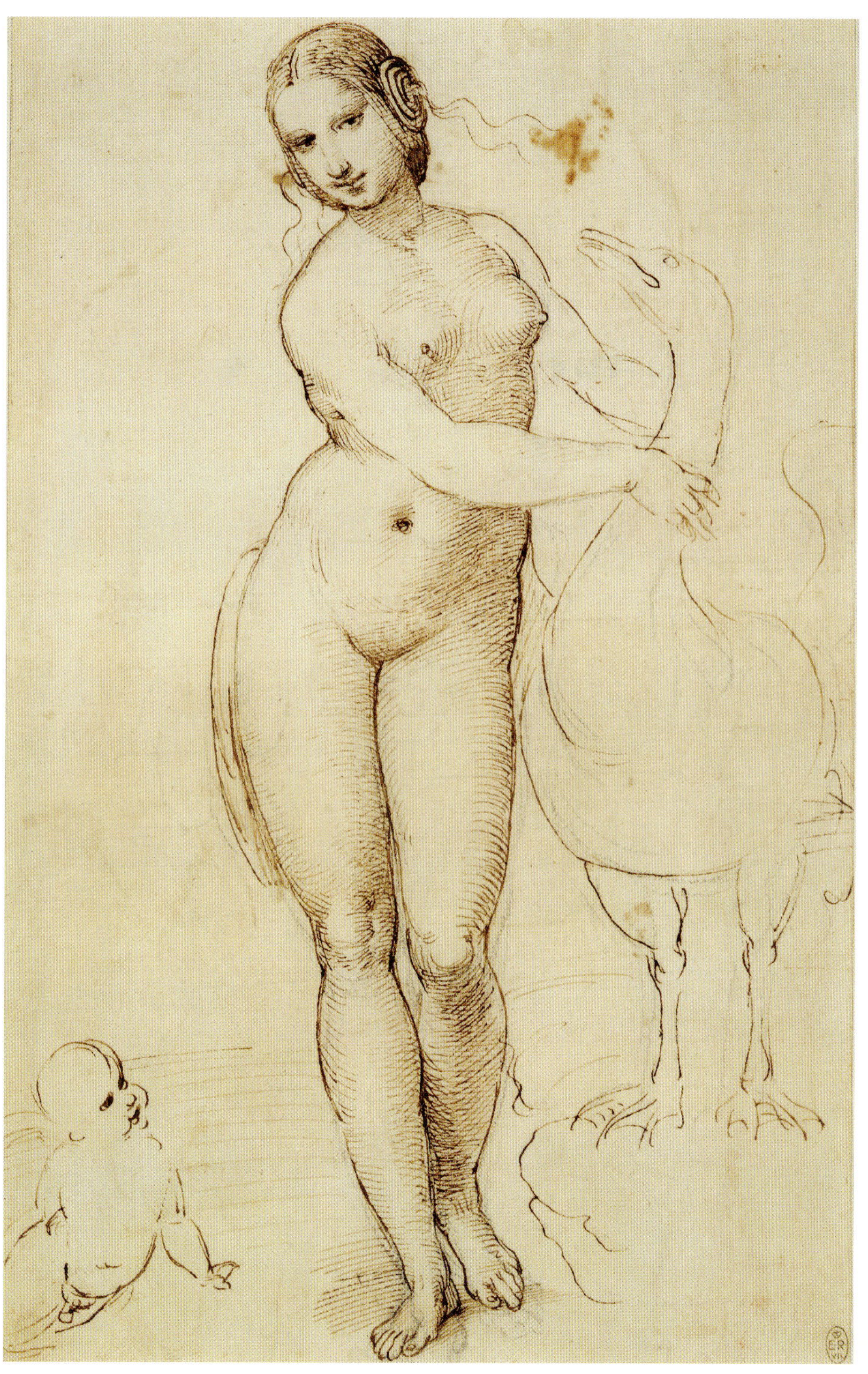

Leda and the Swan, c. 1507
Pen and ink over black chalk underdrawing on paper, 31 x 19.2 cm
(12¼ x 7⅔ in) • The Royal Collection, Windsor

Copied from a painting by Leonardo (now lost), Raphael's drawing concentrates on the voluptuous nude figure of Leda and her spiral movement as she puts her arms around the neck of the swan.

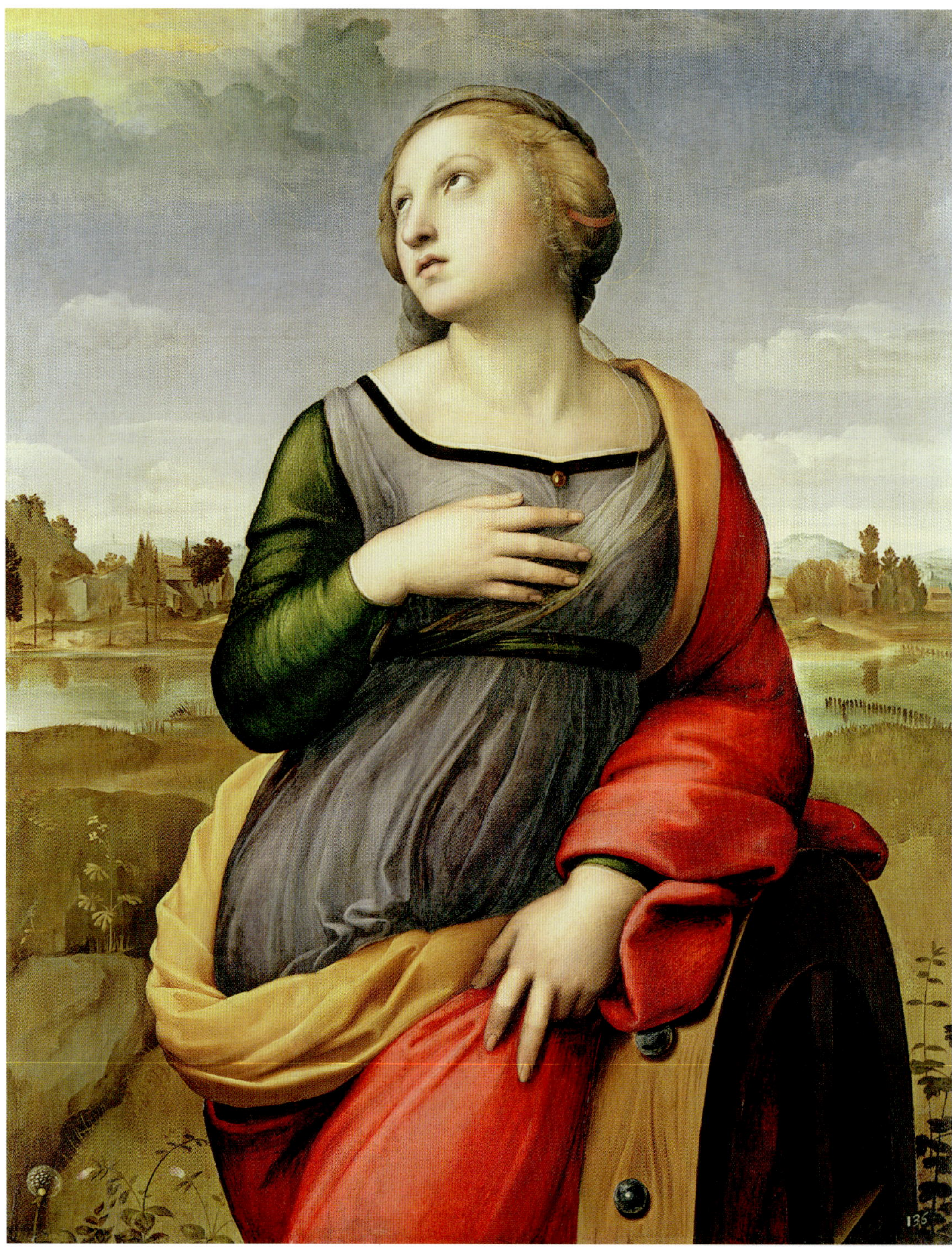

Saint Catherine of Alexandria, *c.* 1507
Oil on poplar, 72.2 x 55.7 (28⅓ x 22 in) • National Gallery, London

Painted at the end of his Florentine period, Raphael again copied Leonardo's standing Leda design (seen in Saint Catherine's twisted pose). Leonardo's influence can also be felt in the picture's colour range.

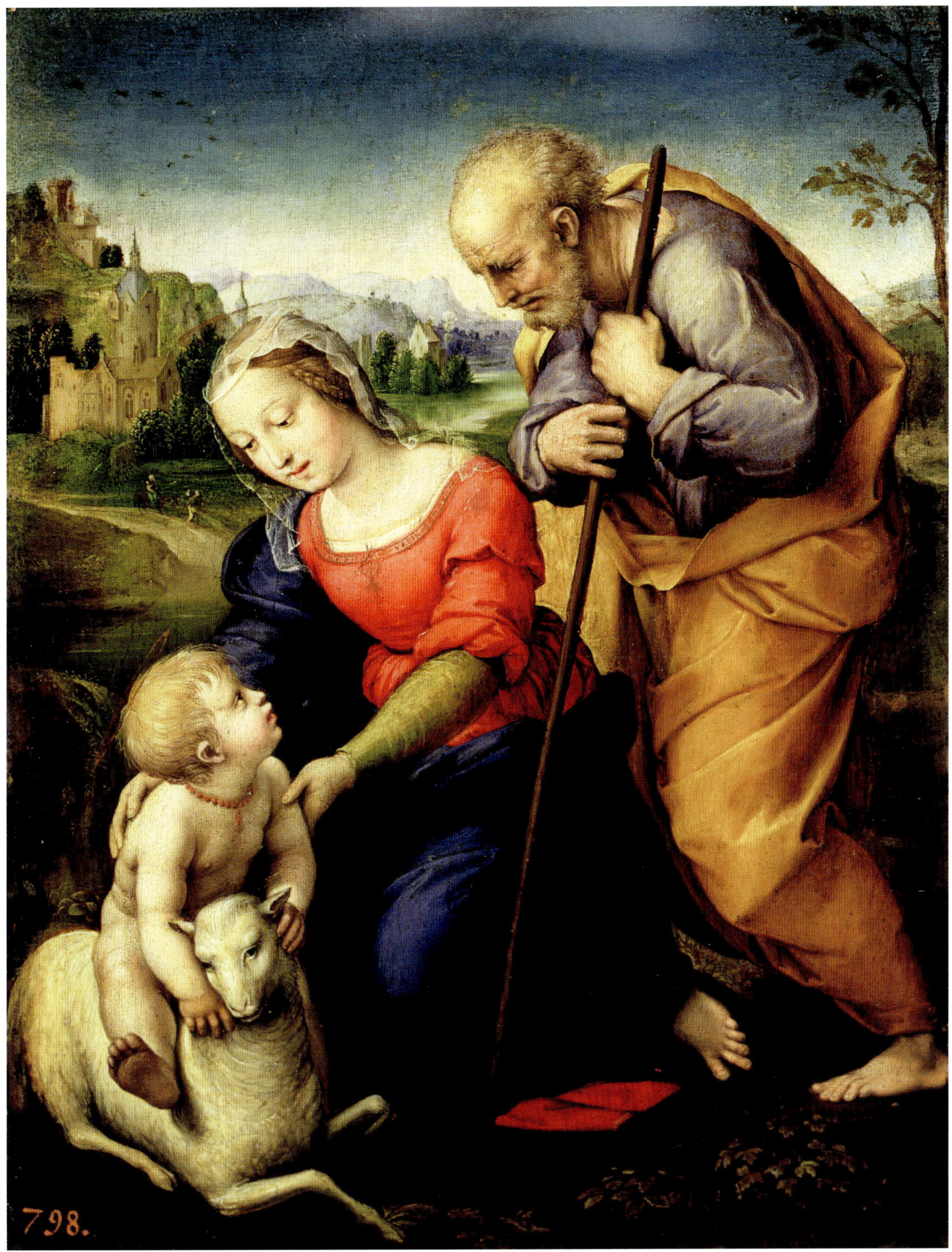

The Holy Family with a Lamb, 1507
Oil on panel, 28 x 21.5 cm (11 x 8½ in) • Museo del Prado, Madrid

Stylistically, this small picture indicates the deep impression Leonardo made on Raphael, but elements of the landscape were taken from Netherlandish engravings and paintings. The Christ Child sits astride a lamb (helped by the Madonna), a symbol of his sacrifice.

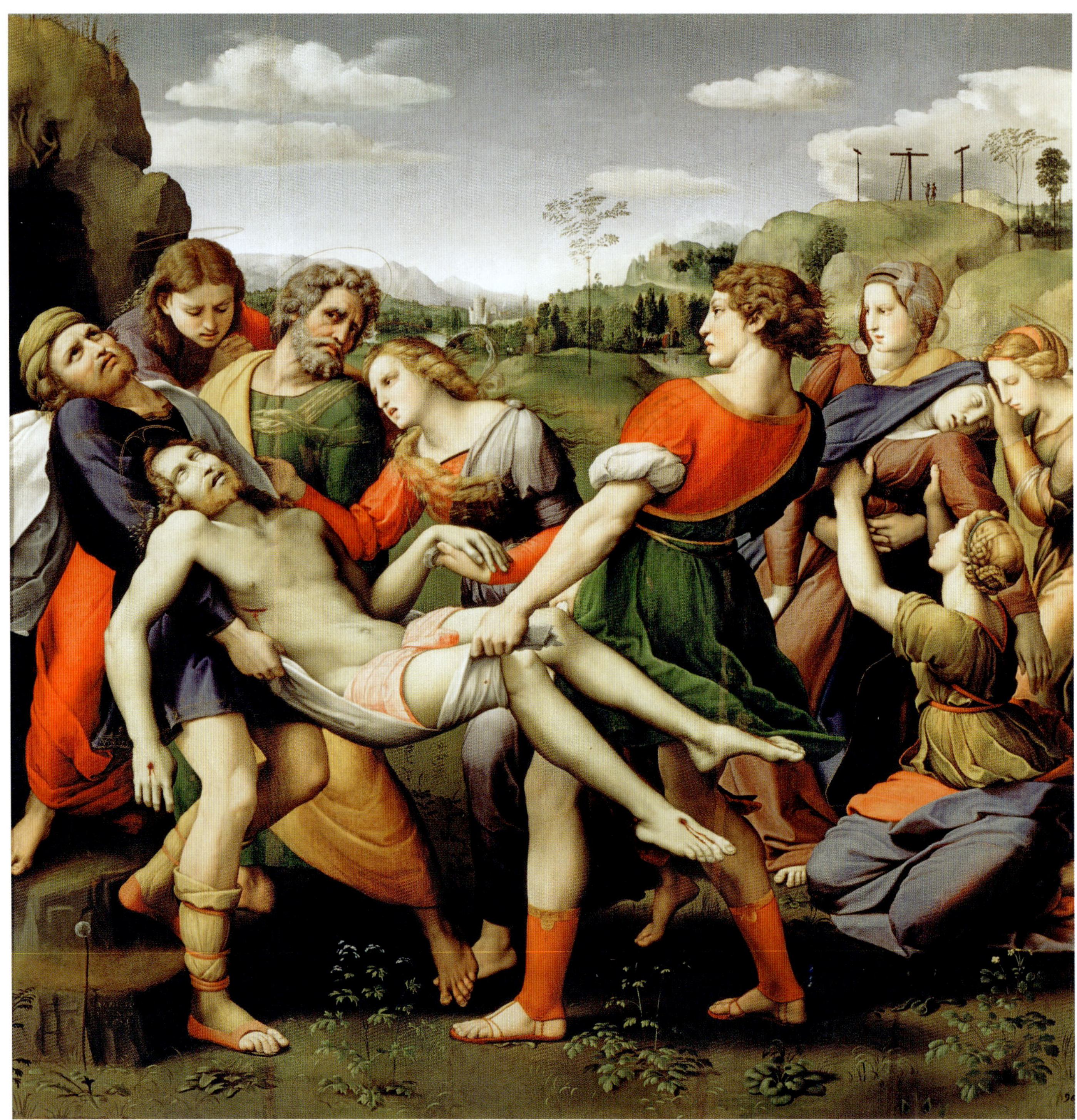

The Deposition (also known as The Entombment), 1507
Oil on wood, 184 x 176 cm (72⅔ x 69⅓ in)
• Galleria Borghese, Rome

This altarpiece reveals the impact on Raphael of the muscular, physically charged and psychologically tense work of the Florentine masters, especially Michelangelo. From the men carrying Christ's body to the swooning Virgin Mary, everyone is in movement.

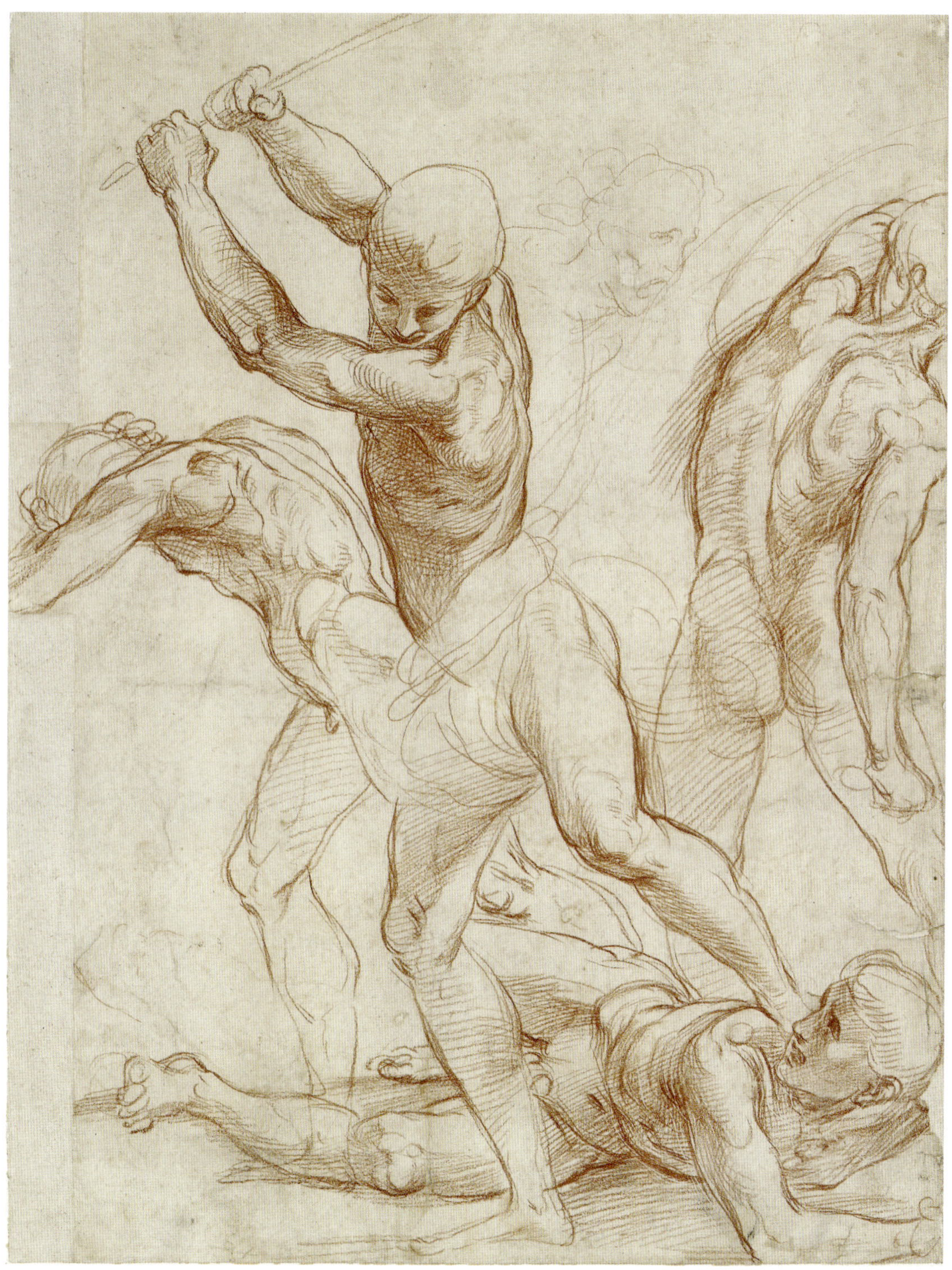

Combat of Nude Men, *c.* **1508–10**
Red chalk on off-white paper, 37.9 x 28.1 cm (15 x 11 in)
• Ashmolean Museum, Oxford

Raphael attempted to create his own version of the heroic nude, and he made a number of drawings of fighting men. He utilized examples from Michelangelo's work and took inspiration from antique Roman relief sculpture.

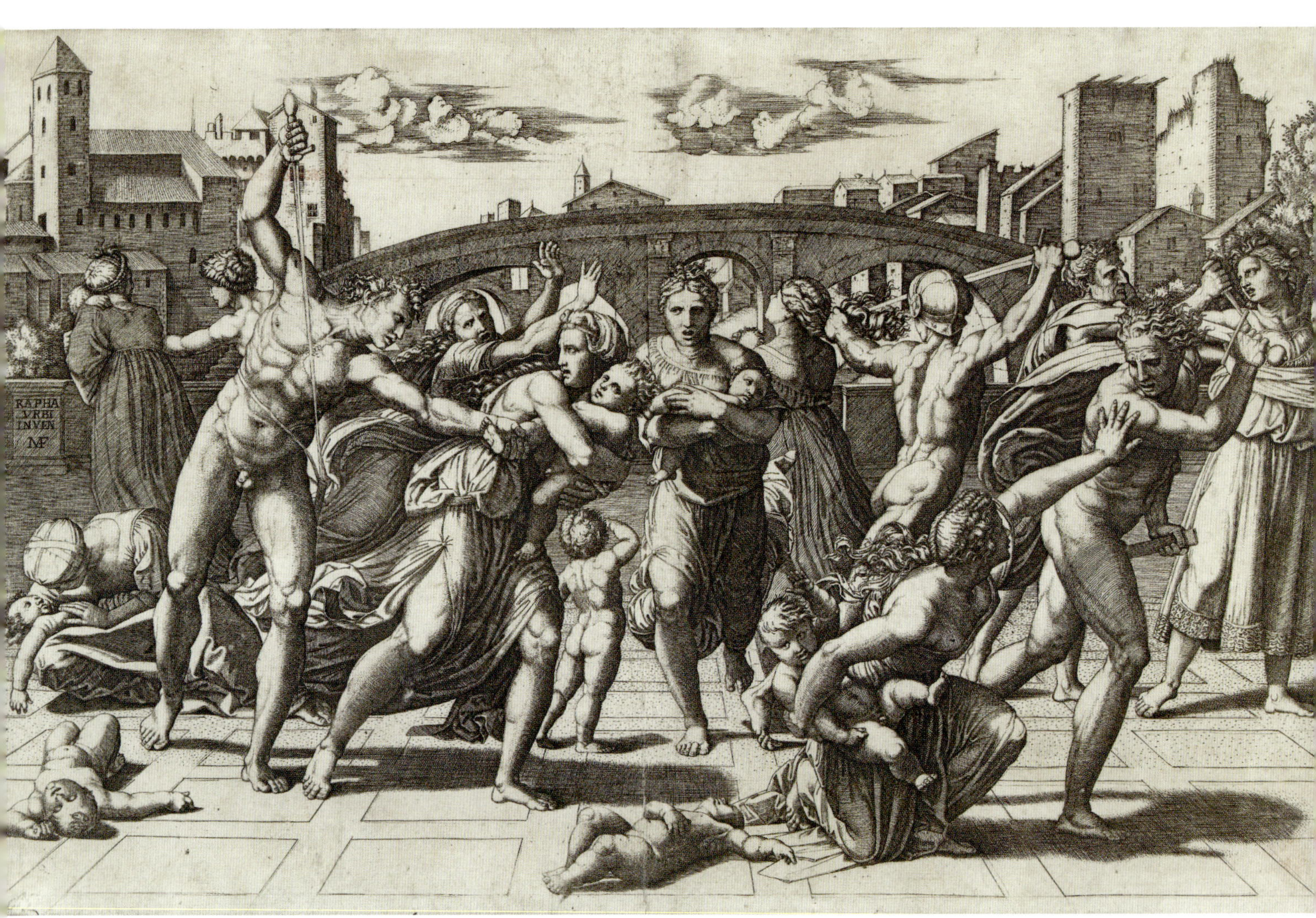

**The Massacre of the Innocents, *c.* 1515, by Marcantonio
Raimondi (*c.* 1480–*c.* 1534) after Raphael**
Engraving on paper, 27.7 x 42.2 cm (11 x 16⅔ in)
• Rijksmuseum, Amsterdam

This scene of climactic violence, full of gestures and expressions of pathos and strife, was one of the
most widely reproduced engravings of the sixteenth century. It established the decade-long, fruitful
collaboration of Raphael and the engraver Raimondi.

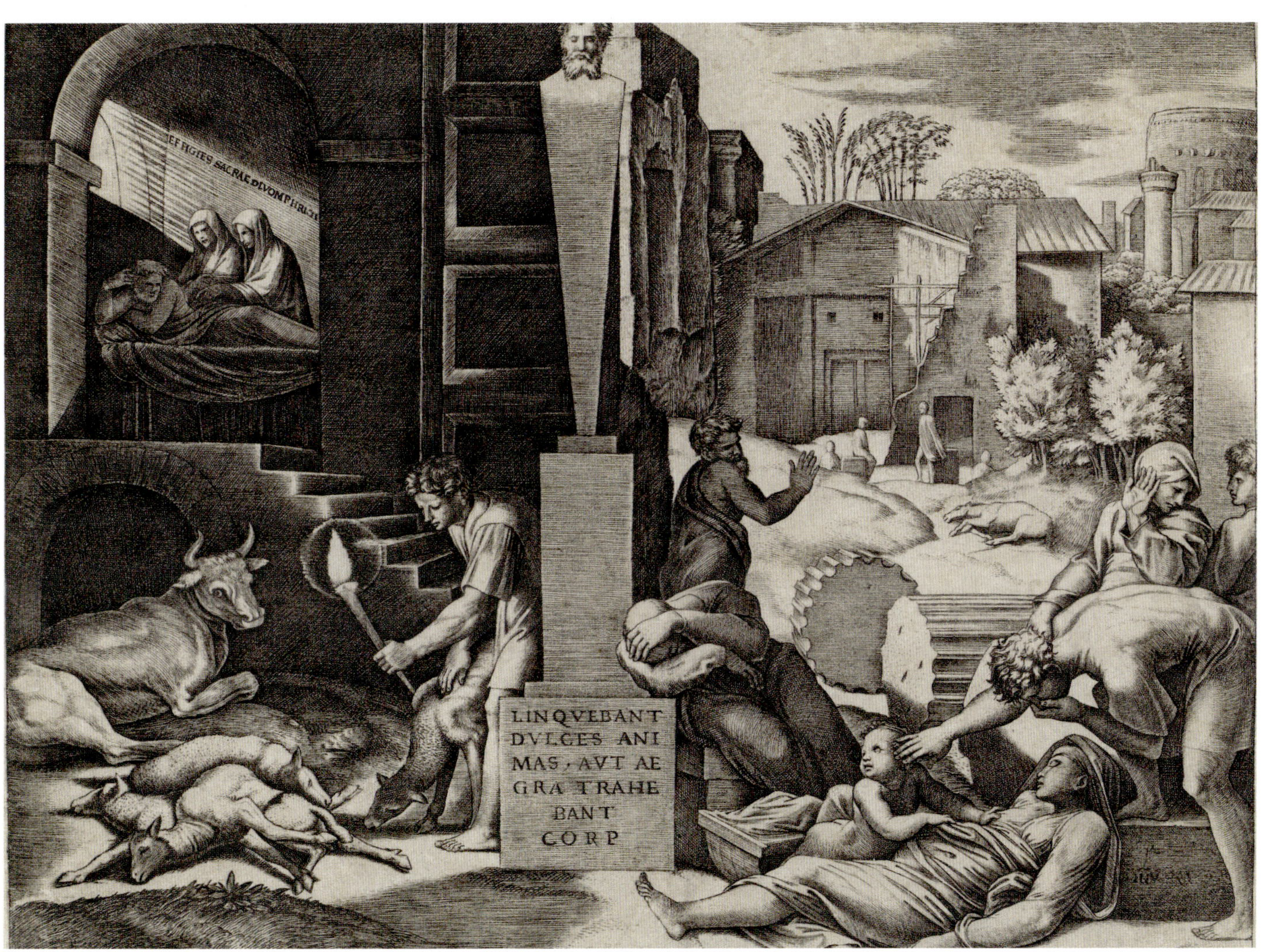

Il Morbetto (The Plague), *c.* **1515–16, by Marcantonio Raimondi after Raphael**
Engraving on paper, 19.5 x 25.2 cm (7¾ x 10 in)
• National Gallery of Art, Washington, DC

Il Morbetto, or the Plague, designed by Raphael and engraved by Raimondi, juxtaposes the pestilence in Crete described in Virgil's (70–19 BC) epic poem *Aeneid* (*c.* 19 BC) with the dire state of Rome's ancient remains in the Renaissance.

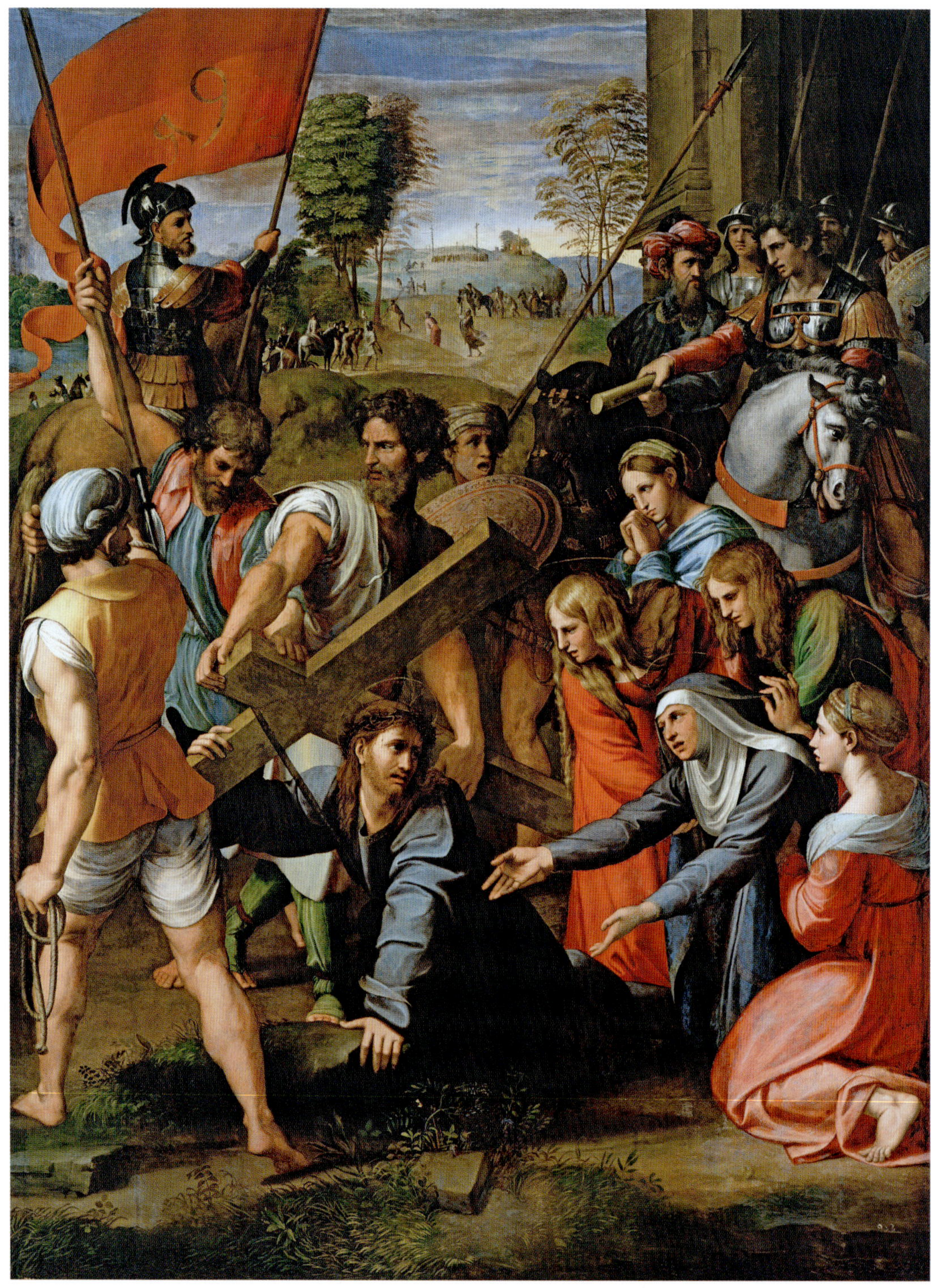

Christ Falling on the Way to Calvary (Lo Spasimo), 1515–16
Oil on panel transferred to canvas, 318 x 229 cm (125¼ x 90¼ in)
• Museo del Prado, Madrid

Taking its name from the Sicilian monastery for which it was painted – Santa Maria dello Spasimo (the Swoon of the Virgin) – this work shows Christ collapsing under the weight of the cross as his anguished mother reaches out in vain.

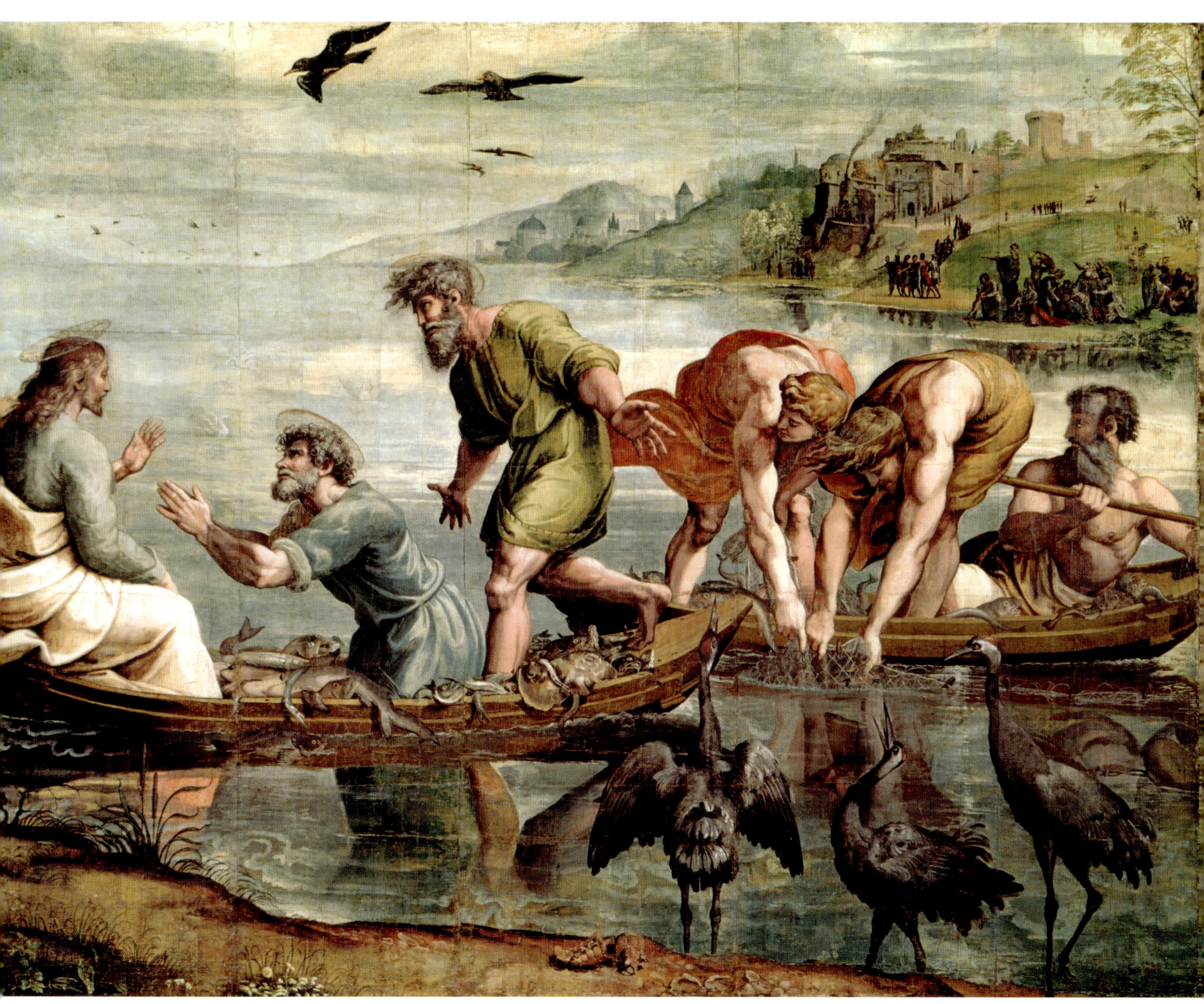

The Miraculous Draught of Fishes (Tapestry Cartoon), 1515–16
Body-colour on paper, mounted on canvas, 319 x 399 cm (125⅔ x 157 in)
• Victoria & Albert Museum, London

Raphael created innovative designs for tapestries (used on special occasions in the Sistine Chapel).
In this cartoon, Christ tells Peter to cast his net into the water, whereupon he and his fellow apostles
(muscular figures) make a miraculous catch.

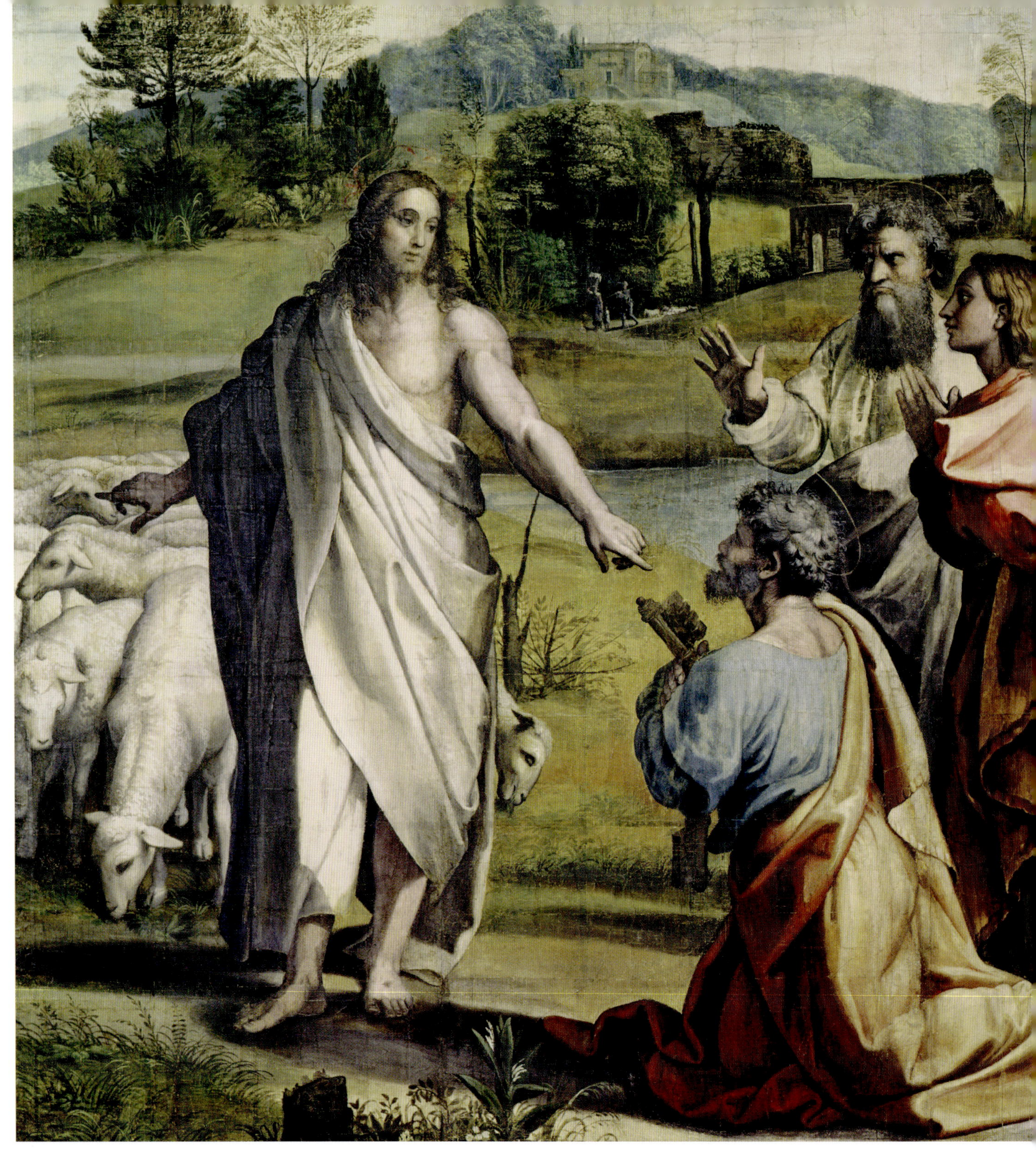

Christ's Charge to Peter (Tapestry Cartoon), 1515–16
Body-colour on paper, mounted on canvas, 343 x 532 cm (135 x 209⅔ in)
• Victoria & Albert Museum, London

Raphael evidently calculated elements of continuity between contiguous tapestries, of which the most obvious is the landscape shared by *The Miraculous Draught of Fishes* and this scene, depicting the dramatic moment when Christ selects Peter to lead his Church.

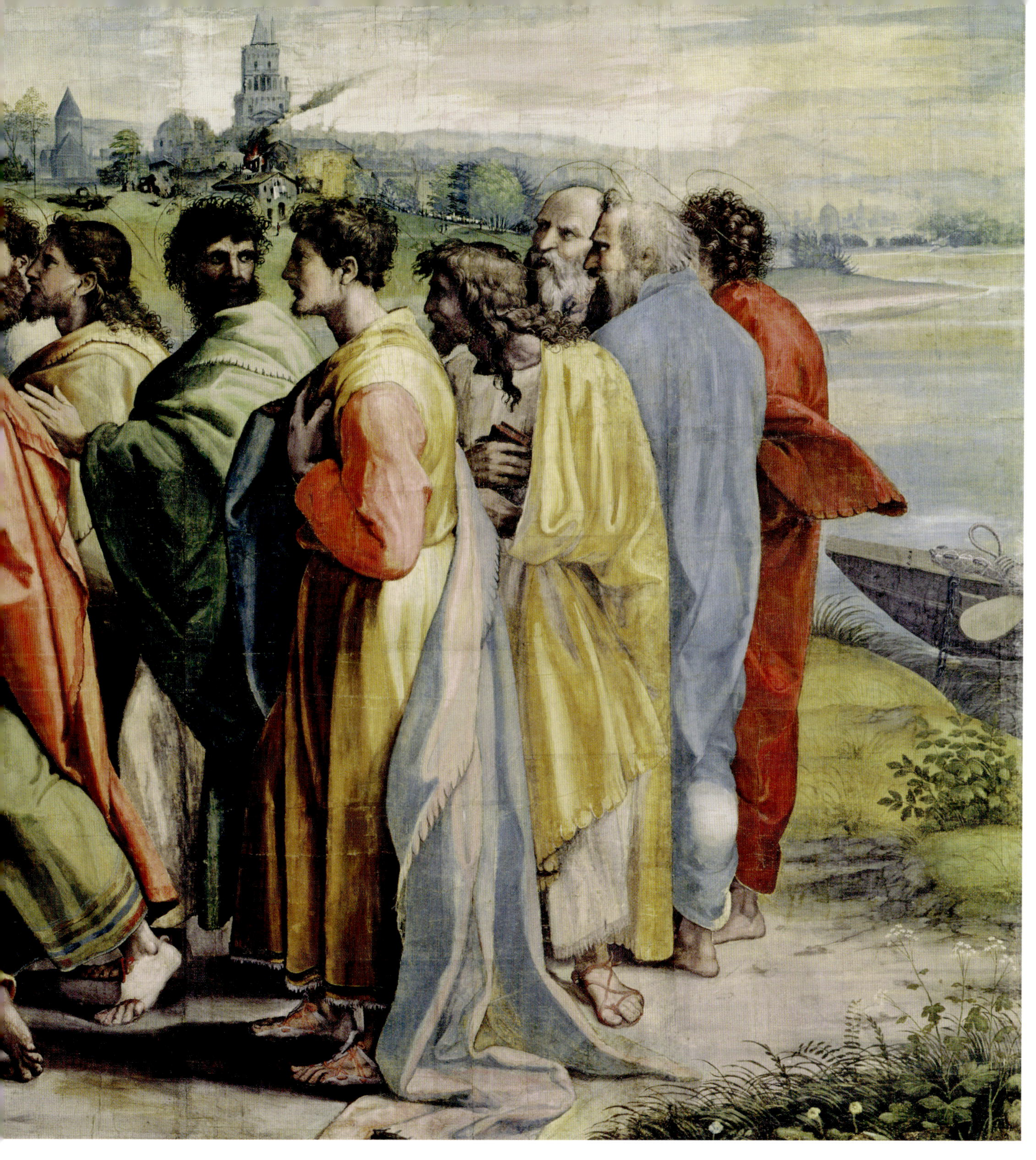

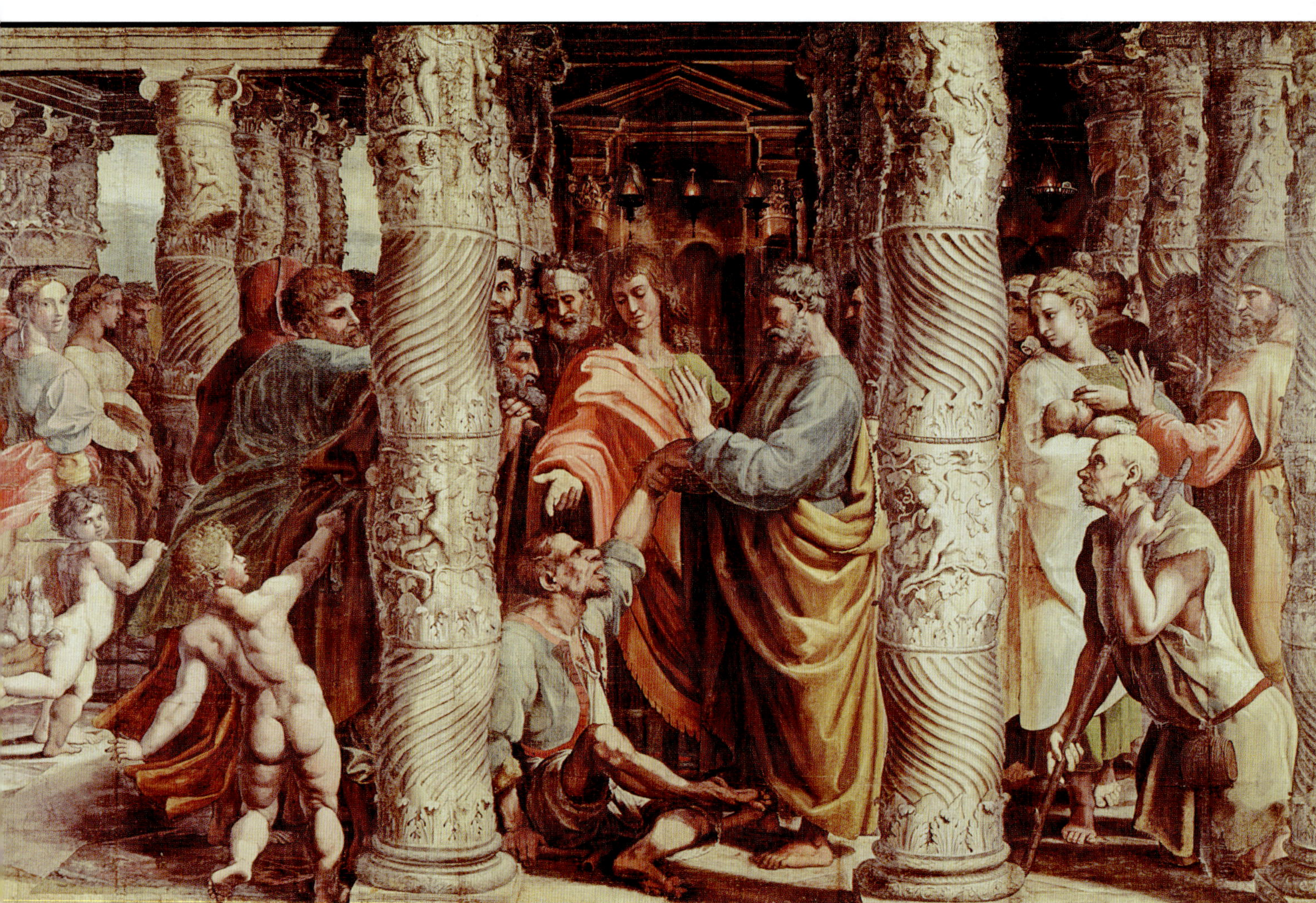

The Healing of the Lame Man (Tapestry Cartoon), 1515–16
Body-colour on paper, mounted on canvas, 342 x 536 cm (134⅔ x 211 in)
• Victoria & Albert Museum, London

Framed by columns based on those in Saint Peter's Basilica (thought to have come from Solomon's Temple in Jerusalem), Peter heals a lame man. The Medici papal patron was attached to images of healing (*medici* is Italian for doctors).

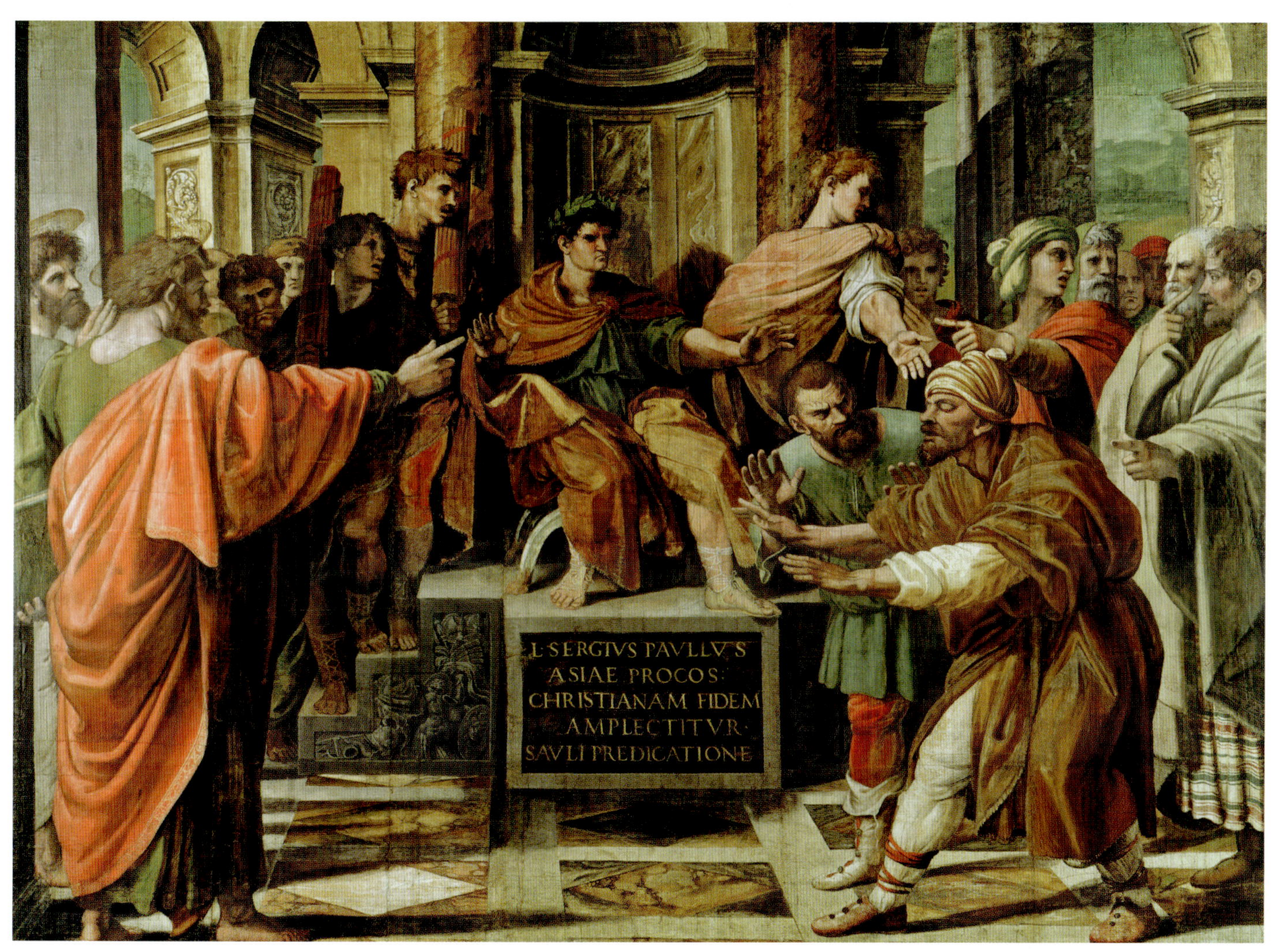

The Conversion of the Proconsul (Tapestry Cartoon), 1515–16
Body-colour on paper, mounted on canvas, 342 x 446 cm (134⅔ x 175⅔ in)
• Victoria & Albert Museum, London

According to Acts 13: 6–12, Elymas, a sorcerer and advisor to the Proconsul Sergius Paulus, ordered that the apostle Paul be punished for his Christian faith. In Paul's first miracle, Elymas is struck blind and the proconsul converts to Christianity.

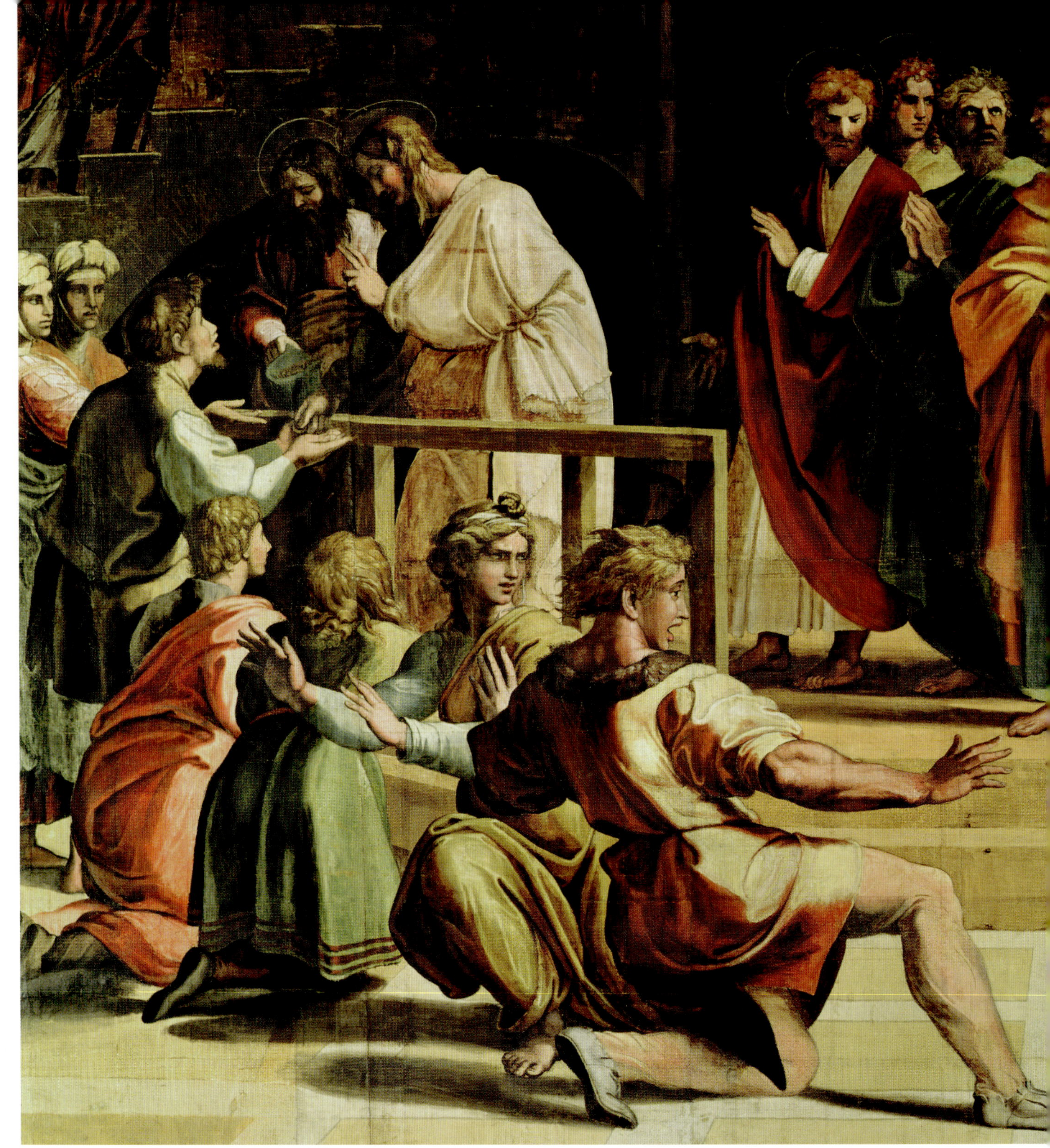

The Death of Ananias (Tapestry Cartoon), 1515–16
Body-colour on paper, mounted on canvas, 342 x 532 cm (134⅔ x 209⅔ in)
• Victoria & Albert Museum, London

Ananias (completed by Raphael) kept back some of the proceeds from his land instead of giving the profits to the poor and was rebuked by Peter. Here, he falls to the ground, dying, surrounded by onlookers (designed by Raphael's assistants).

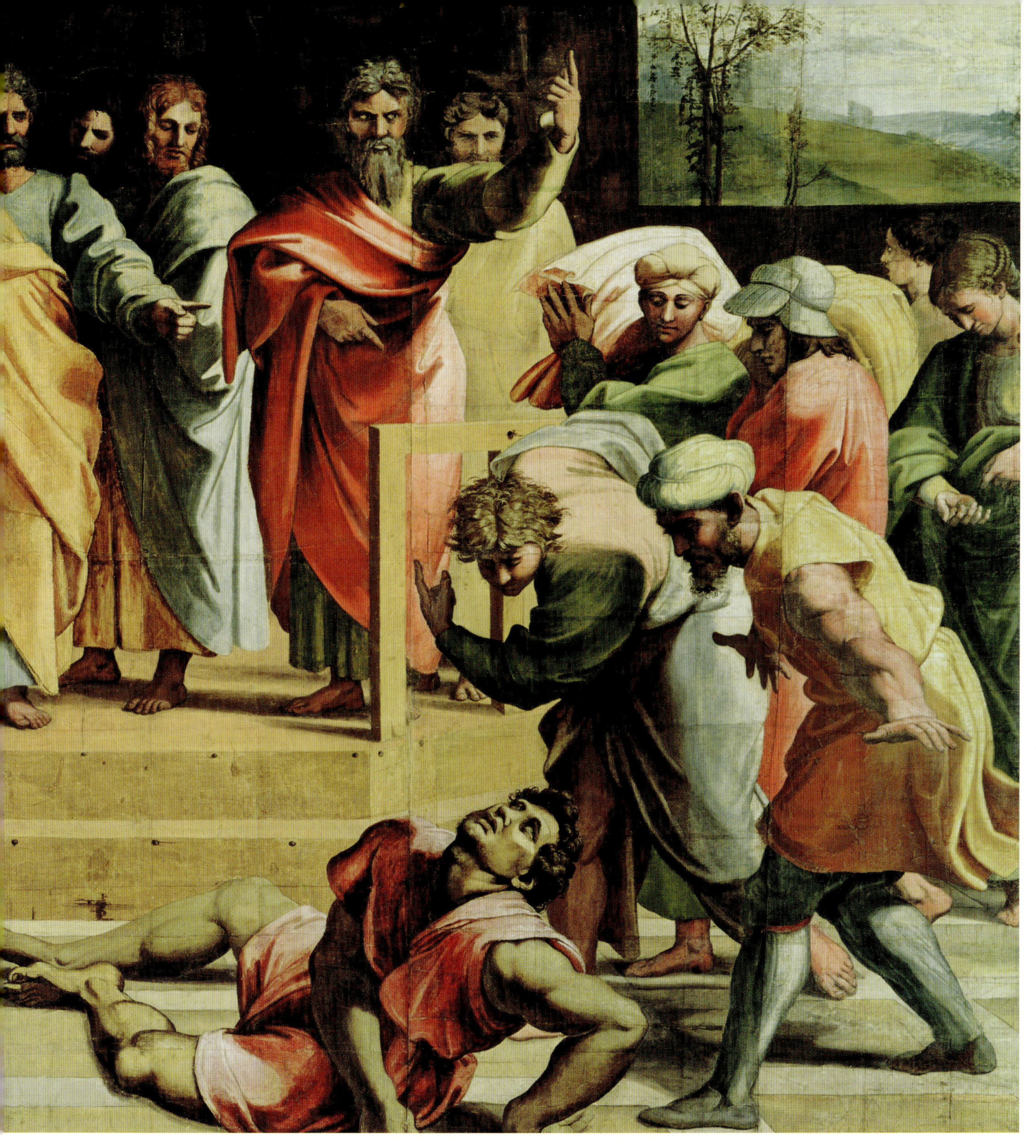

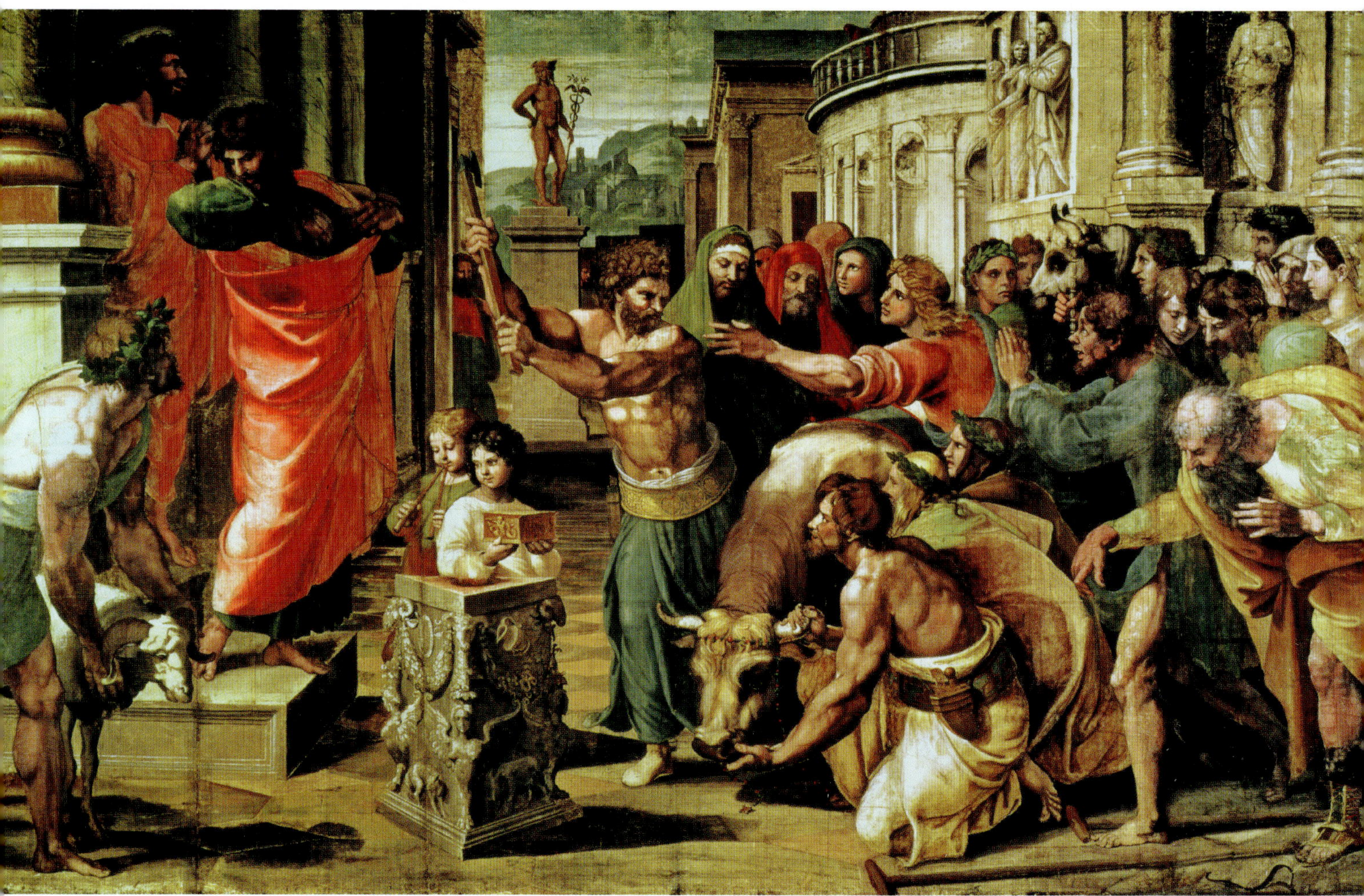

The Sacrifice at Lystra (Tapestry Cartoon), 1515–16
Body-colour on paper, mounted on canvas, 347 x 542 cm (137 x 213⅔ in)
• Victoria & Albert Museum, London

Containing an expressive energy, this crowd scene shows how, after healing a lame man in the city of Lystra, the people mistake Paul and Barnabas for the gods Jupiter and Mercury and offer them a pagan sacrifice.

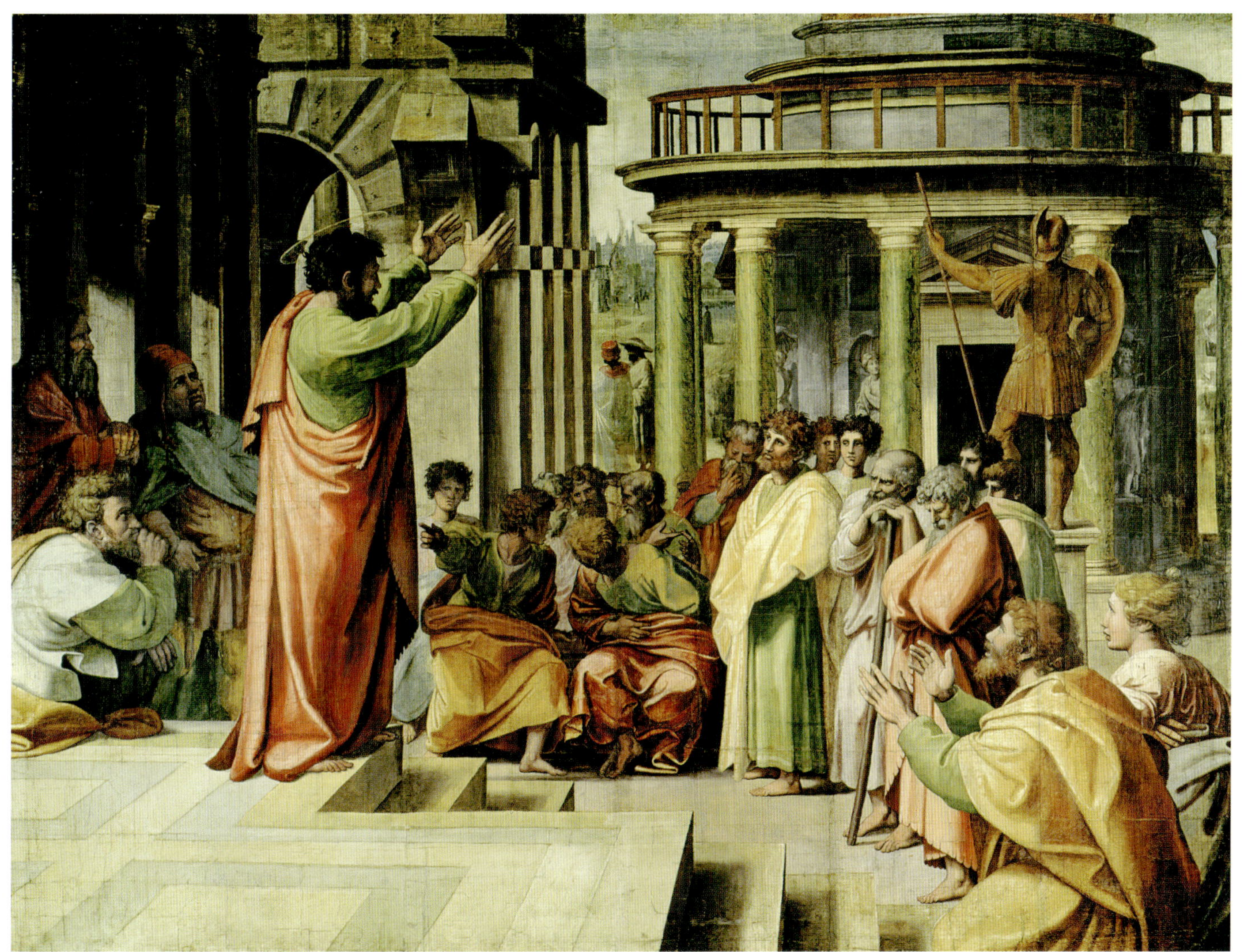

Paul Preaching at Athens (Tapestry Cartoon), 1515–16
Body-colour on paper, mounted on canvas, 343 x 442 cm (135 x 174 in)
• Victoria & Albert Museum, London

Paul stands in Athens in the area where the ruling council meet and preaches against worshipping false idols, represented here by the Classical statue (of Mars or Achilles) and the round temple in the background.

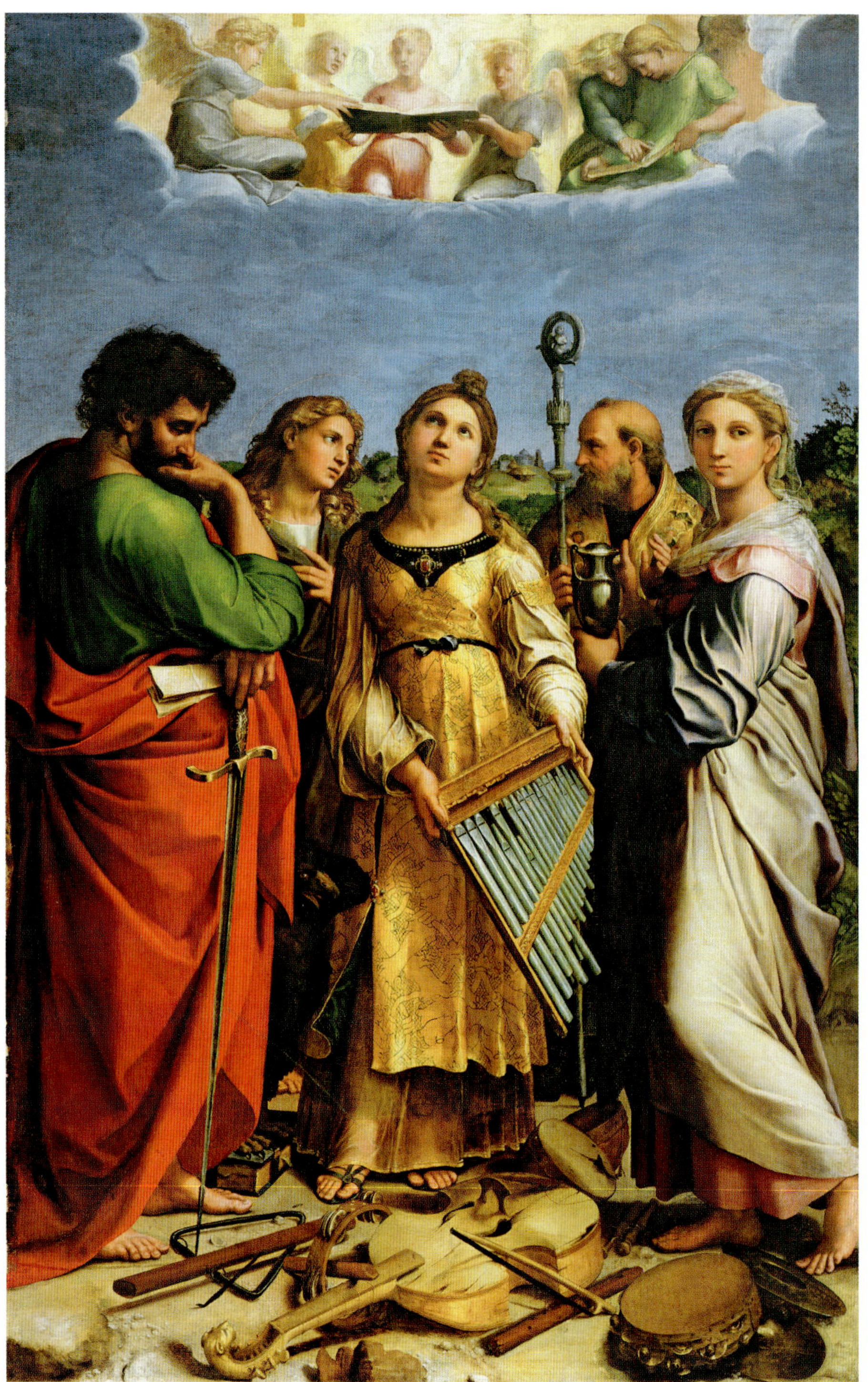

The Ecstasy of St Cecilia, *c.* 1518
Oil on panel transferred to canvas, 220 x 136 cm (86⅔ x 53½ in)
• Pinacoteca Nazionale, Bologna

Variously dated to 1515, 1516–17 and 1518, this altarpiece shows Saint Cecilia standing between saints Paul, John the Evangelist and Augustine, and Mary Magdalene. One of Raphael's assistants may have painted the broken, discarded musical instruments on the ground.

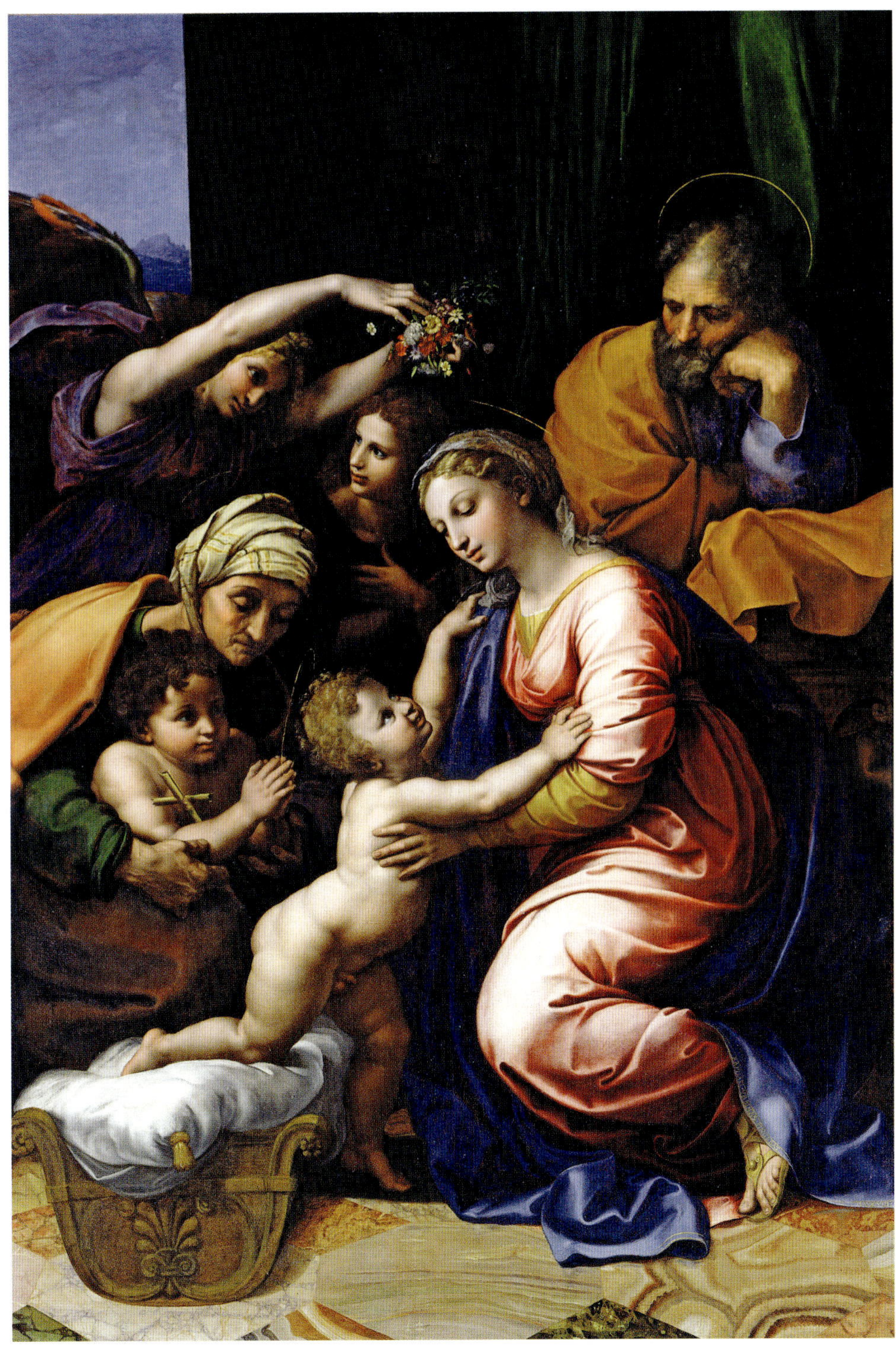

The Holy Family of Francis I, 1518
Oil on wood transferred to canvas, 207 x 140 cm (81½ x 55 in)
• Musée du Louvre, Paris

Although signed by Raphael, the artist delegated most of the work on this altarpiece to his assistants. It was commissioned by Pope Leo X as a gift for Claude (1499–1524), wife of Francis I of France (1494–1547).

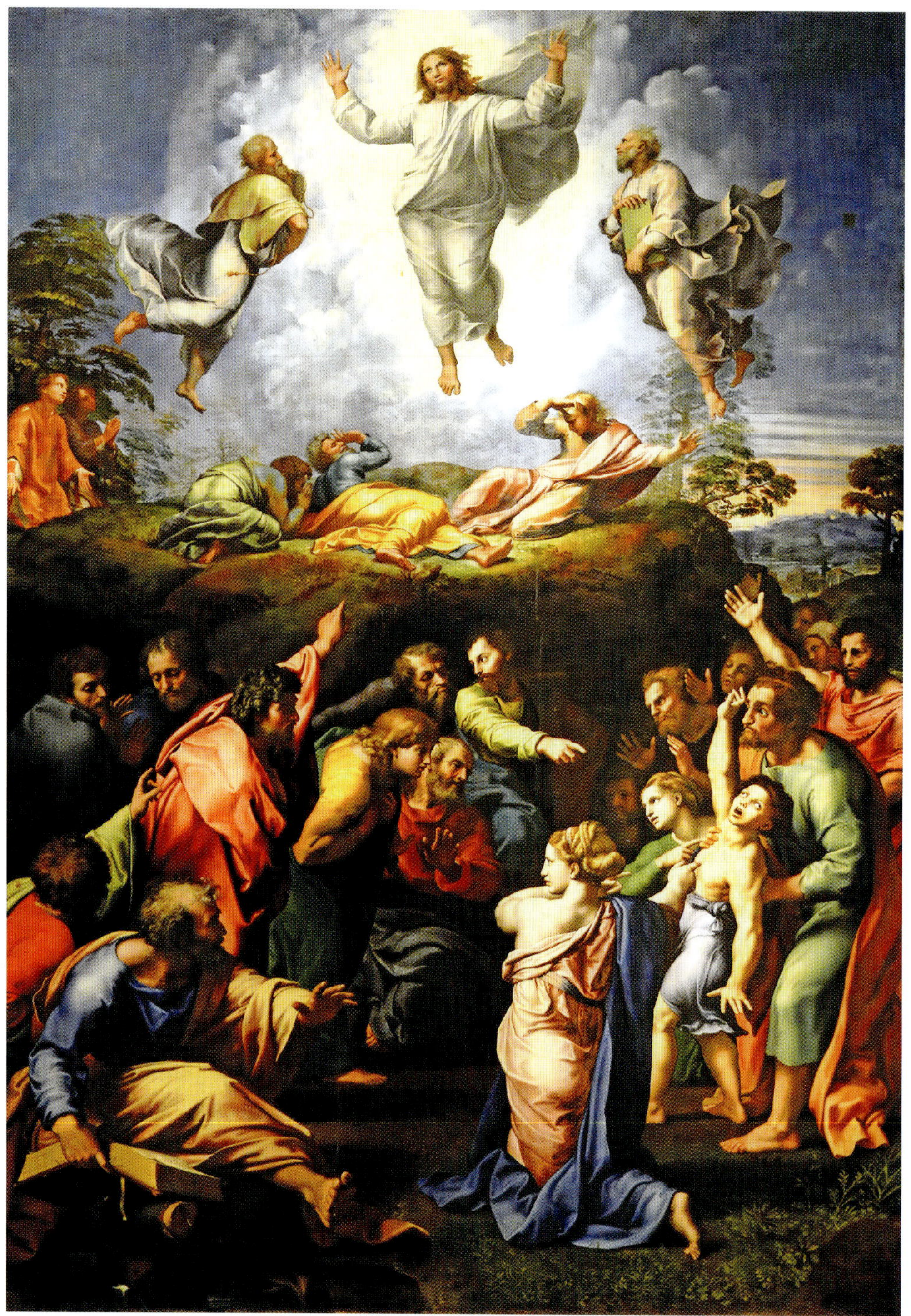

The Transfiguration, 1516–20
Tempera on wood, 405 x 278 cm (159⅔ x 109⅔ in)
• Pinacoteca Vaticana, Rome

Raphael's last painting combines two biblical scenes: a boy being exorcised of his demons and the Transfiguration of Christ. According to one sixteenth-century writer, the artist worked 'with all possible concentration' on the face of Christ.

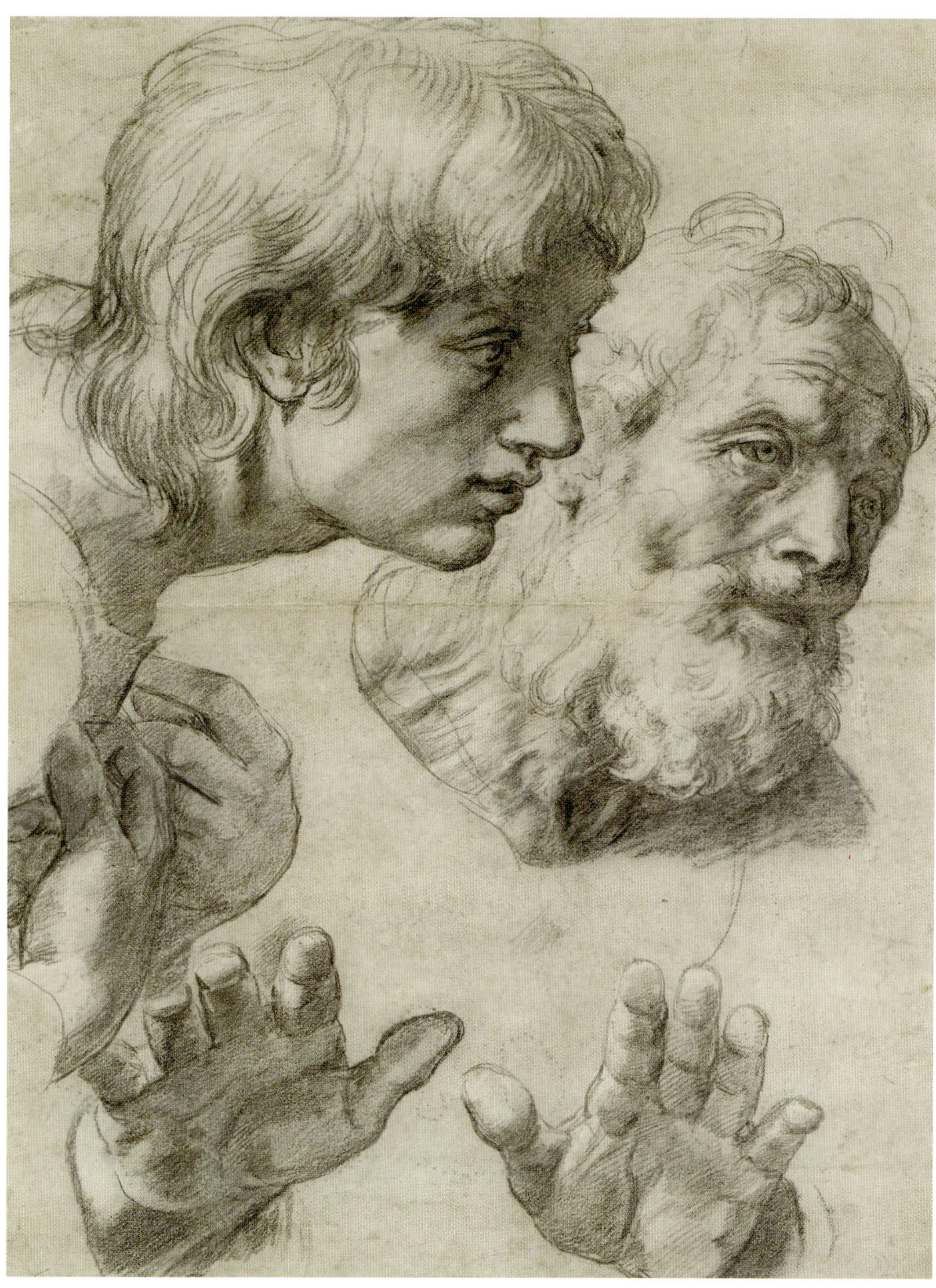

**Studies of the Heads and Hands of two Apostles for
The Transfiguration, 1516–20**
Black chalk with white chalk highlights on paper, 49.9 x 36.4 cm (19⅔ x 14⅓ in)
• Ashmolean Museum, Oxford

Arguably the most impressive of all Raphael's drawings, this set of preparatory studies contrasts the reactions of an old man (with taut sinews on his neck and furrows on his questioning brow) with a beautiful youth, who leans forward.

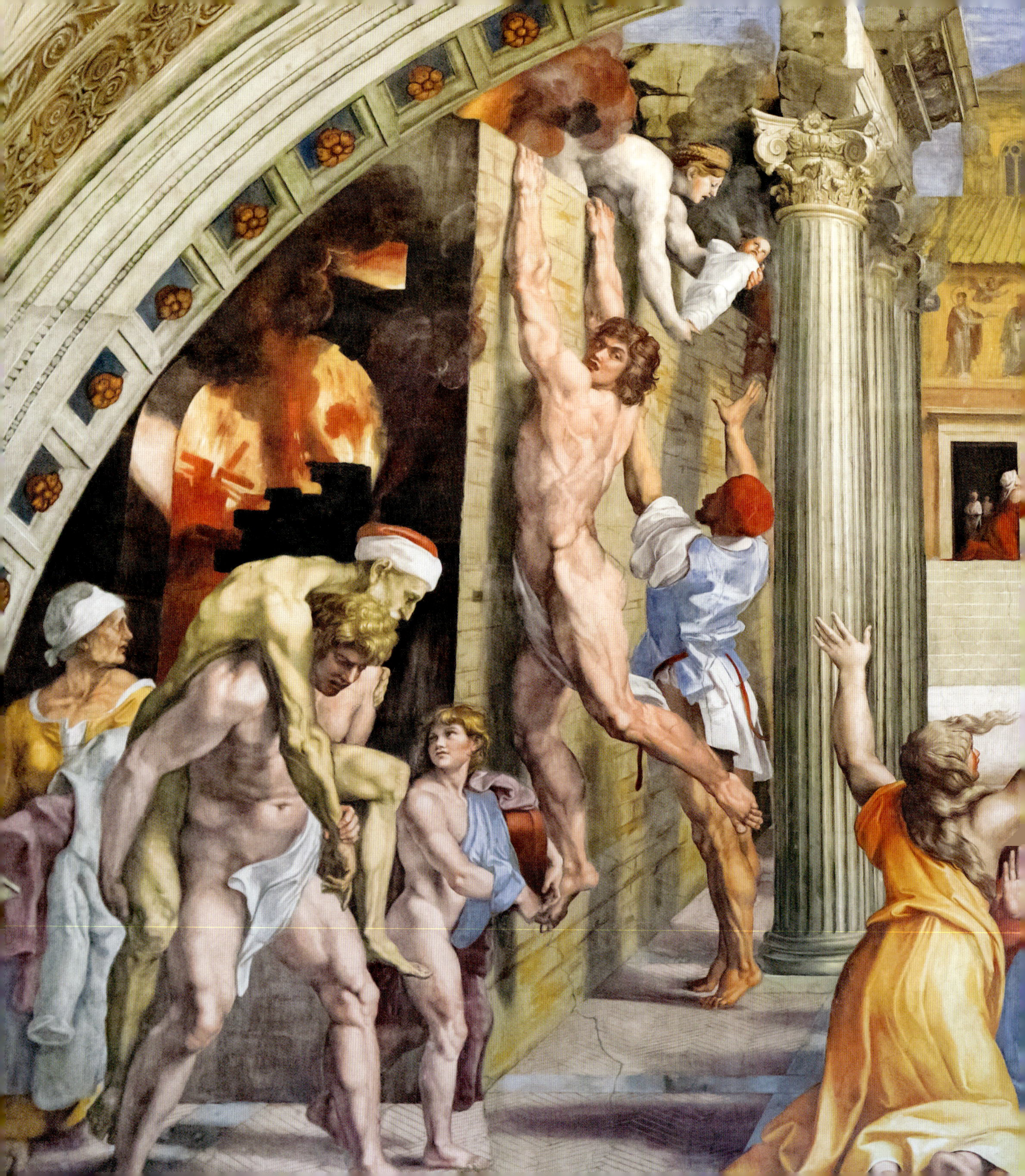

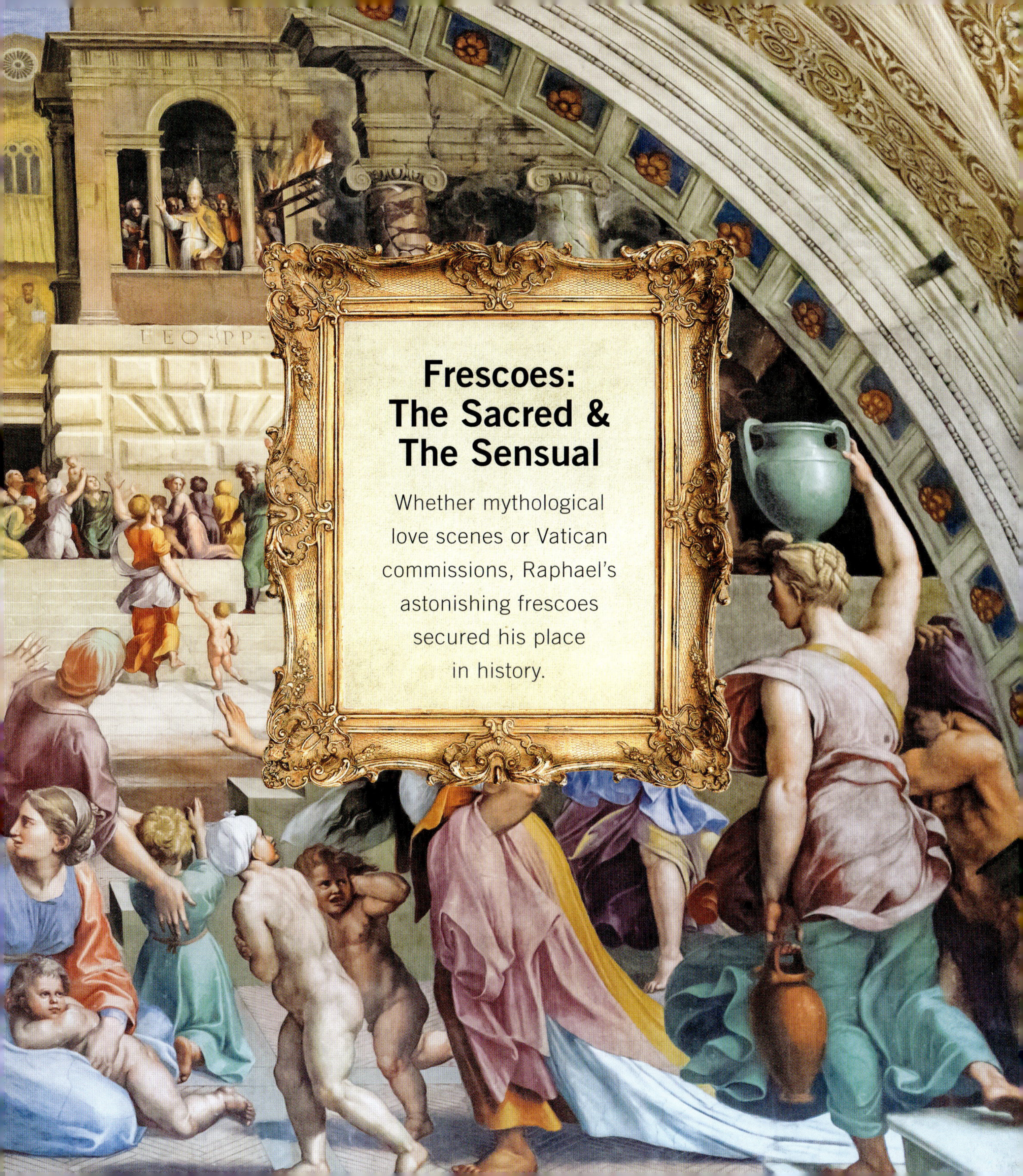

Frescoes: The Sacred & The Sensual

Whether mythological love scenes or Vatican commissions, Raphael's astonishing frescoes secured his place in history.

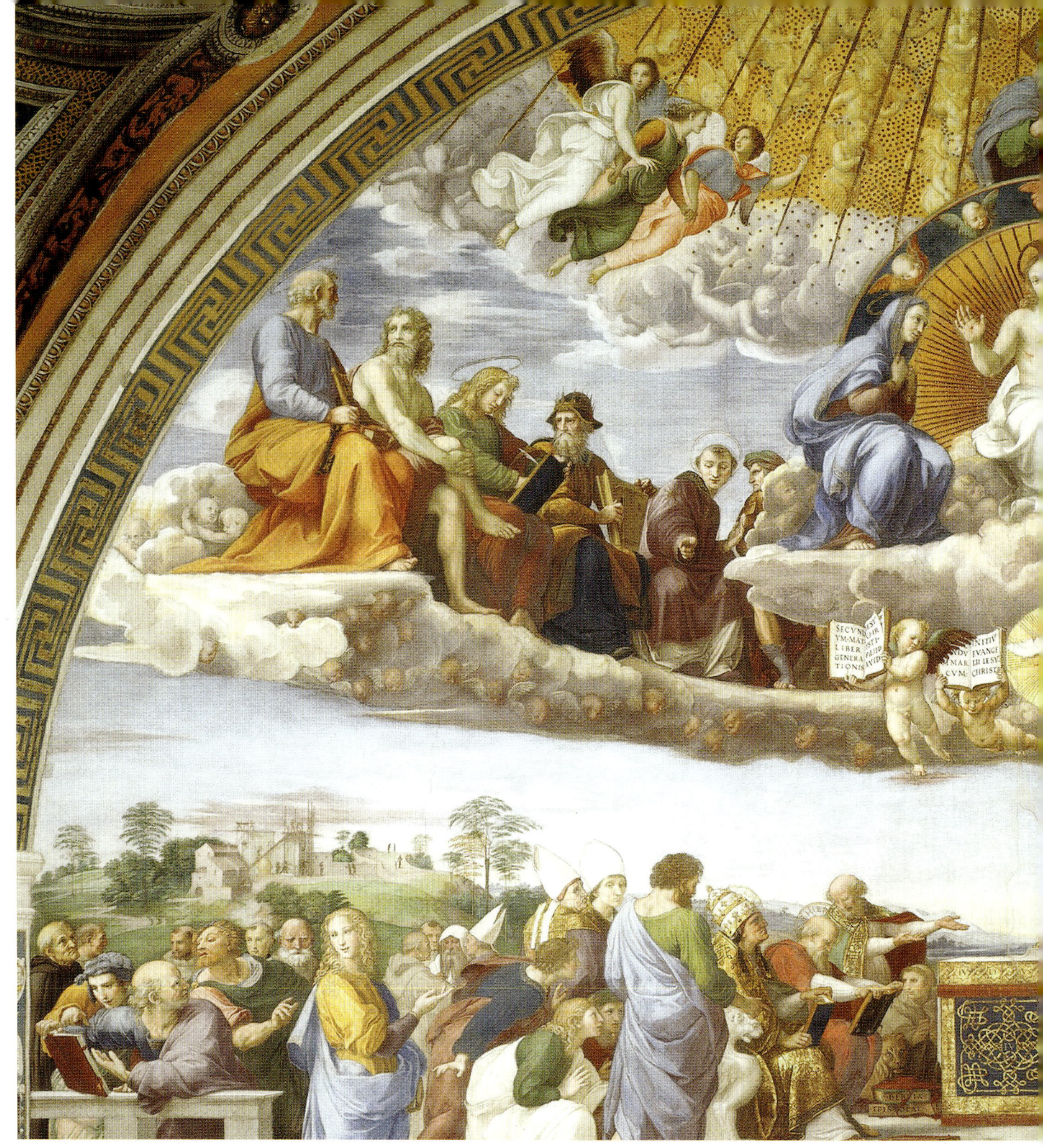

The Disputation of the Holy Sacrament (Disputa), 1509–11
Fresco, 500 x 770 cm (197 x 303¼ in)
• Stanza della Segnatura, Vatican Museums, Rome

Representing divine truth, this fresco was commissioned by Pope Julius II as part of a project to paint the walls of the Stanza della Segnatura, the pope's apartments in the Vatican (now referred to as the 'Raphael Rooms').

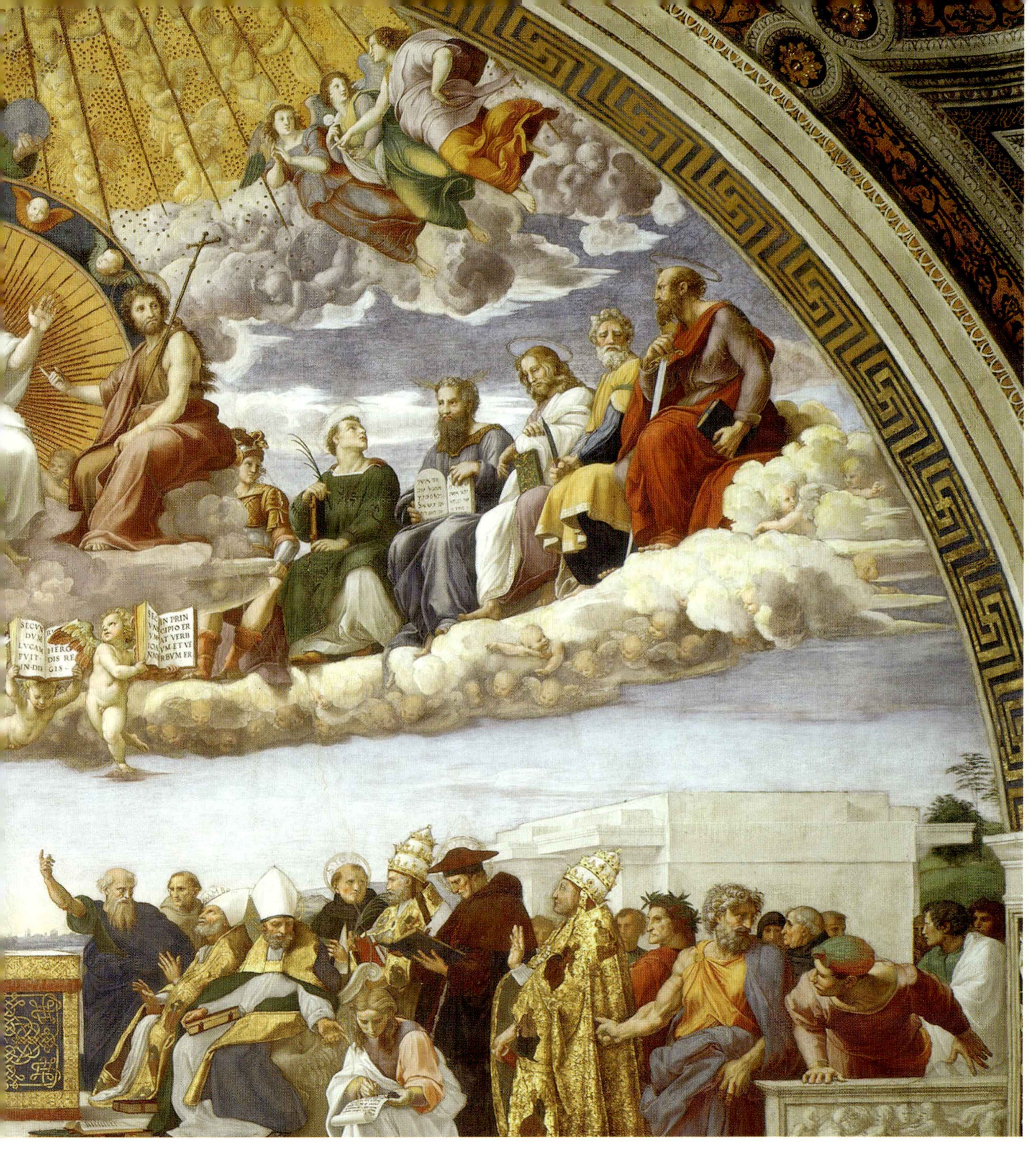

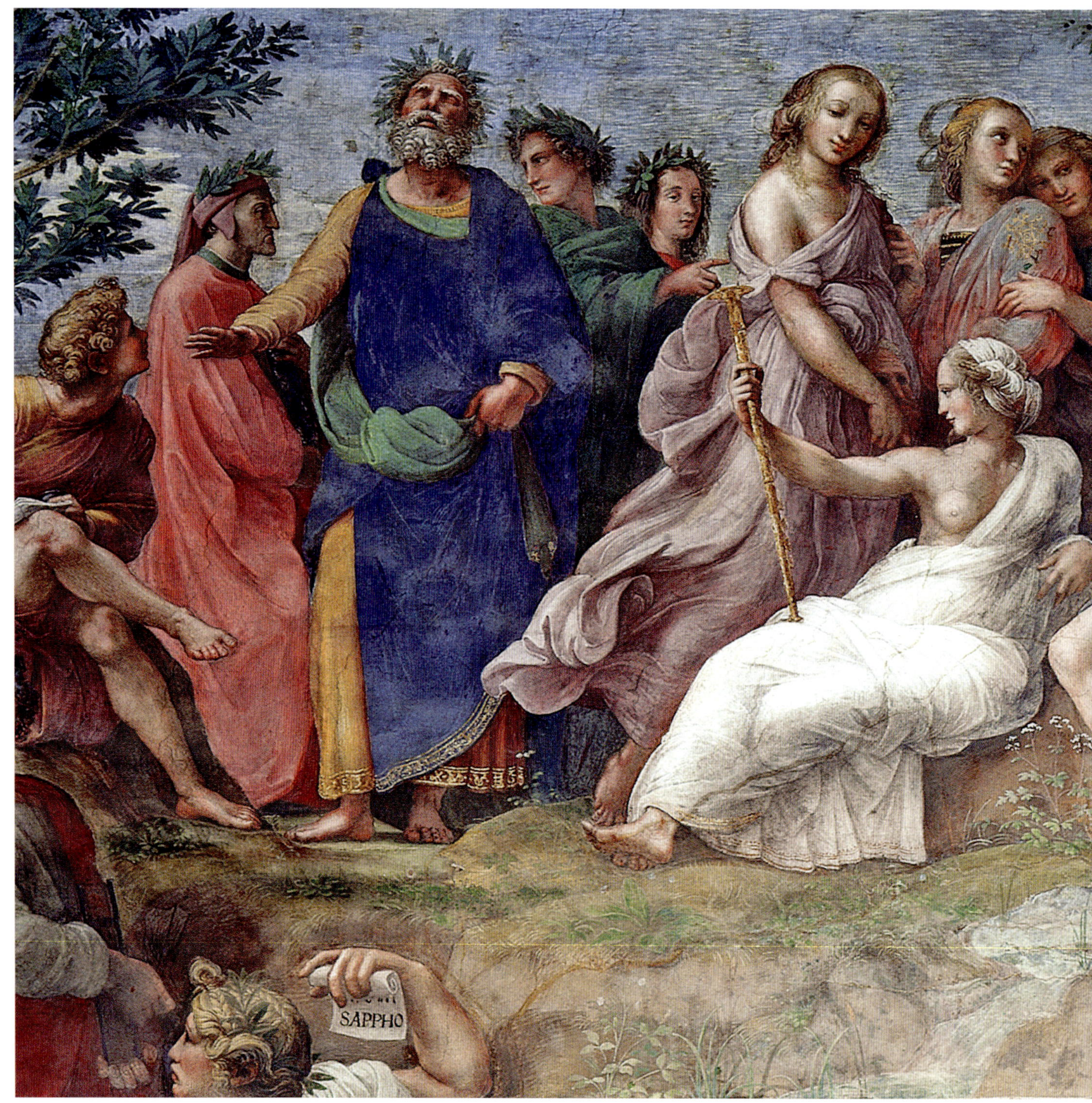

The Parnassus, 1509–11
Fresco, 670 cm (264 in) wide
• Stanza della Segnatura, Vatican Museums, Rome

According to Classical myth, Mount Parnassus was the home of Apollo, the nine Muses (depicted here with voluptuous forms and softly undulating drapery) and poetry. The harmoniously organized composition includes a series of ancient and contemporary poets.

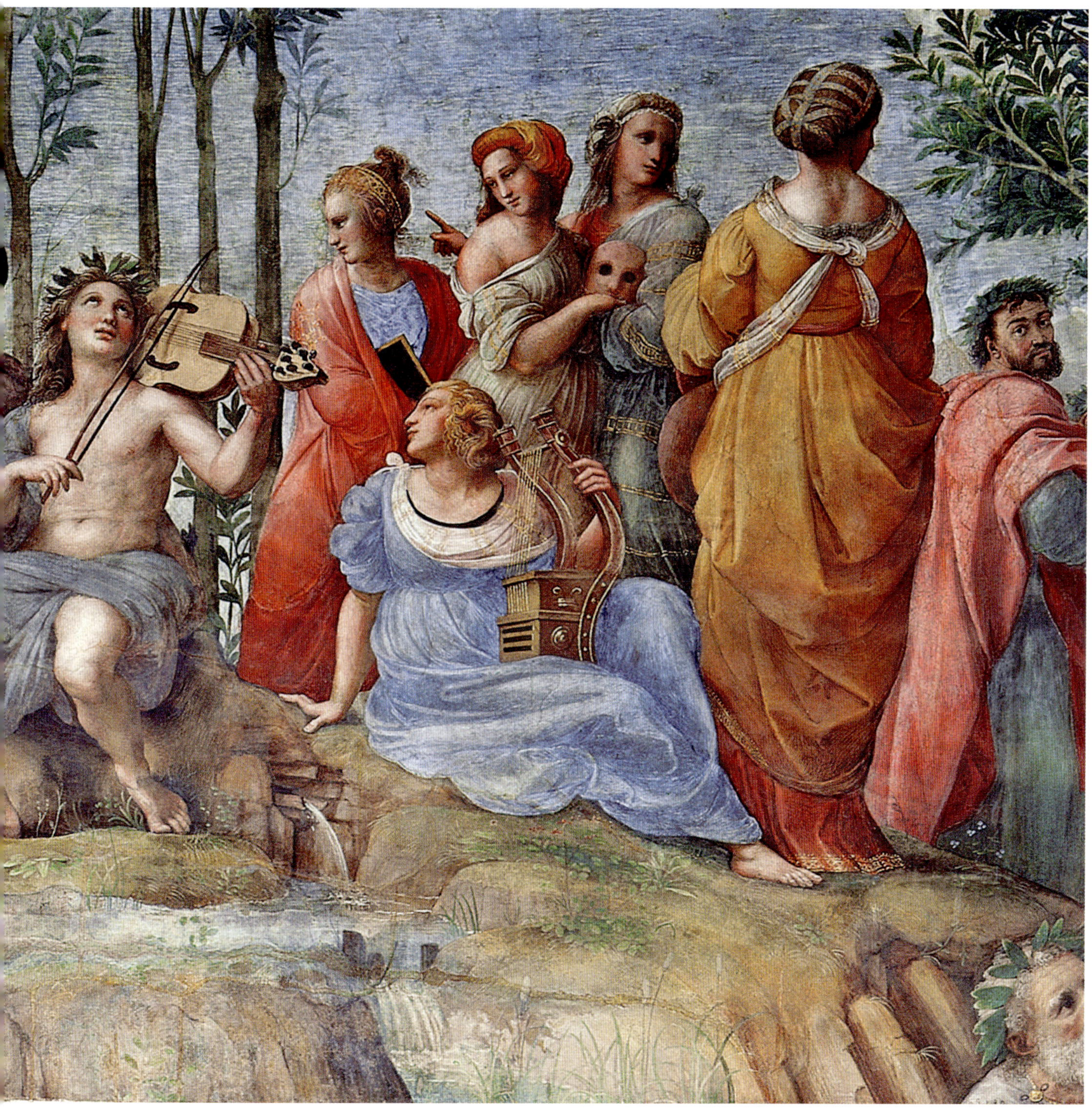

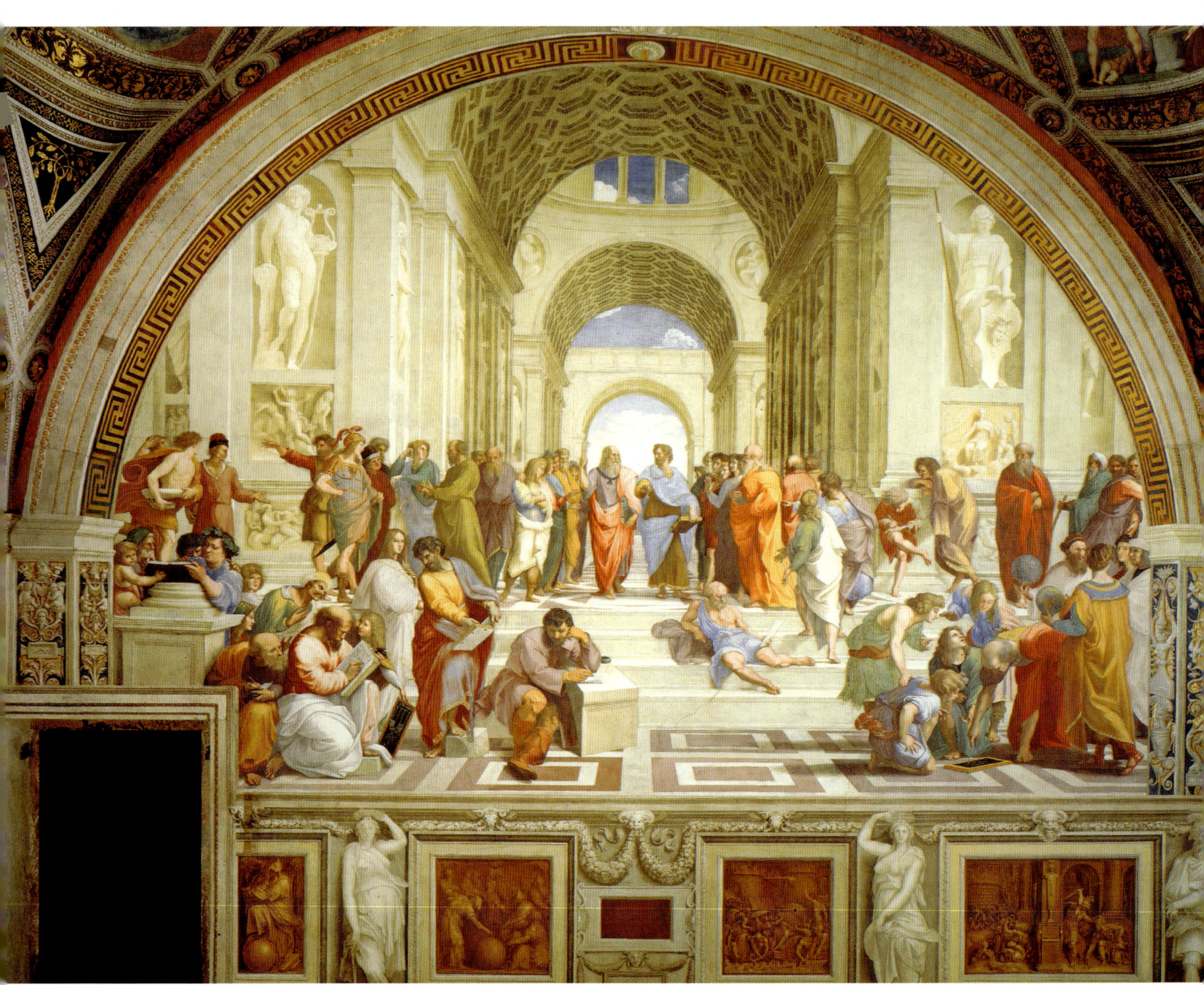

The School of Athens, 1509–11
Fresco, 500 x 770 cm (197 x 303¼ in)
• Stanza della Segnatura, Vatican Museums, Rome

Often regarded as Raphael's greatest masterpiece, this complex scene (in which the artist used perspective based on geometry and optics) contains an extraordinary cast of characters debating different philosophical propositions. Raphael himself appears at the fresco's right edge.

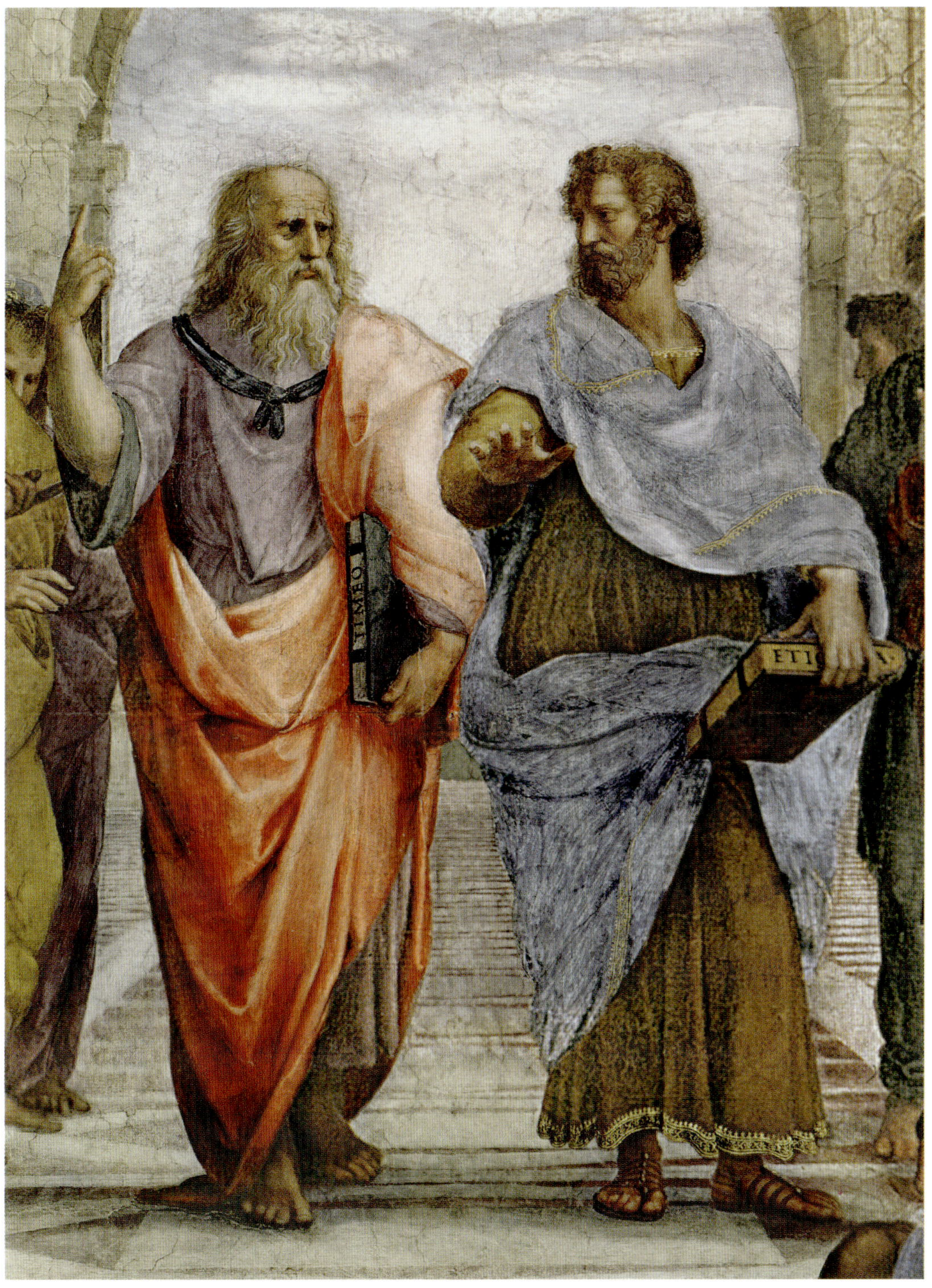

**Plato and Aristotle,
detail from The School of Athens, 1509–11**
Fresco • Stanza della Segnatura, Vatican Museums, Rome

Aristotle (right) holds his book (*Ethics*, written *c.* 340 BC) and converses with his teacher, the white-bearded Plato, whose *Timaeus* (written *c.* 360 BC) is tucked under his arm. The latter may be a portrait of Leonardo.

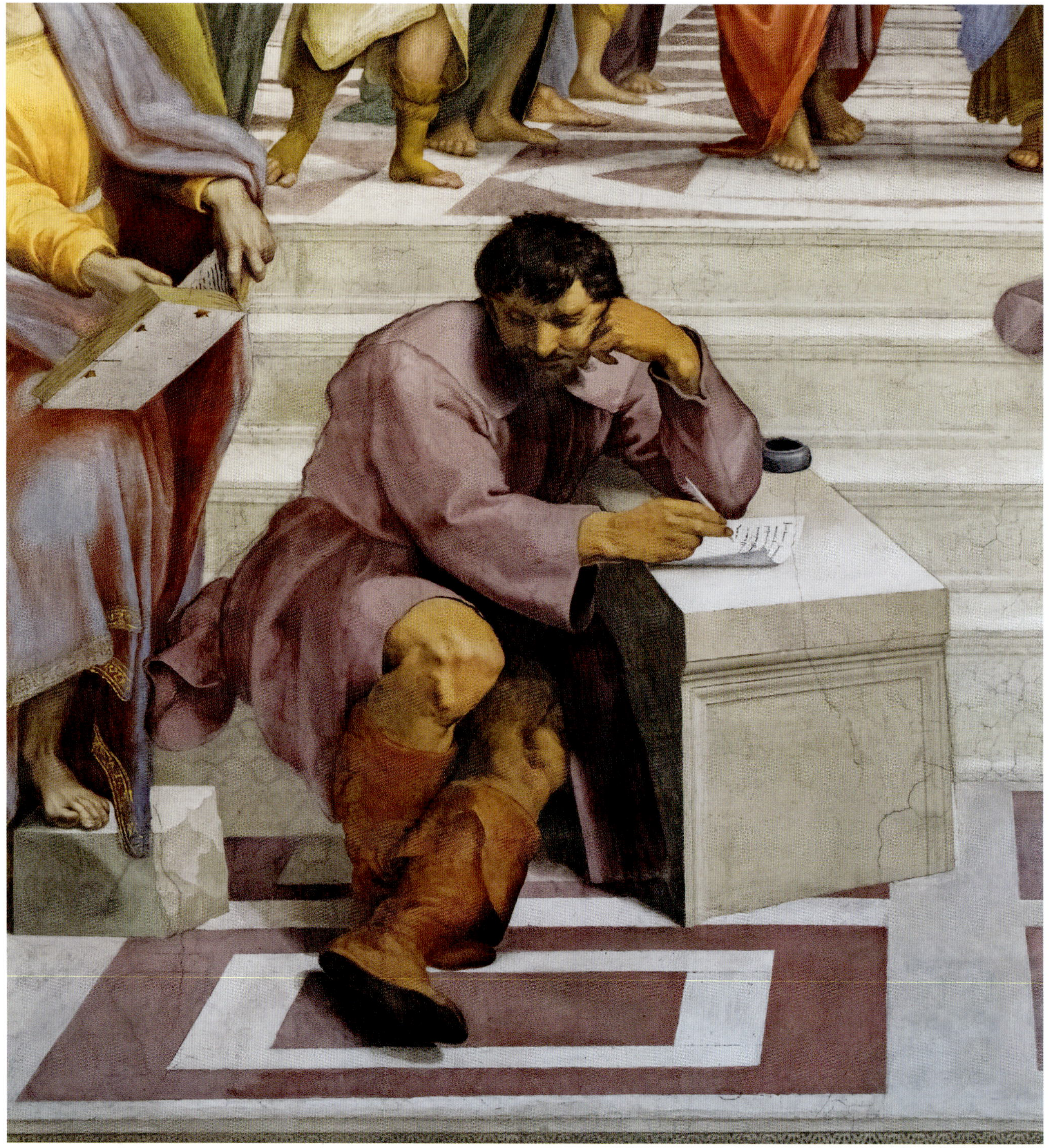

Heraclitus, detail from The School of Athens, 1509–11
Fresco • Stanza della Segnatura, Vatican Museums, Rome

Raphael painted Michelangelo's features on to the figure of the philosopher Heraclitus (legendary for his sour temper and scorn for rivals). Raphael added this figure after he had completed the main fresco, painting on a freshly applied section of plaster.

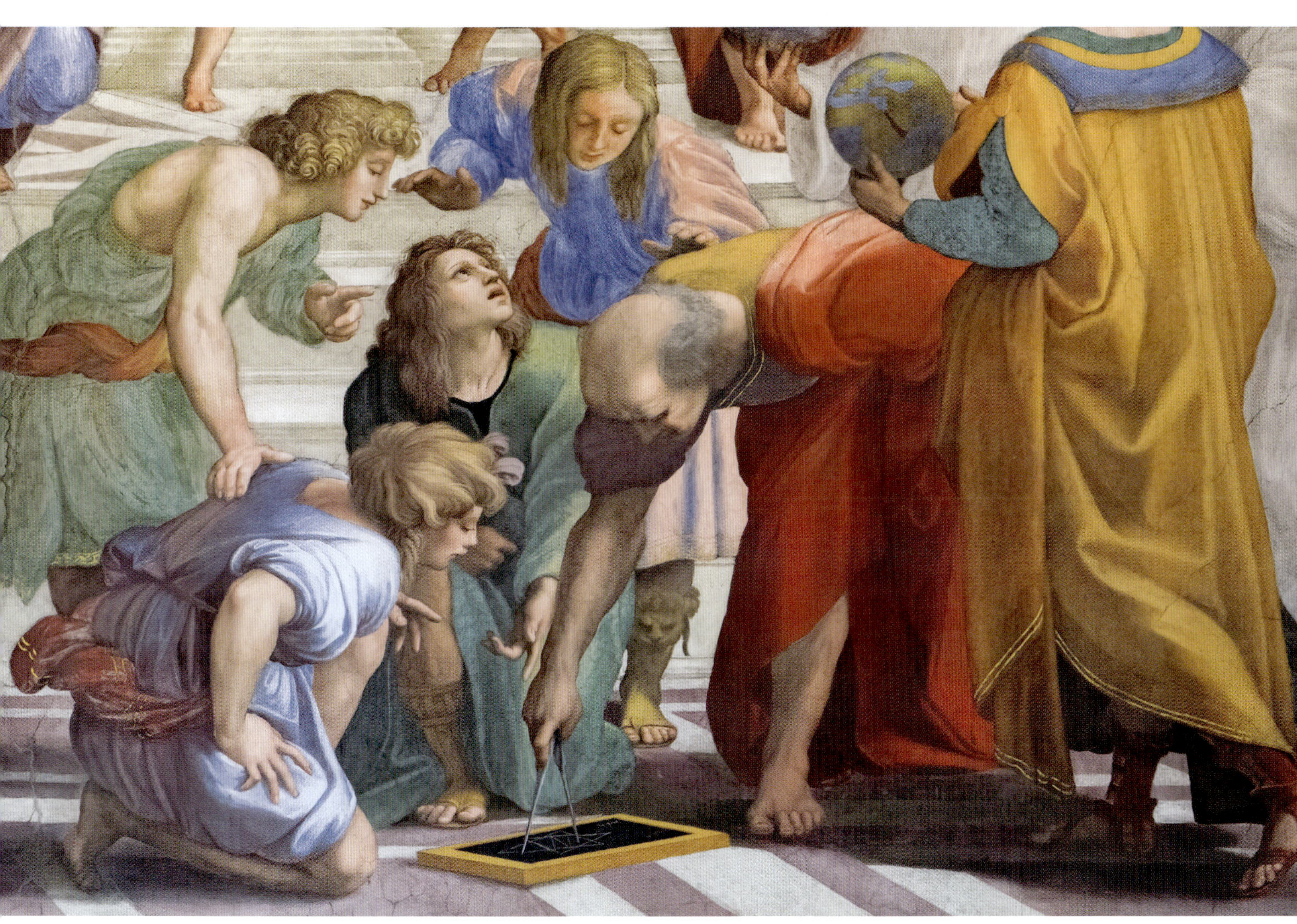

Euclid, detail from The School of Athens, 1509–11
Fresco • Stanza della Segnatura, Vatican Museums, Rome

Raphael depicted his friend Donato Bramante, the chief architect in Rome, as the Greek mathematician Euclid (or Archimedes, *c.* 287–*c.* 212 BC). He is shown, compass in hand, demonstrating a theorem to his fascinated students.

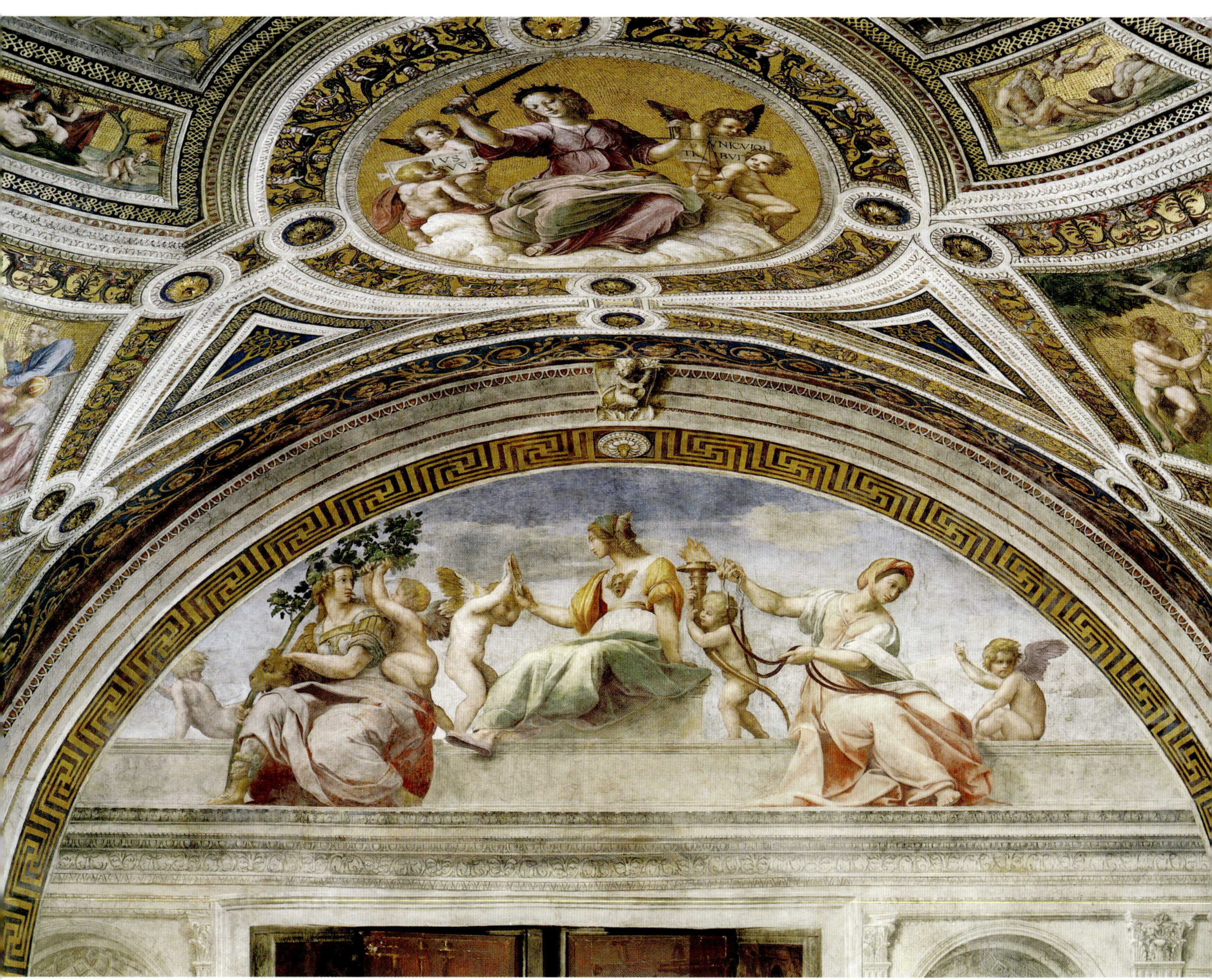

The Cardinal and Theological Virtues, 1509–11
Fresco, 660 cm (260 in) wide
• Stanza della Segnatura, Vatican Museums, Rome

Raphael's modelling of the forms of the three cardinal virtues (Fortitude, Prudence and Temperance) suggests Michelangelo's influence. These figures are attended by five cherubs, three of whom depict the theological virtues of Charity, Hope and Faith.

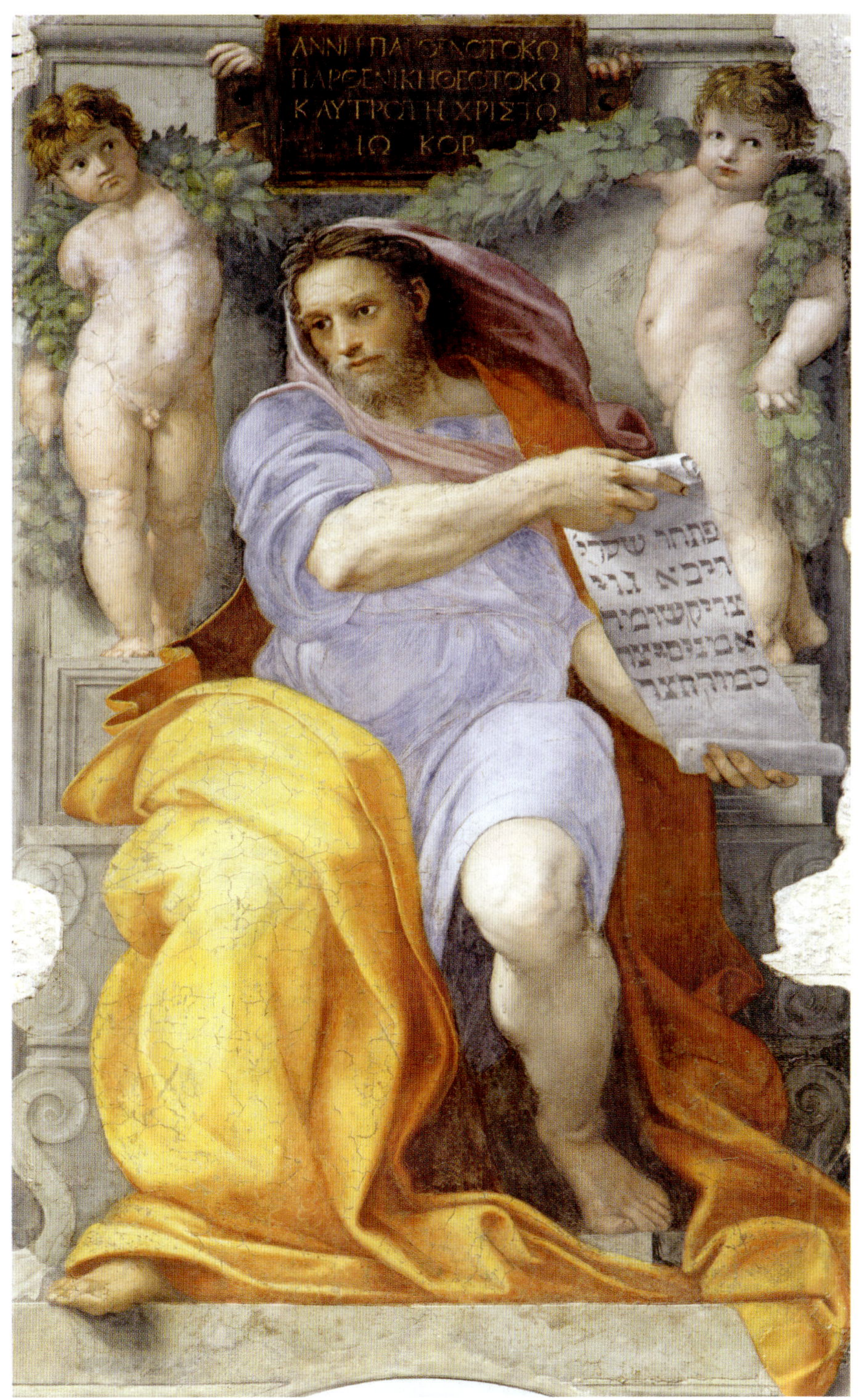

The Prophet Isaiah, 1512
Fresco, 250 x 155 cm (98⅔ x 61 in) • Basilica di Sant'Agostino, Rome

This fresco is transparently an homage to the prophets in Michelangelo's Sistine Chapel ceiling in its composition, the sweeping grandeur of the figure's gesture and even the acidic hues of the drapery.

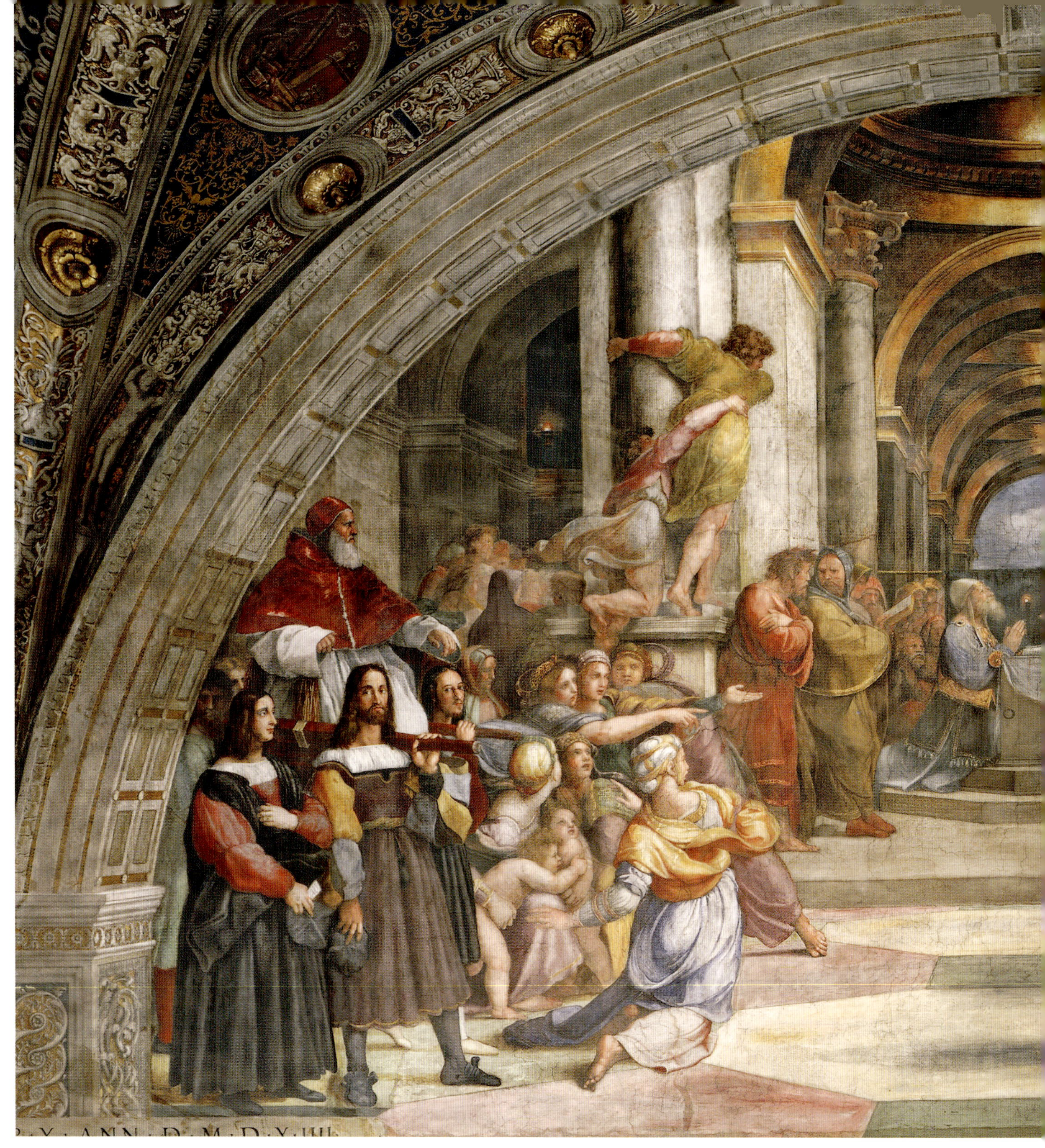

The Expulsion of Heliodorus from the Temple, 1512–14
Fresco, 750 cm (295⅓ in) wide
• Stanza di Eliodoro, Vatican Museums, Rome

This dramatic fresco shows Heliodorus being driven out of the Temple in Jerusalem (having attempted to seize its treasure) by a horseman and two youths. Pope Julius II witnesses the scene from his portable throne.

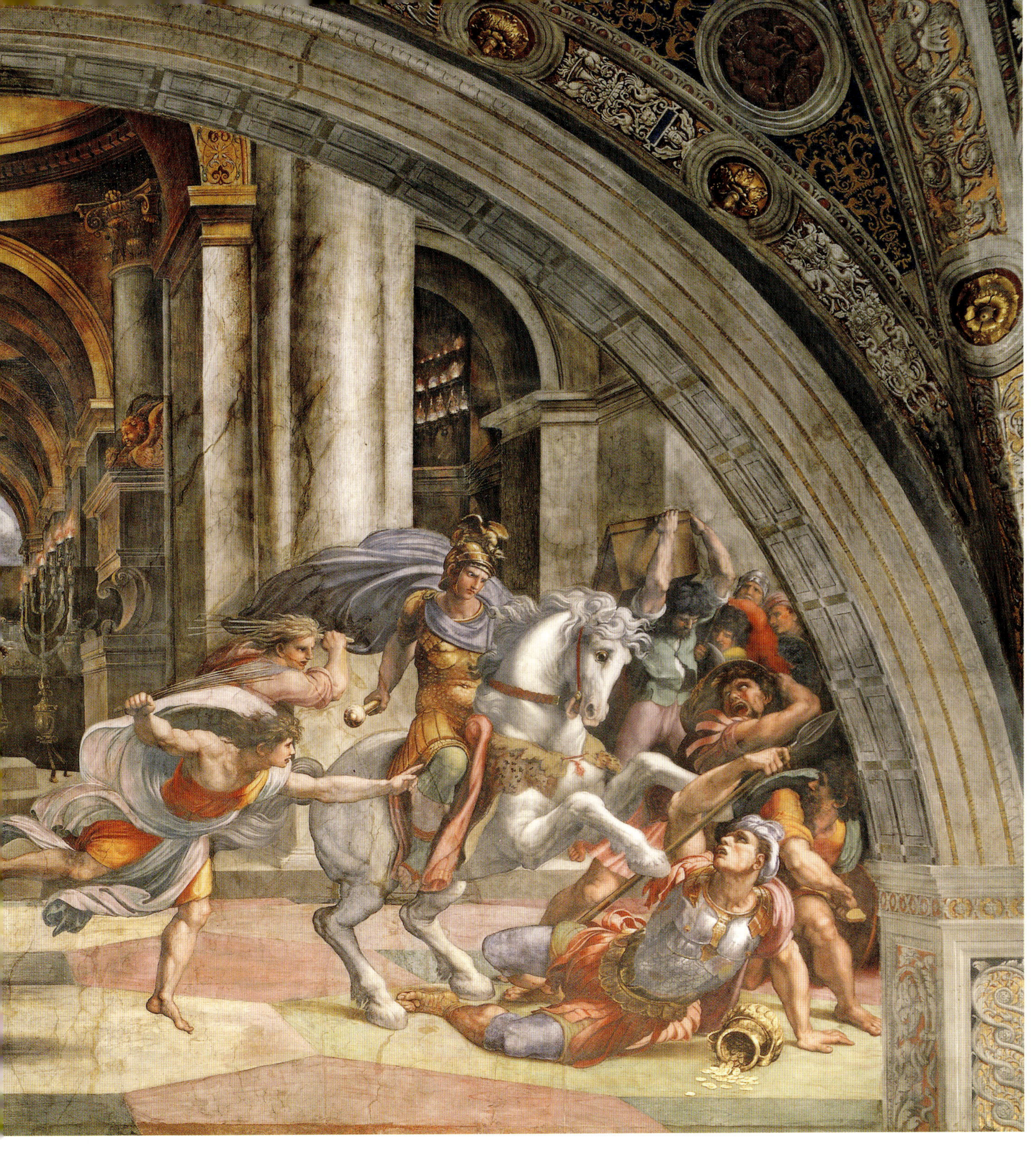

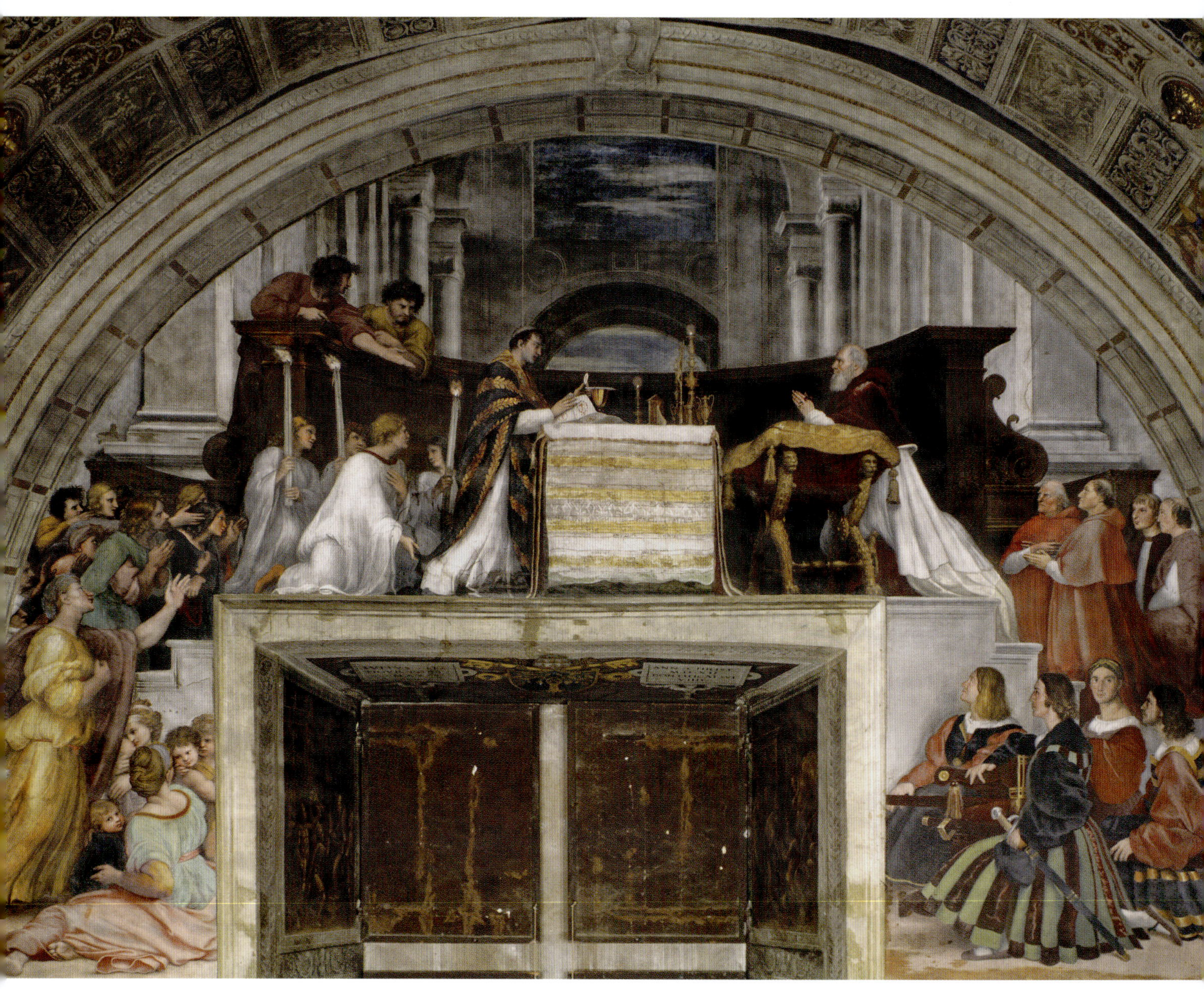

The Mass at Bolsena, 1512–14
Fresco, 660 cm (260 in) wide
• Stanza di Eliodoro, Vatican Museums, Rome

Pope Julius II, shown venerating the *corporale* (communion cloth) of Bolsena, also participates in a medieval miracle – the bleeding wafer confirmed a Bohemian priest's faith in transubstantiation (the belief that Christ's body and blood are present in the Eucharist).

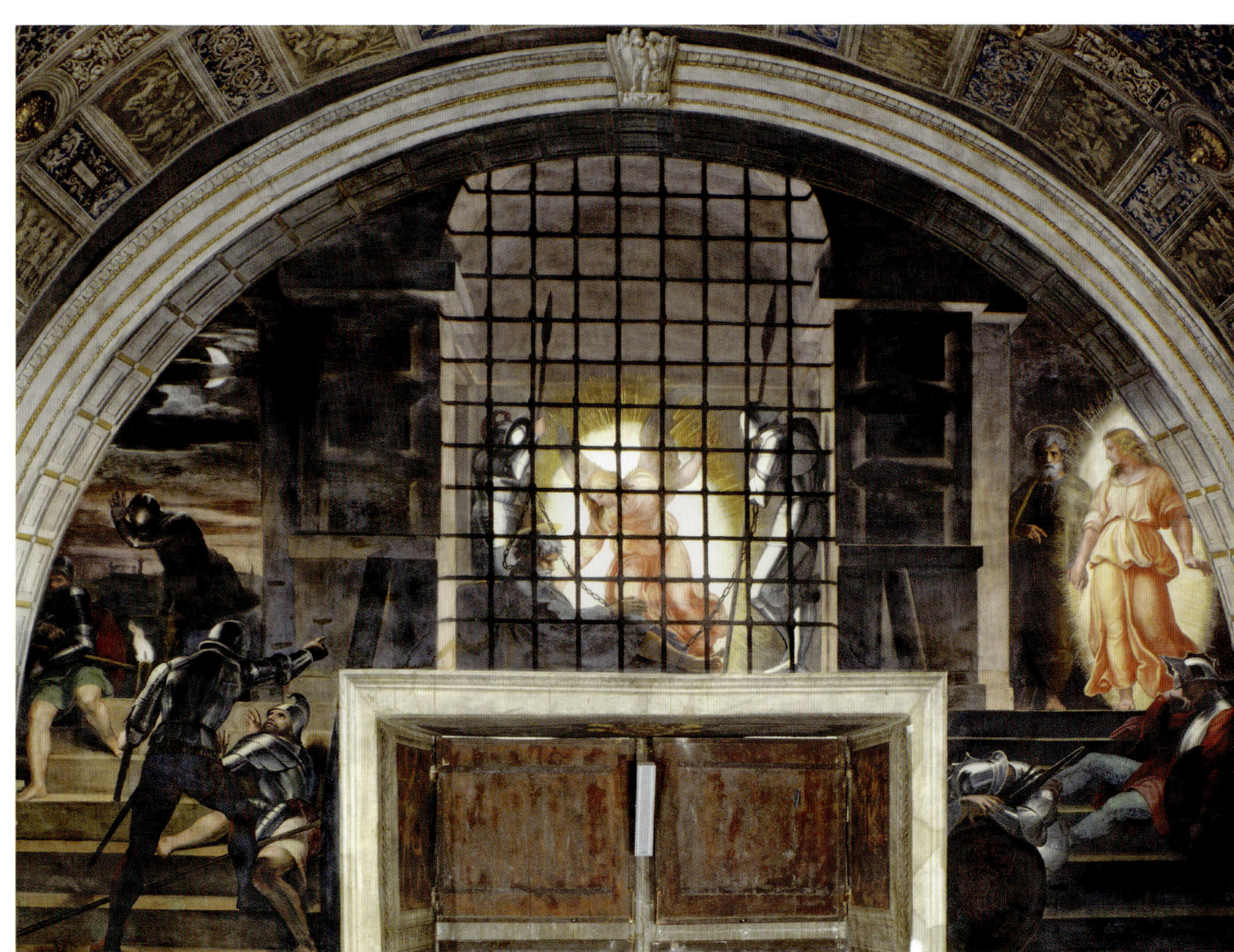

The Liberation of Saint Peter, 1514
Fresco, 560 cm (220½ in) wide
• Stanza di Eliodoro, Vatican Museums, Rome

Raphael played with effects of light and colour in this nighttime scene. The fresco shows Peter miraculously being delivered from prison by an angel, while guards lie sleeping (as described in the Acts of the Apostles).

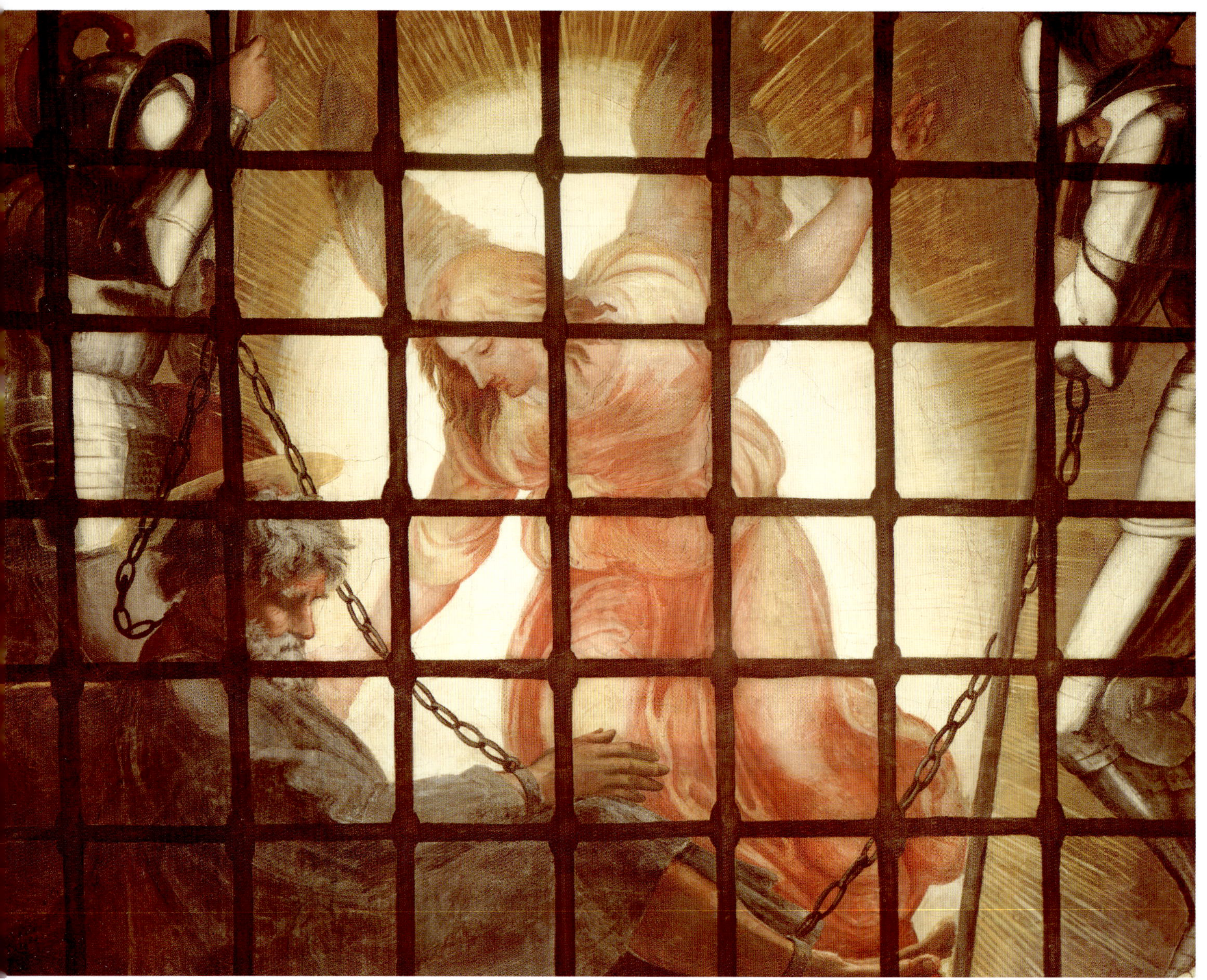

**The Angel Wakes Saint Peter,
detail from The Liberation of Saint Peter, 1514**
Fresco • Stanza di Eliodoro, Vatican Museums, Rome

One sixteenth-century viewer, marvelling at Raphael's rendering of the angel's 'dazzling splendour', noted that 'the arms of the soldiers shine resplendent … their burnished lustre seems more lifelike than if they were real, although they are only painted'.

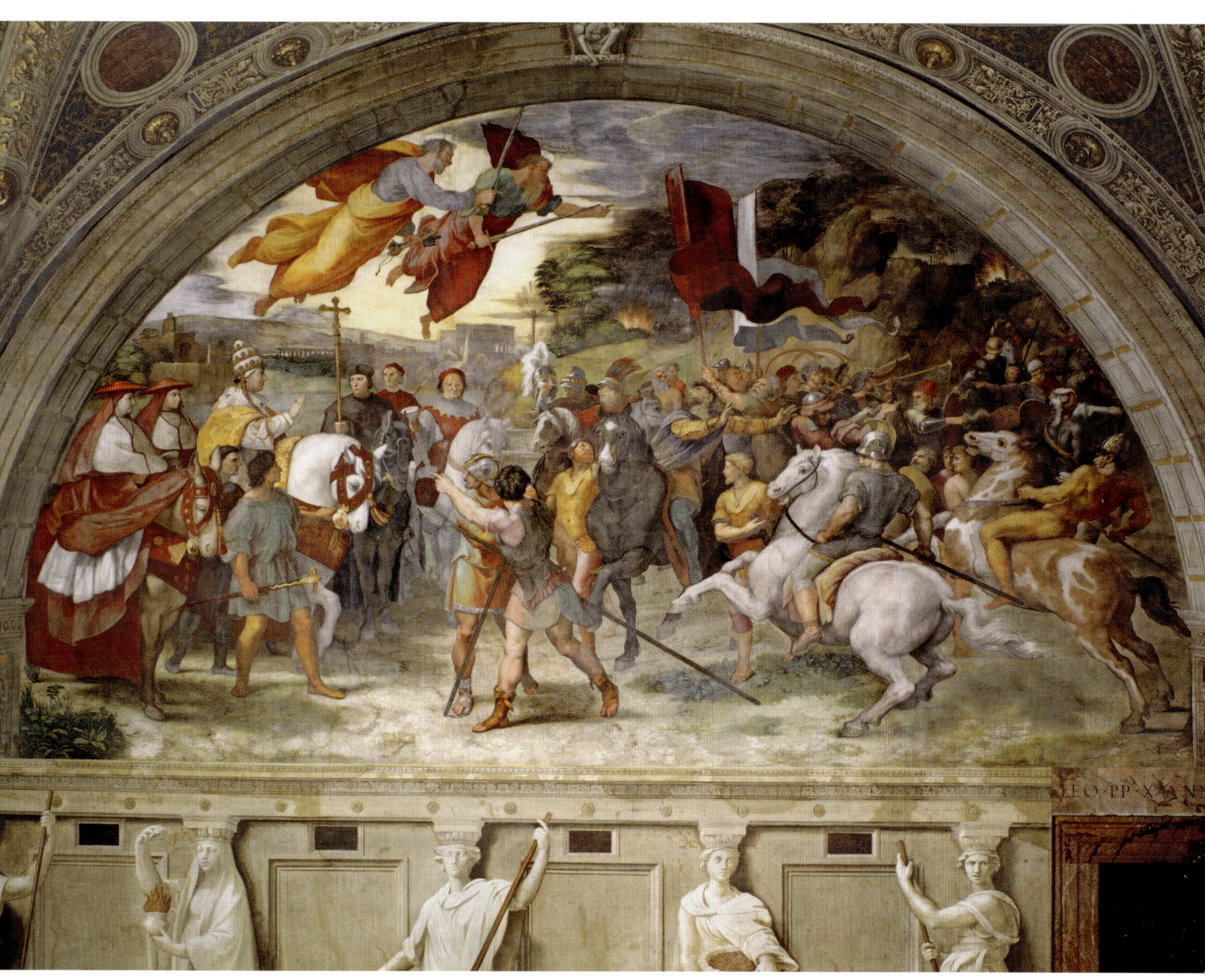

The Meeting of Leo the Great and Attila, 1514
Fresco, 500 x 750 cm (197 x 295⅓ in)
• Stanza di Eliodoro, Vatican Museums, Rome

Raphael, with the help of his assistants, portrayed the moment in AD 452 when Pope Leo the Great managed, thanks to an apparition of saints Peter and Paul, to prevent Attila (ruler of the Huns) from invading Italy.

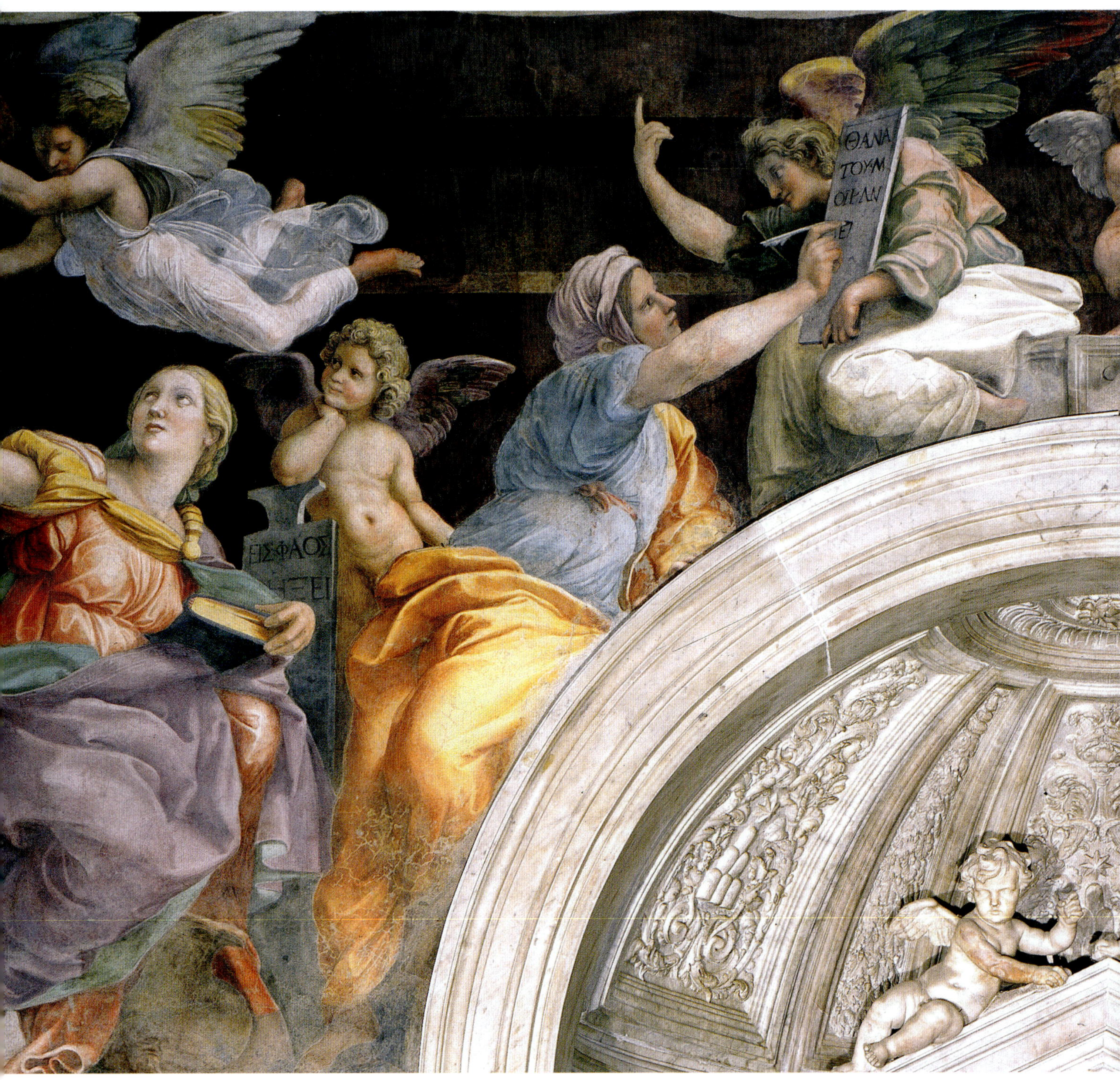

Sibyls Receiving Instruction from Angels, 1514
Fresco, 615 cm (242 in) wide • Santa Maria della Pace, Rome

Raphael co-opted Michelangelo's Sistine Chapel ceiling sibyls and prophets for his sibyls (Cumaean, Persian, Phrygian and Tiburtine) and angels painted above the entrance arch of the banker Agostino Chigi's private chapel.

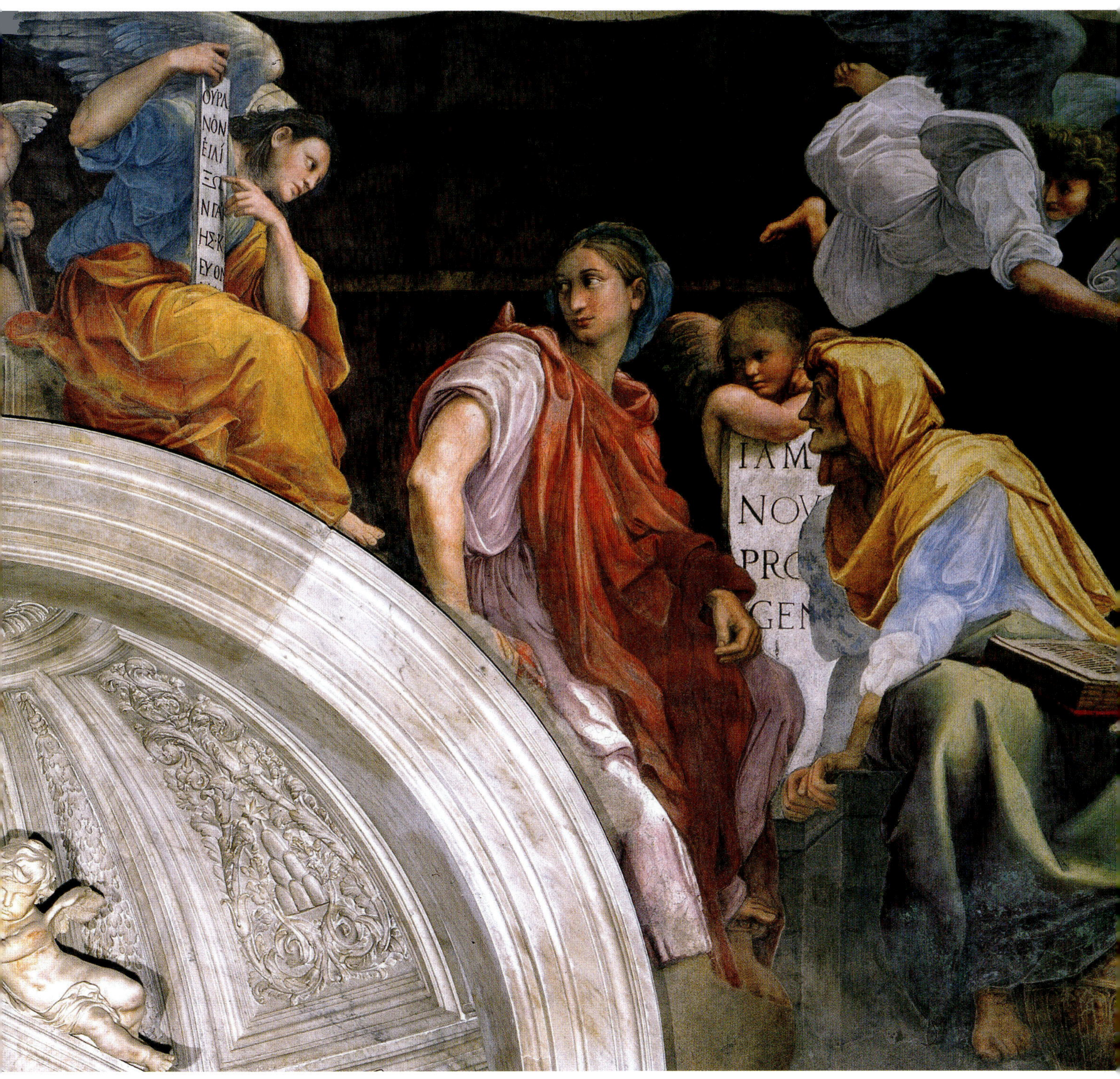
OYPA
NON
E IA
EI
N IA
H E K
EY ON

IAM
NOV
PRO
GEN

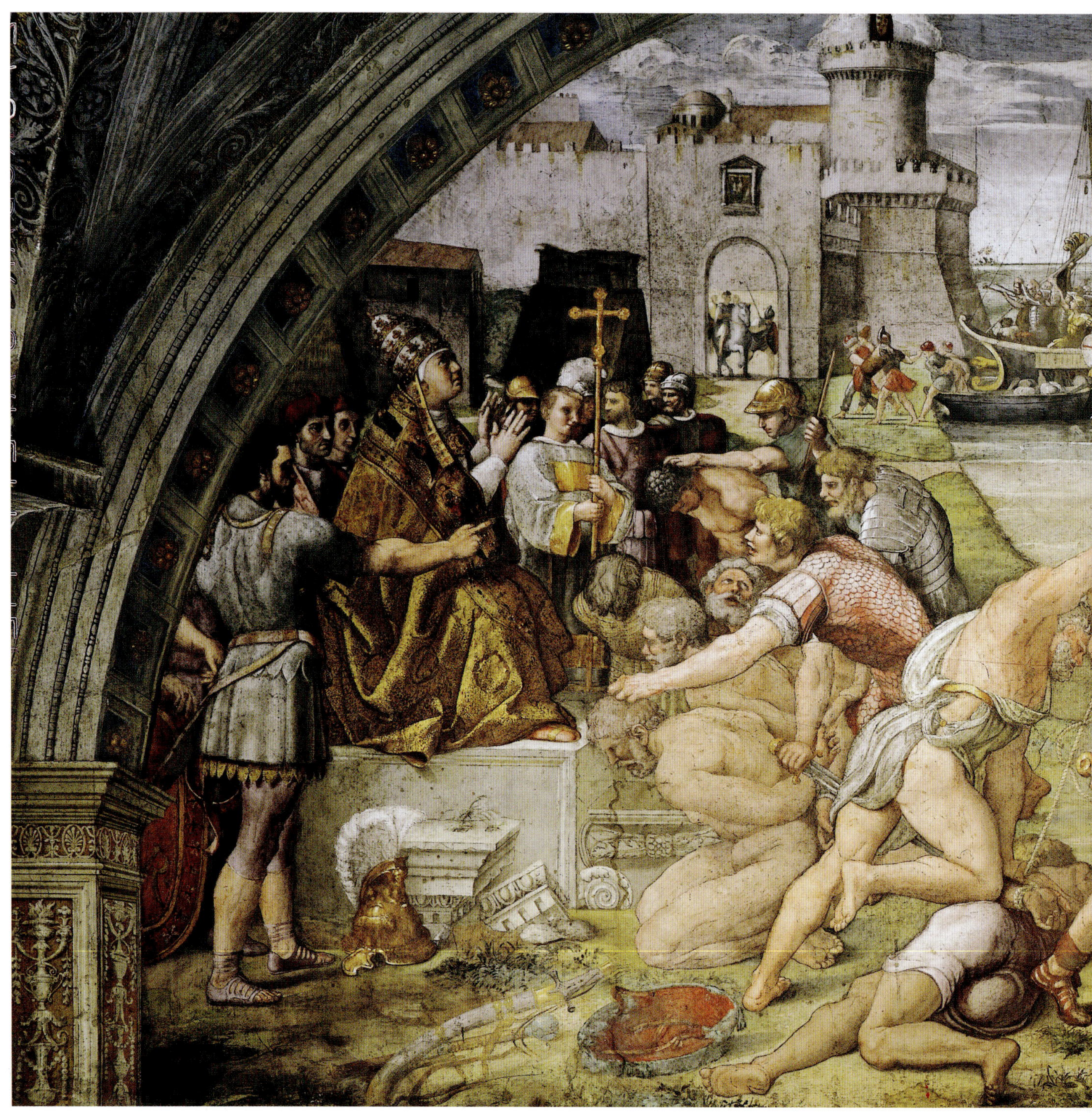

The Battle of Ostia, 1514–17, by Giulio Romano (*c.* 1499–1546)
Fresco, 770 cm (303¼ in) wide • Stanza dell'Incendio di Borgo, Vatican Museums, Rome

Raphael provided some figure studies, but Giulio Romano was entrusted with the cartoon and execution of this fresco. It refers to a naval battle between the Arab fleet and papal forces in AD 849.

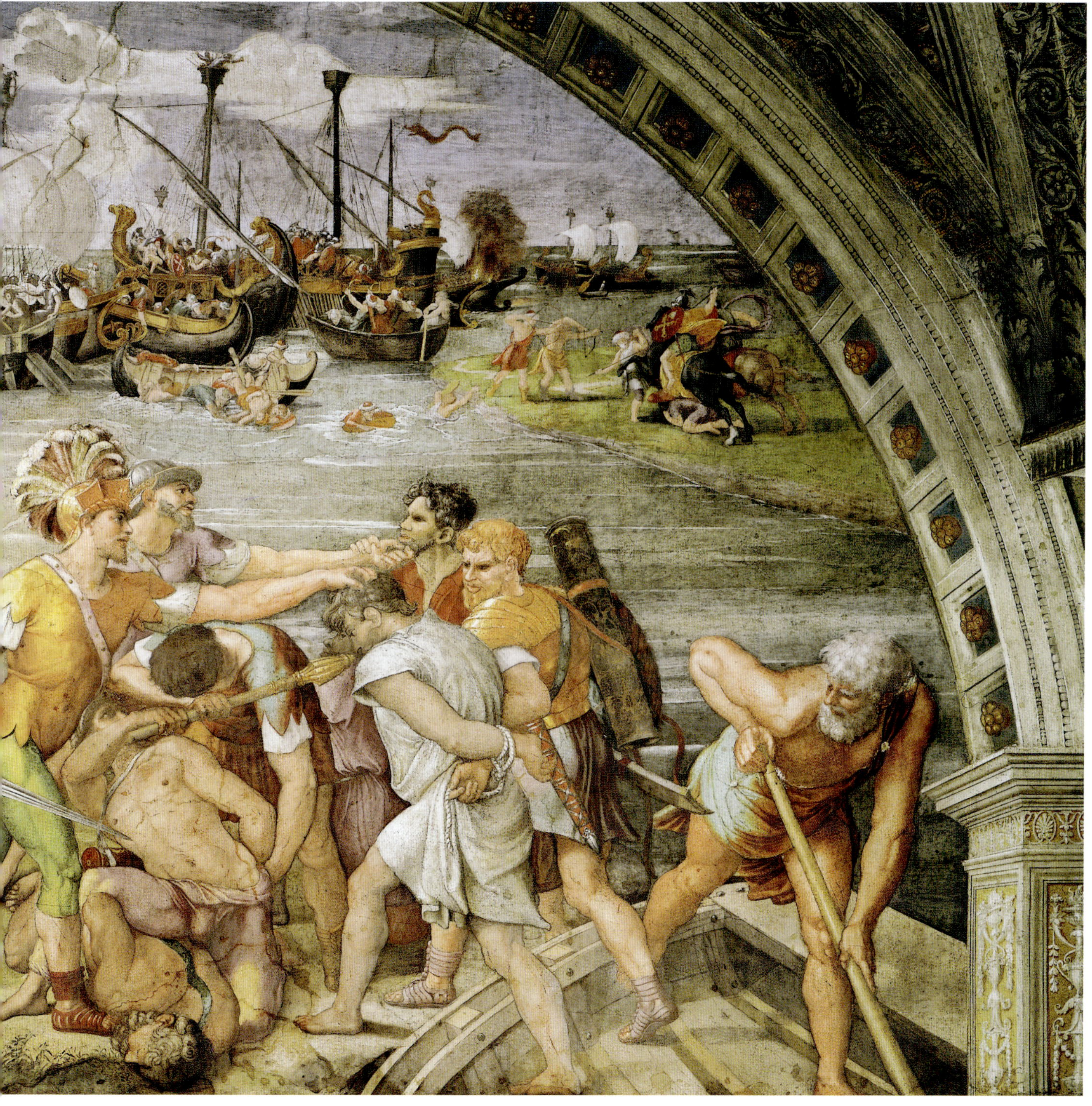

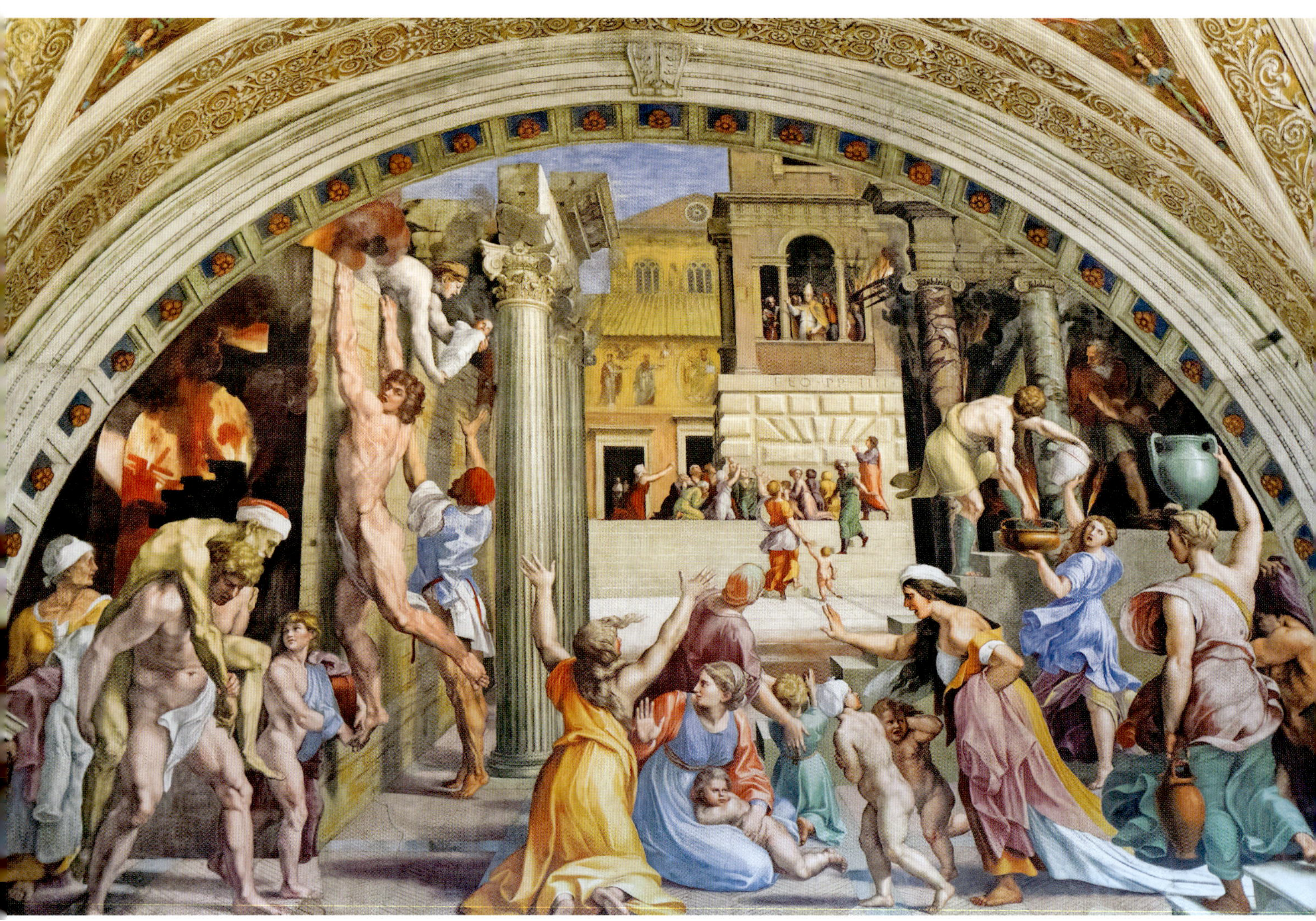

Fire in the Borgo, 1514–17
Fresco, 670 cm (264 in) wide
• Stanza dell'Incendio di Borgo, Vatican Museums, Rome

This scene of catastrophe, designed and painted largely by Raphael himself, is an allegory of Pope Leo X putting out the flames of war, just as Pope Leo IV had miraculously extinguished the fire in a district of Rome in AD 847.

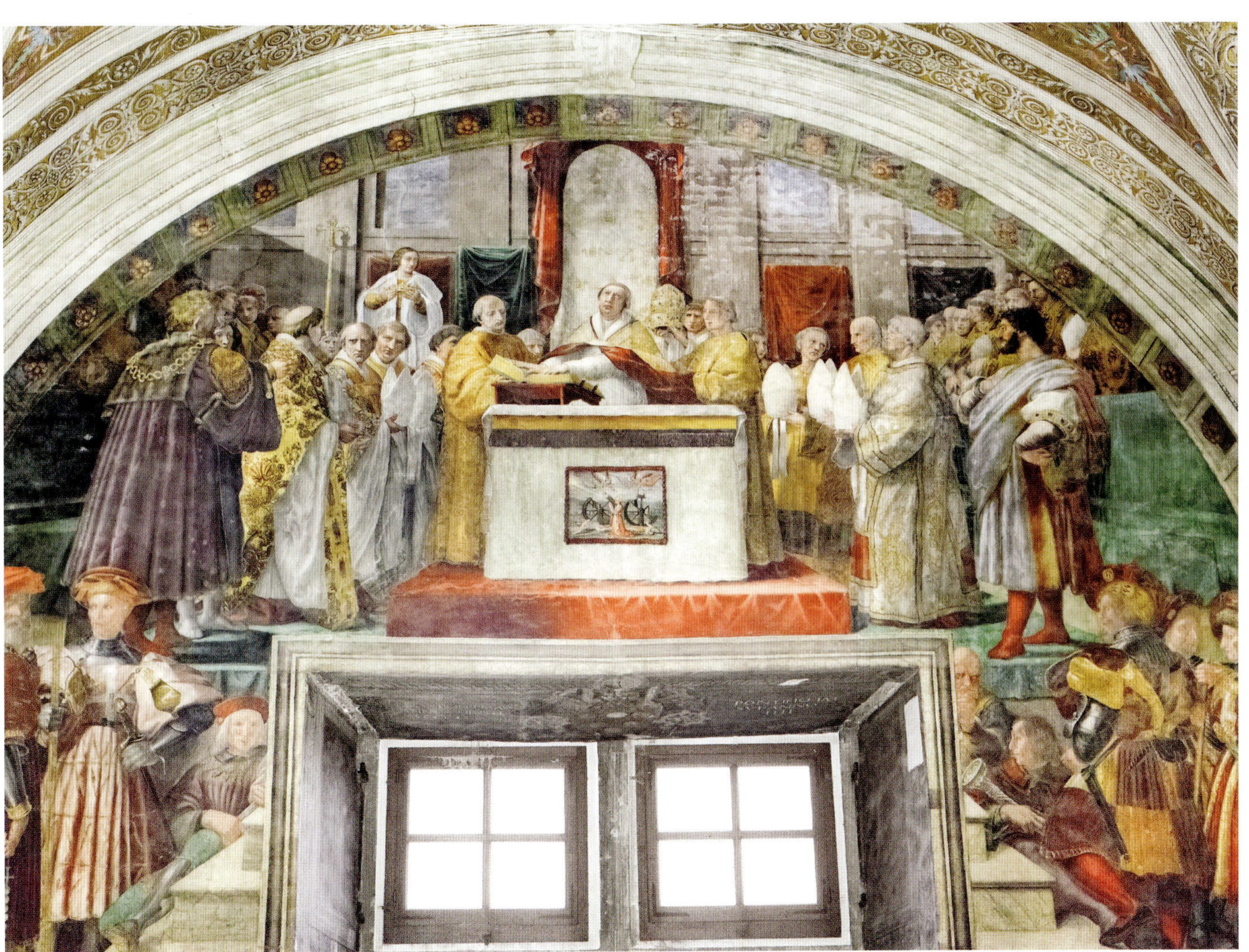

**The Oath of Leo III, 1514–17,
by Perino del Vaga (Pietro Buonaccorsi, 1501–47)**
Fresco, 770 cm (303¼ in) wide
• Stanza dell'Incendio di Borgo, Vatican Museums, Rome

Painted by a member of Raphael's studio, in this fresco Pope Leo III (looking remarkably like Leo X) is taking the oath of purification, having been falsely accused of misconduct in AD 800.

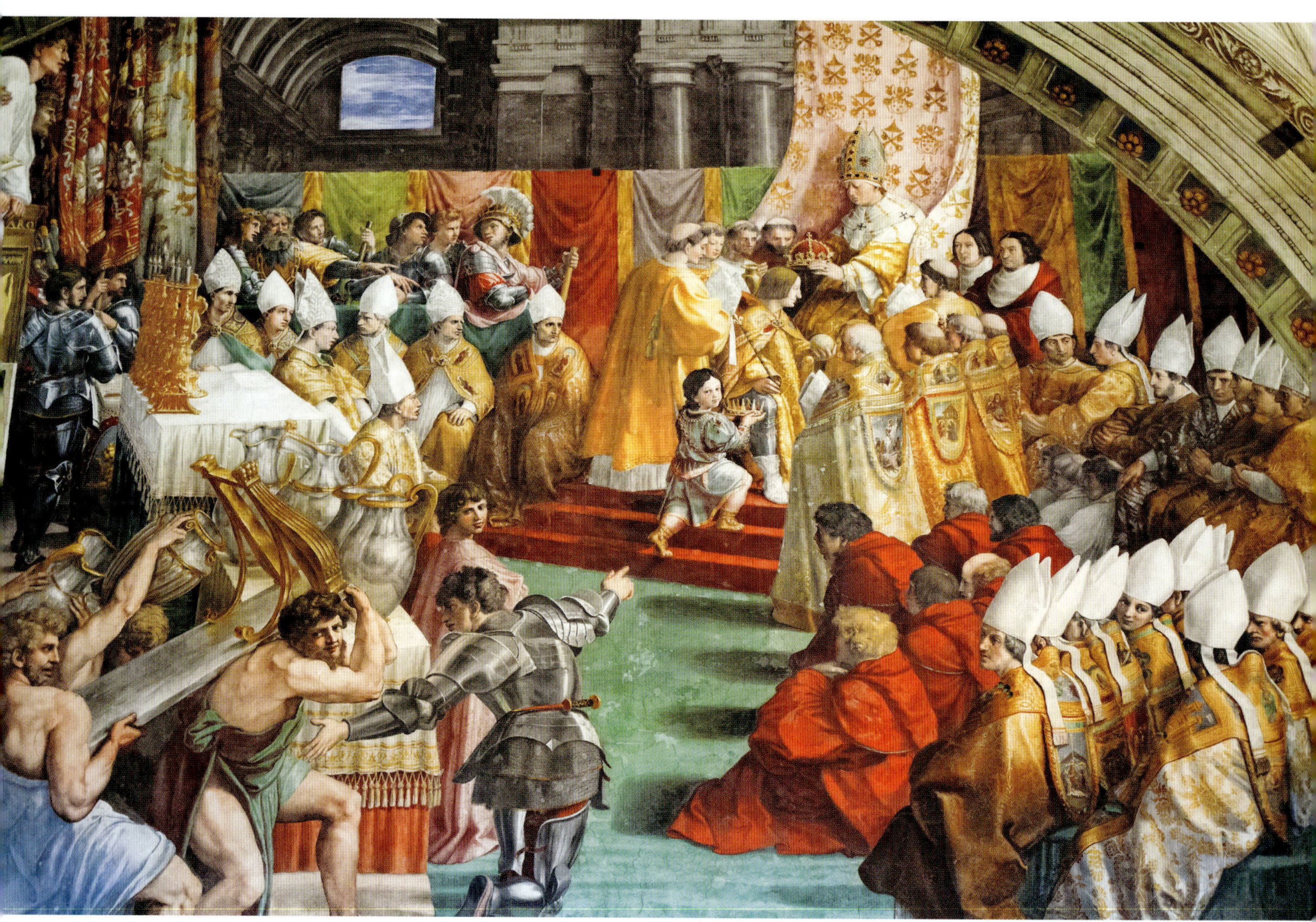

**The Coronation of Charlemagne (detail), 1514–17,
by Gianfrancesco Penni (*c.* 1496–1528)**
Fresco, 670 cm (264 in) wide
• Stanza dell'Incendio di Borgo, Vatican Museums, Rome

Raphael probably designed this composition, but the fresco was painted by his pupil Gianfrancesco Penni. It shows Charlemagne (a portrait of the French king, Francis I) being crowned by Pope Leo III in AD 800.

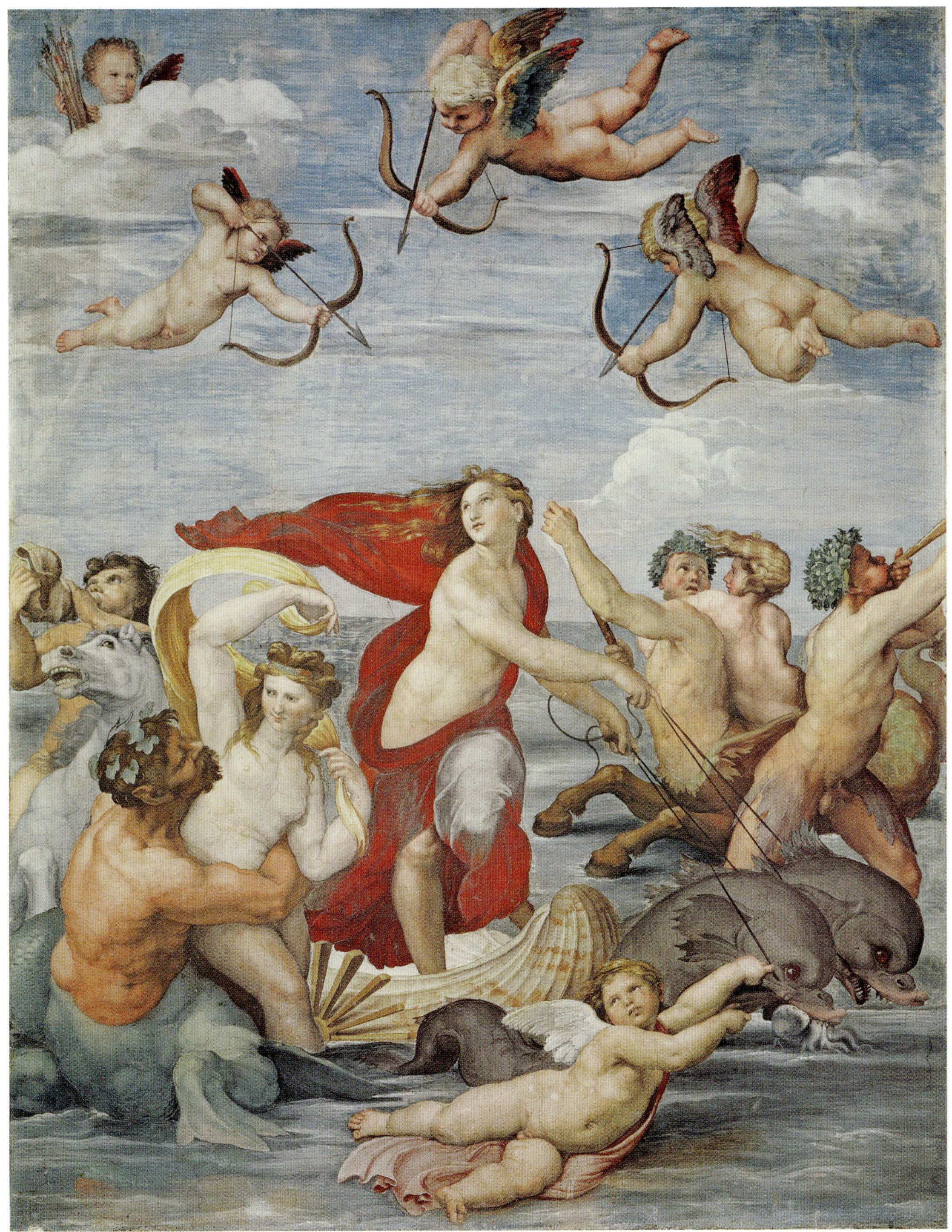

The Triumph of Galatea, 1514
Fresco, 295 x 225 cm (116 x 89 in)
• Loggia di Galatea, Villa Farnesina, Rome

Raphael based his image of Galatea not on any specific model, but on 'a certain idea' he had formed in his mind of perfect beauty – he created the nymph's body out of qualities he had seen in various women.

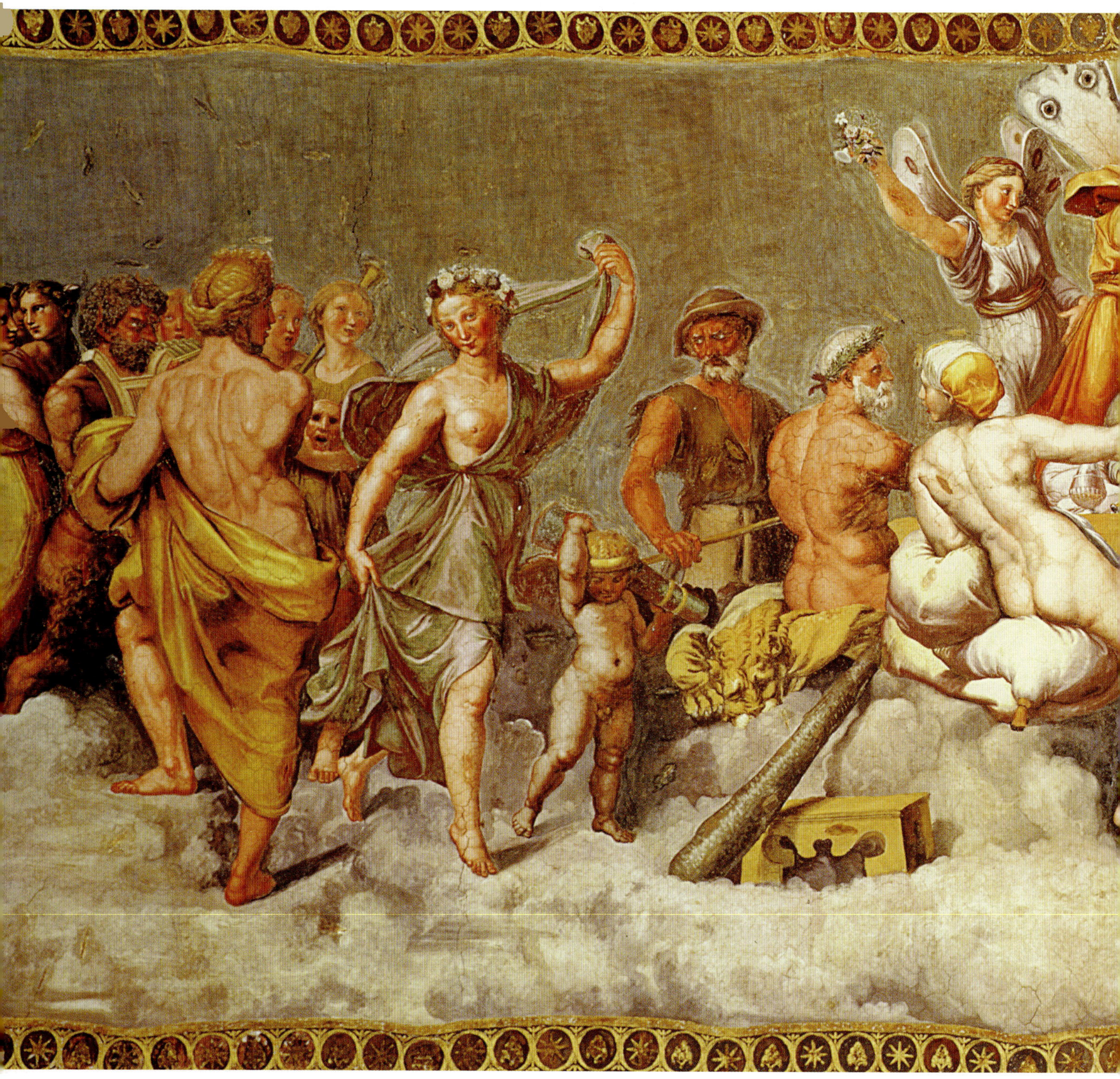

**The Banquet of the Gods (Wedding Feast of Cupid and Psyche),
1517–18, by Gianfrancesco Penni, Giulio Romano and
Giovanni da Udine (1487–1564), from designs by Raphael**

Fresco, dimensions unknown • Loggia di Amore e Psiche, Villa Farnesina, Rome

Painted by Raphael's workshop, this fictive tapestry on a loggia ceiling of Agostino Chigi's villa depicts the gods (arranged like relief sculpture) at the nuptial feast of Cupid and Psyche. The loggia started a wave of mythological decoration.

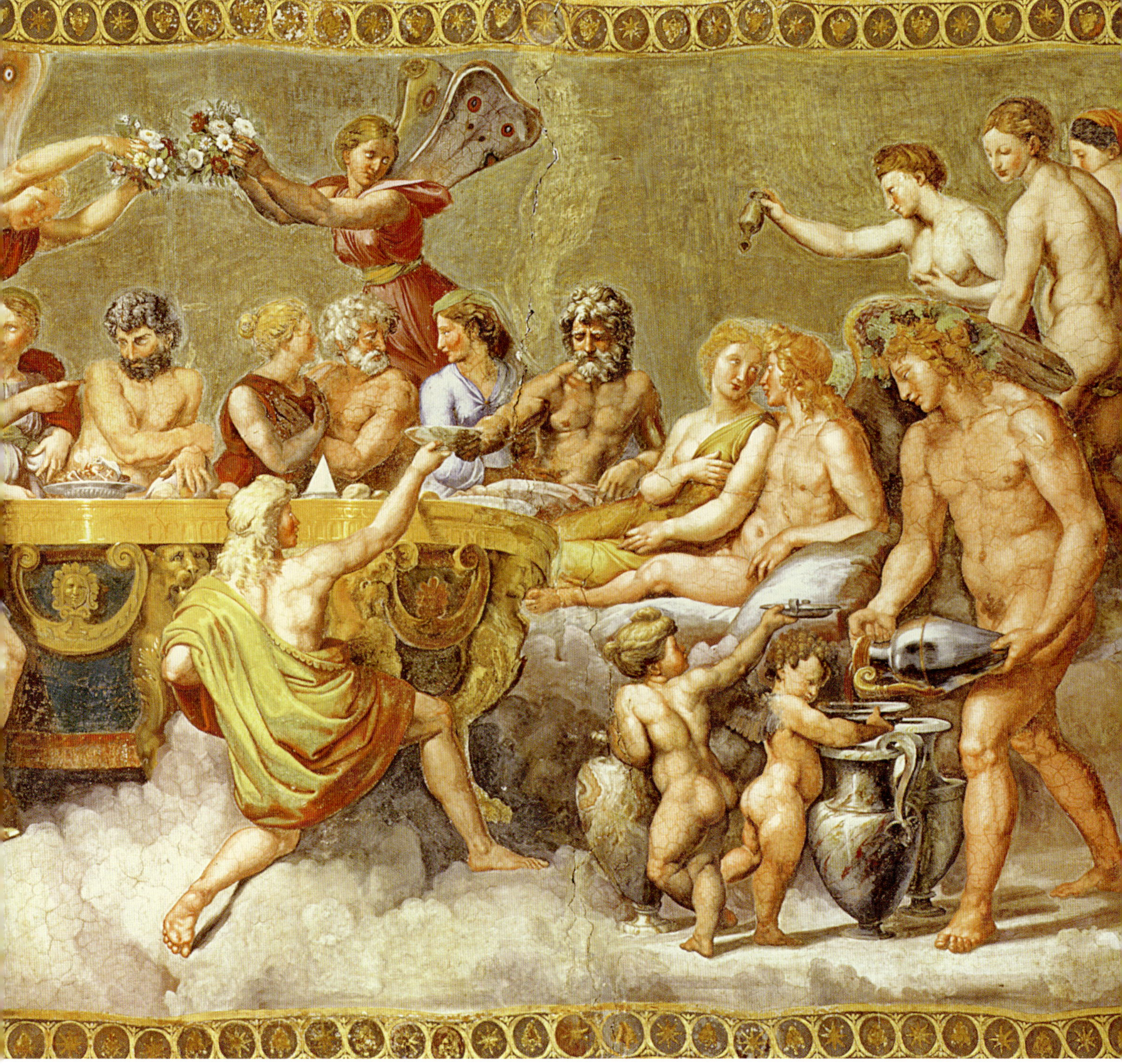

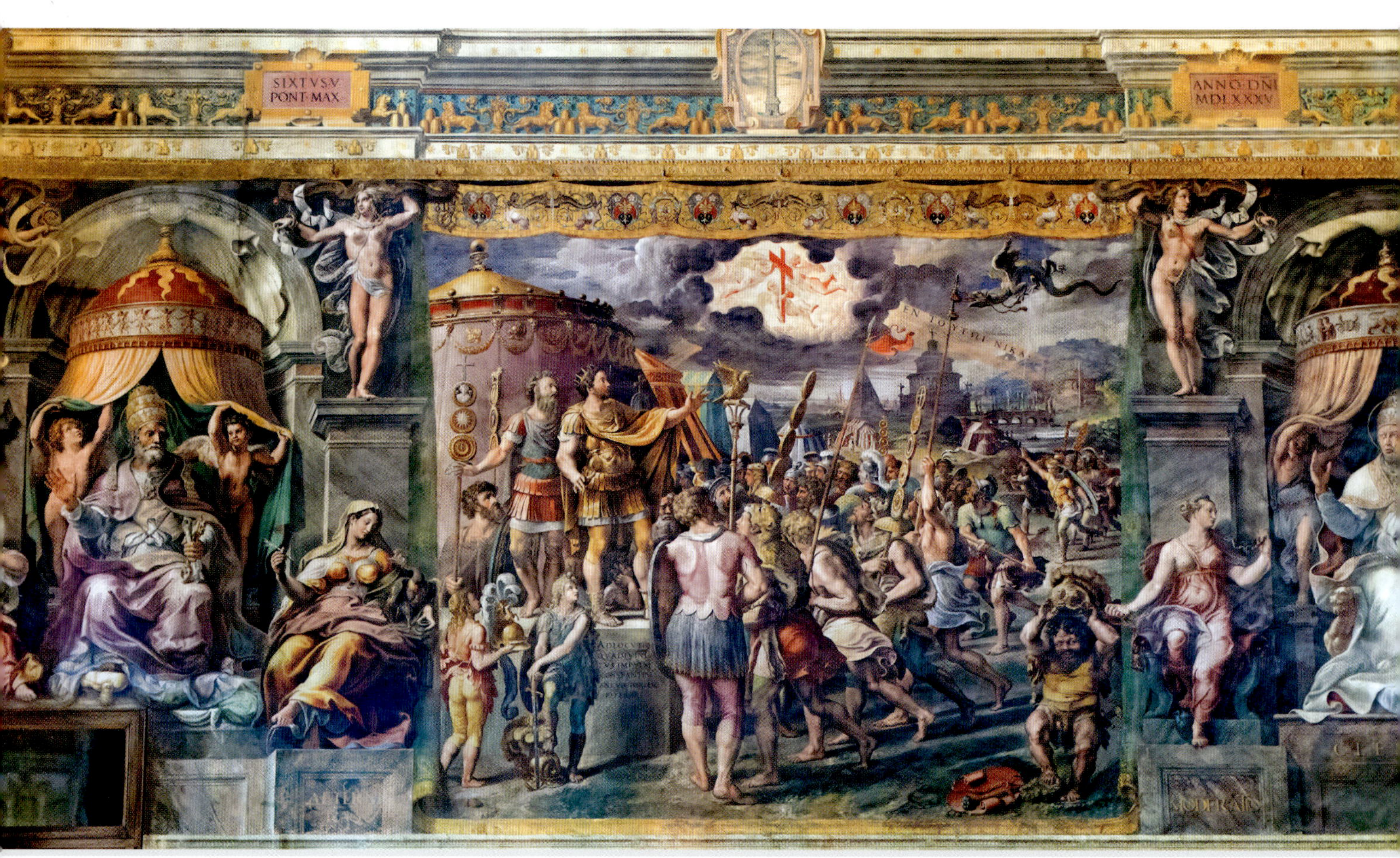

The Vision of the Cross, 1520–24, by Gianfrancesco Penni
Fresco, dimensions unknown
• Sala di Costantino, Vatican Museums, Rome

Surviving drawings suggest Raphael played some part in designing this narrative (completed by his assistant). It shows a vision of the cross appearing to Constantine on the eve of battle, with the words 'In this sign thou shalt conquer.'

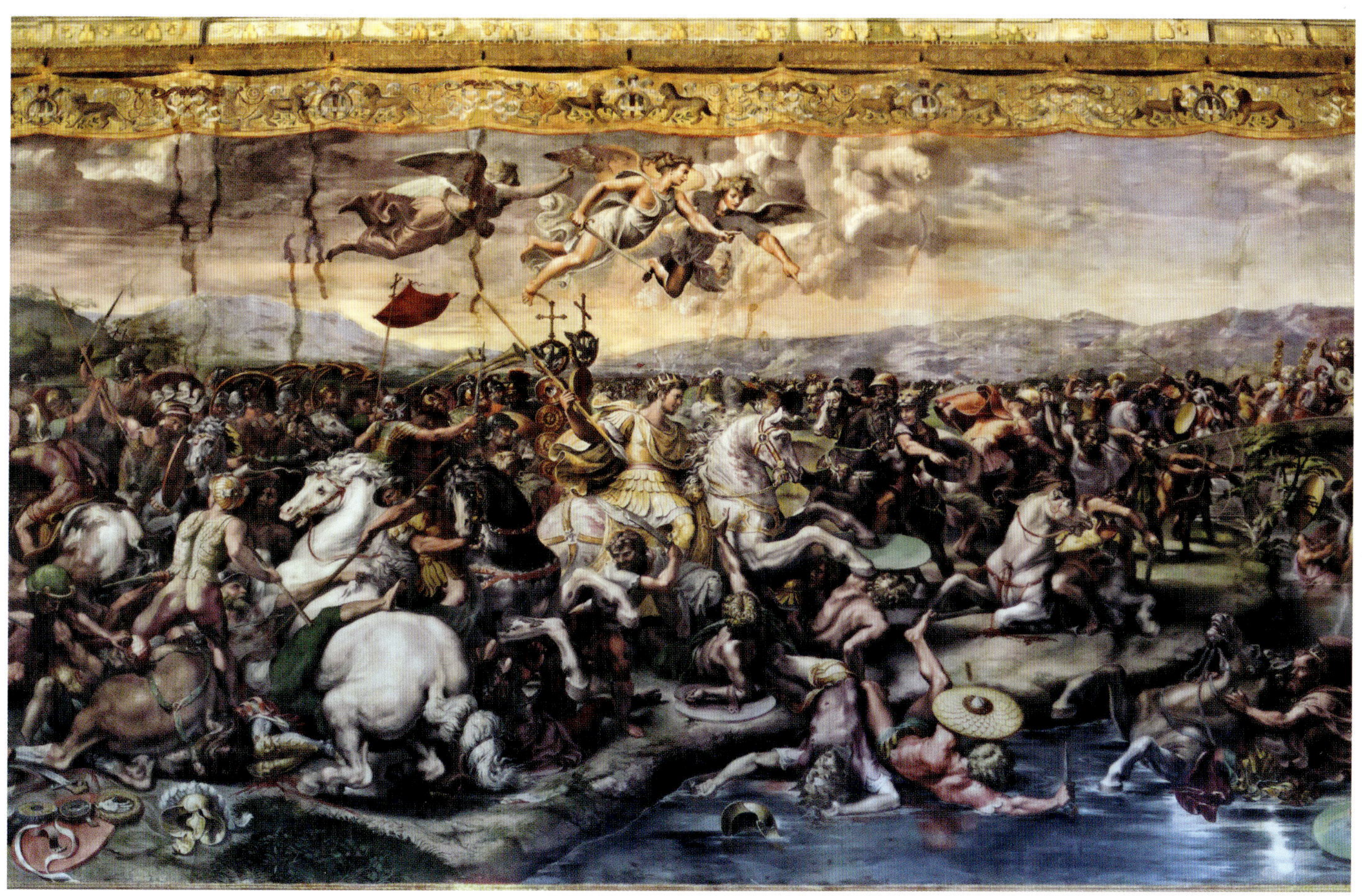

The Battle of the Milvian Bridge, 1520–24, by Giulio Romano

Fresco, dimensions unknown

• Sala di Costantino, Vatican Museums, Rome

Raphael utilized a relief on the triumphal Arch of Constantine (AD 315) in Rome for the basic composition of this image. Executed by his pupil Giulio Romano, it shows Constantine's victory over Maxentius (*c.* AD 276–312) in AD 312.

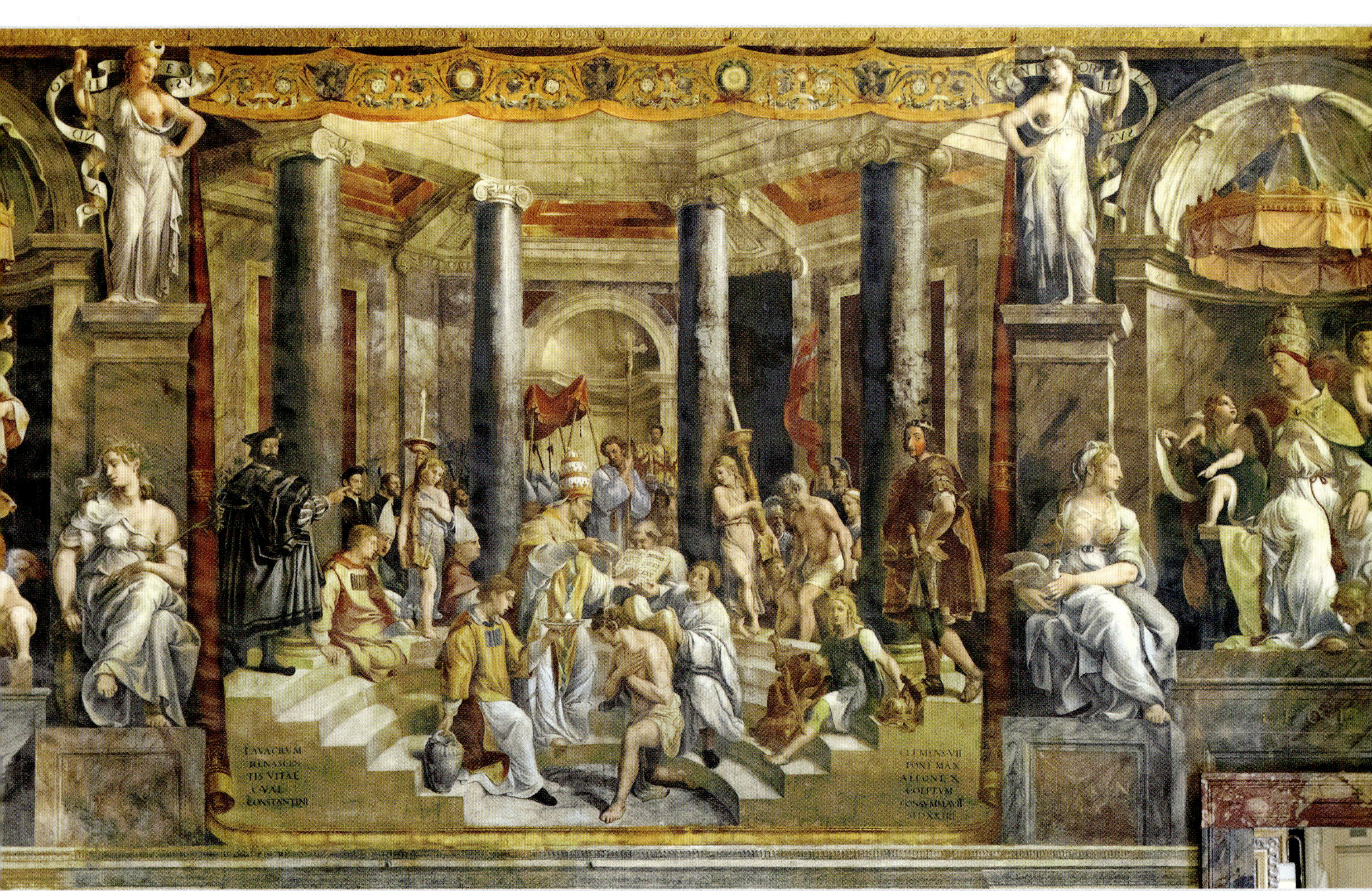

The Baptism of Constantine, 1523–24, by Gianfrancesco Penni
Fresco, dimensions unknown
• Sala di Costantino, Vatican Museums, Rome

Work did not begin on this fresco until 1523 under the reign of Pope Clement VII, whose features were given to Pope Sylvester (reigned AD 314–335), depicted in the act of baptizing the emperor Constantine.

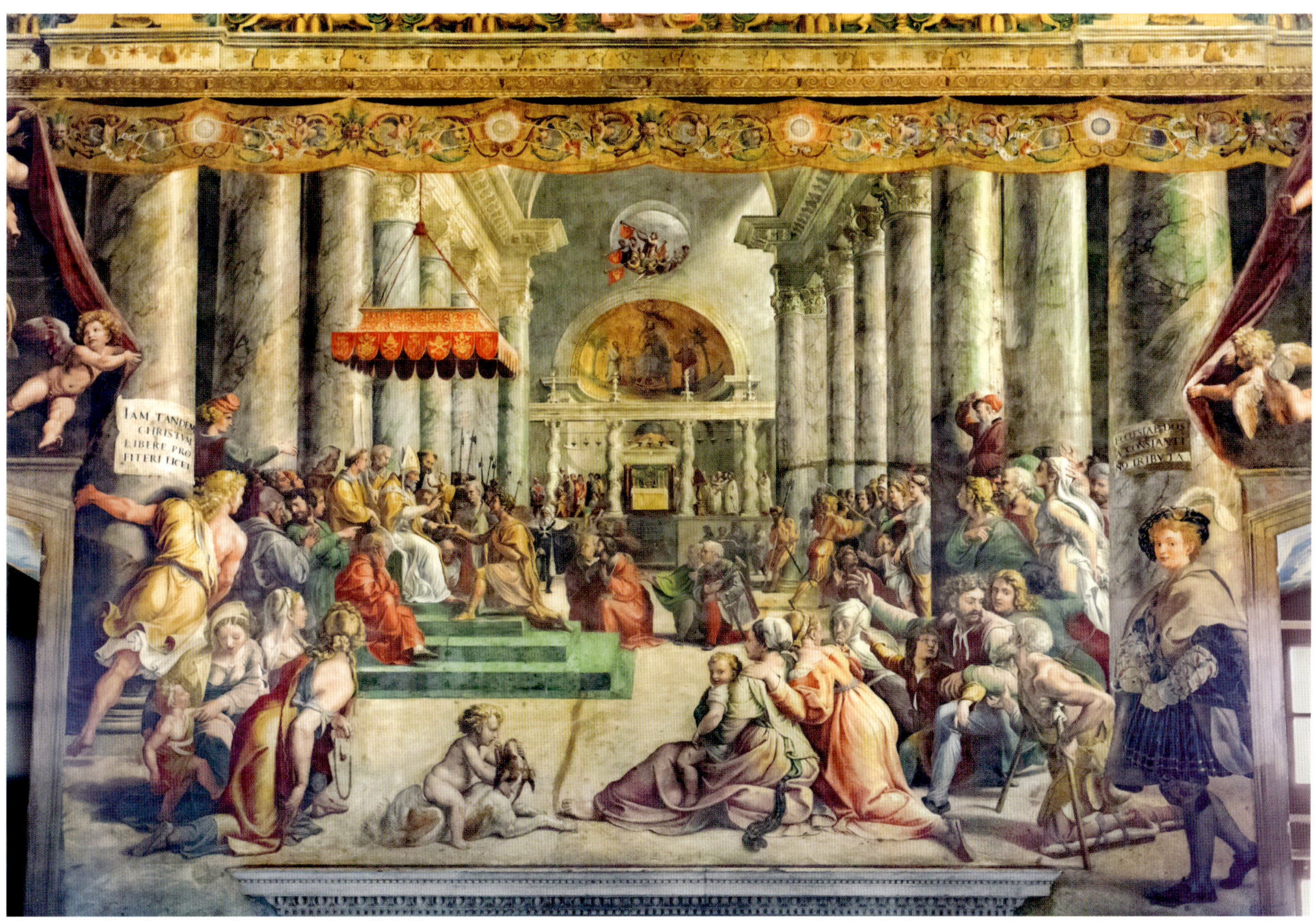

**The Donation of Constantine, 1523–24,
by Gianfrancesco Penni or Giulio Romano**

Fresco, dimensions unknown • Sala di Costantino, Vatican Museums, Rome

Constantine kneels before Pope Sylvester and offers him the city of Rome, symbolized through the exchange of a gold statue. Pope Clement VII wanted to make clear that he considered the papal claim to temporal power historically justified.

Indexes

Index of Works

Page numbers in *italics* refer to illustration captions.

General Index

Page numbers in *italics* refer to illustration captions.

A

Alberti, Leon Battista 9
De Pictura (*On Painting*) 13
Antonio da Sangallo the Younger 24
Apuleius *The Golden Ass* 21
archaeology 24
architecture 24
Ariosto, Ludovico 15
Aristotle 15

B

Baccio d'Agnolo 10
Baglioni, Atlanta 13
Baroque 19
Bastiano da Sangallo ('Aristotle') 10
Bellini, Giovanni 7
Bembo, Pietro 25
Bibbiena, Bernardo Dovizi da 21
Boccaccio, Giovanni 15
Bologna 19
Botticelli, Sandro 6
Bramante, Donato 14, 15, 16, 24
Brunelleschi, Filippo 9

C

Canigiani, Domenico 12
cartoons 11, 22–23, 24–25, 26
Castiglione, Baldassare *The Book of the Courtier* (*Il Libro del Cortegiano*) 22
Chigi, Agostino 9, 20–21
Cimabue (Cenni di Pepo) 6
Città di Castello 7, 9
Clement VII, Pope 24
Constantine the Great 25–26
Coronation of Saint Nicholas of Tolentino (1501) 7
Correggio (Antonio Allegri) 26

D

d'Este, Isabella 25
dall'Olio, Elena Duglioli 19
Dante Alighieri 15
de Grassis, Paris 22
Delacroix, Eugène 26
Domus Aurea (Golden House) 20
Donatello (Donato di Niccolò di Betto Bardi) 9, 10
Doni, Agnolo 12
drawings 11
Dürer, Albrecht 18

E

engravings 18–19
Euclid 15
Evangelista da Pian di Meleto 7

F

Florence 6, 7, 9–11, 13, 14, 16
Fra Bartolommeo (Baccio della Porta) 10–11, 13, 15

G

Ghiberti, Lorenzo 9
Ghirlandaio, Ridolfo 10
Giovanni da Udine (Giovanni Nanni) 17, 21, *120*
Giulio Romano (Giulio Pippi) 17, 21, 26, *114*, *120*, *123*, *125*

H

Hamilton Bible 22
Heraclitus 16

J

Julius II (Giuliano della Rovere), Pope 14–16, 22
Justus of Ghent 7

L

Leo X (Giovanni de'Medici), Pope 16, 20, 22, 23, 24
Leonardo da Vinci 6, 7, 10, 11, 12, 14, 15, 21, 27
Battle of Anghiari, The (1504–05) 10
Benois Madonna (1478) 12
Mona Lisa (c. 1503–05) 12, 22
Tratta della Pittura 12
Luti, Margherita 22

M

Mannerism 19
Mantegna, Andrea 7, 13
Masaccio (Tommaso di Ser Giovanni di Simone) 10
Medici, Giulio de 24
Michelangelo Buonarroti 6, 16–17, 20, 21, 22, 24, 25, 27
Battle of Cascina 10
David (1501–4) 10
Doni Tondo (1505–06) 13
Pietà (1498–99) 13–14
Saint Matthew (c. 1506) 13
Montefeltro, Federico da 7
Montefeltro, Guidobaldo da 9

N

Nasi, Lorenzo 12
Nero 20

O

Orvieto Cathedral 8

P

painting techniques 12–13
Penni, Gianfrancesco 17, 21, 26
Perugia 6, 7, 8, 10, 13
Perugino (Pietro Vannucci) 7, 8–9, 11, 12, 14
Betrothal of the Virgin (*Lo Sposalizio*) (1500–04) 9
Lamentation over the Dead Christ (1495) 13
Petrarch (Francesco Petrarca) 15
Picasso, Pablo 26, 27
Piccolomini, Francesco 9
Piero della Francesca 7
Pinturicchio (Bernardino di Betto) 9
Pius II, Pope 9
Pius III, Pope 9
Plato 15
Pliny the Younger 24
Poliziano, Angelo 21
portraits 22
prints 18–19
Pucci, Antonio 19

R

Raimondi, Marcantonio 18–19
Raphael (Raffaello Santi/Sanzio) 6
arrival in Rome 14
artist's workshop 17–18
cartoons and tapestries 22–23
changing tastes 26–27
competing with Perugino 8–9
drawings 11
early life 7
engravings and prints 18–19
final flourish 24–25
Florence 9–10
Florentine friends 10–11
from Leonardo to Michelangelo 13–14
from painter to architect and archaeologist 24
Madonna paintings 11–12, 19
magisterial creative outpouring 14–15
money and mythology 20–21
musical altarpiece 19
painting political concerns 15–16
painting techniques 12–13
passion and death 25–26
prince of painters 27
Raphael's Bible (decorations for papal loggia) (1518–19) 20
rivals 16–17
Siena 9
skilful portraitist 22
working for a Medici Pope 20
young master 7–8
Renaissance 6, 7, 9–10, 18, 27
High Renaissance 17, 22
Reni, Guido 17
Renoir, Pierre-Auguste 26
Romanticism 26
Rome 6, 9, 14, 19, 24, 27
artist's workshop 17–18
Vatican 14–16, 20, 21, 25–26
Villa Farnesina 20–21
Rovere, Giovanna Feltria della 9
Rubens, Peter Paul 26

S

Santi, Giovanni 7
Santi, Raffaello *see* Raphael
Savonarola, Girolamo 10
Sebastiano del Piombo (Sebastiano Luciani) 21
Raising of Lazarus, The (1517–19) 24–25
Siena 6, 9
Signorelli, Luca 7
End of the World (1499–1502) 8
Last Judgement (1499–1502) 8
Soderini, Piero 9–10
Strozzi, Maddalena 12

T

Taddei, Taddeo 12
tapestries 22–23
Titian (Tiziano Vecellio) 6

U

Urbino 6, 7, 10, 13, 14

V

van Aelst, Pieter 23
van der Weyden, Rogier 7
van Eyck, Jan 7
Vasari, Giorgio *Lives of the Artists* 6, 7, 9, 10, 12, 13, 14, 15, 16–17, 18, 19, 22, 24, 25, 27
Vatican 14–16, 21, 25–26
Velázquez, Diego 26
Venice 16
Verrocchio, Andrea del 12–13
Villa Farnesina 20–21
Villa Madama, Rome 24
Vitruvius 24

W

workshop 17–18

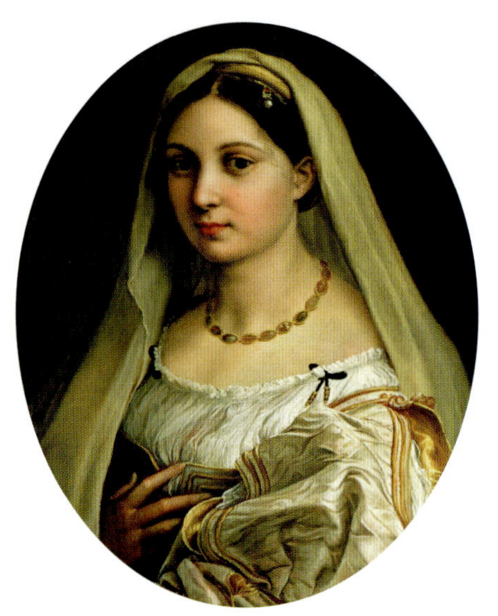

Masterpieces of Art
FLAME TREE PUBLISHING

A new series of carefully curated print and digital books covering the world's greatest art, artists and art movements.

If you enjoyed this book please sign up for updates, information and offers on further titles in this series at

blog.flametreepublishing.com/art-of-fine-gifts/